JUNIOR GUNNERS

Edited by

Andy Lamb

LEGAL NOTICE

BOY SERVICE IN THE ROYAL ARTILLERY

Memories of being in the Boys' Battery, Boys' Regiment,
Junior Leaders Regiment, RA and the Army Foundation College

1937 – 2009

Copyright © 2018

Love @ Best Wishes from Andy

1

BOY SERVICE IN THE ROYAL ARTILLERY

Memories of being in the Boys' Battery, Boys' Regiment,
Junior Leaders Regiment, RA and the Army Foundation College

1937 – 2009

Acknowledgements

Thanks are due to:

Johnny Seaton, Jack Williams, Keith Reeve, Soldier Magazine,
Michael John Nicholson, Fran Horton, Mike Luscombe, Denis Law,
Phil Hatch, Simon Hutt and Lt Kidane Cousland for their accounts of
training in RA boy and junior service, and permission to produce
them in this book.

Thanks are due to:

Pete A Nicholas, Steve Collins, David Dufall, Robert Sheddon Teddy
McKenzie and many others too numerous to mention for their
encouragement in this project.

Thanks are due to:

Mick McTiernan, Kirsty Greenwood and Robert Sheddon for their
help in editing the text.

FORWARD

As someone who, in 1954, joined the Royal Artillery as a boy-soldier
I regard it as an honour to write this Forward and it has given me
great and nostalgic pleasure to do so, particularly as I know two of
the writers.

As the author says in his Introduction, boys have served in the Army
since time immemorial. For instance, they are mentioned by
Shakespeare (Henry V, Acr 3, Sc 1; and Henry VI Part 1, Act 4, Sc
6). We know that boy soldiers served in fighting units throughout the
19th century and until 1915, when a public outcry about their casualty
rate caused them to be withdrawn into non-operational posts. But
they remained extant.

Boy service in the Royal Artillery continued (at Woolwich) until
disbanded in 1939. In 1941, however, a boys battery was re-
introduced and it served at the RA Depot, Woolwich, until 1949
when it moved to Kinmel Park, Rhyl. In 1952 The Boys Battery
moved from Rhyl to Bradbury Lines, Hereford, and was expanded
into a two-battery Regiment soon after. Each regiment or corps of
the Army had a boys unit and that was mirrored in both the Royal
Navy and RAF.

In 1957 the War Office (as it then was) thought it right to improve
both the training and the image of boy soldiering in the Army. As a
result, the name of The Boys Regiment RA was changed to the Junior
Leaders Regiment RA and the training and husbandry of boys took a
distinct turn for the better. In 1958 the Regiment was moved to
Bramcote, in Warwickshire. The accounts in this book start at
Woolwich and take the reader forward from there, by personal
experiences, written and presented (I am pleased to see) in the
vernacular, through to the Army-wide abolition of boy service in
1993. Each contributor gives a highly subjective view of Army life

as it affected him and his reaction to it, together with his thoughts, feelings and ideals at the time he spent as a boy soldier or as a permanent staff member. Lieutenant Colonel Nicholson, writing of his time in the Regiment as a captain gives a light-hearted account of life 'behind the scenes'.

I personally recall that, at the time individual boys spent in the Regiment many were home sick, many resented it and wished they had not joined, and many found barrack-room life and the training very hard and testing to take. Some of that is reflected in these accounts. On the other hand, I know of some who regarded life in the Regiment as being better than at home or, particularly, than in a children home. Having said all that, I have to report that having, since then, met very many ex-boys over the years not one of them has denied that boy service did him the world of good and many (myself included) say that they could not have achieved in life whatever they did without that upbringing. Boy service did an immense amount of good for the Army because most warrant officers and sergeants messes had a disproportionate number of ex-boys as members. The system also hugely benefitted society at large by instilling discipline and courtesy into boys, many of whom had been semi-wild.

My personal view is that those in the government and the Civil Service who, for short-term financial savings, brought to an end boy service, nation-wide, did the country as a whole an enormous disservice and caused long-term damage. Happily, the mistake was soon felt but because governments and civil servants don't admit to mistakes, there was no going back. Instead their solution was to create The Army Foundation College at Harrogate (a single unit for all cap badges). It thrives and continues to turn out the future warrant officers and sergeants and some commissioned officers for the backbone of the Army. Long may it and boy service flourish. Onward and upward.

Robert Sheddon

(Shrapnel Troop, Hereford, 1954 – 1956

Colonel

INTRODUCTION

Historical Context

Throughout history and in many cultures, children have been extensively involved in military campaigns.

The earliest mentions of minors being involved in these ways come from antiquity. There is evidence of children serving in the ancient Greek and Egyptian armies. The Greek/Roman historian, Plutarch, in his essay *Parallel Lives* (about 100AD), reported regulations required that youths serving in the Roman army had to be at least sixteen years of age.

It is probably true to say that youths served in the English and British armed forces since the formation of the New Model Army in 1645. Children served in the British army during the 18th and 19th century, usually as drummers or orderlies. In the early days, boys as young as 10 served in this capacity.

Reporting in his letter to *'Gunner Magazine'*, Colonel Bob Shedden cites the example of a 16-year-old boy serving as a Battery Commander's trumpeter in 1804. Another example exists in the Museum of Army Music at Kneller Hall there is a music notation book that had been found next to the body of a young drummer on the battlefield at Waterloo. It is estimated that he was 14 years old.

Boys were serving in the Royal Artillery up to, and during, World War 2.

"Boys of good character between the ages of 12 and 17 years may be specially enlisted for the purpose of being employed as trumpeters, buglers or bandsmen. The number of boys will not exceed four per battery ..."

Volunteer Regulations 1901

The Military Service Bill was enacted in 1914 and specified that men were liable to be called up from the age of 18. However, it is known that many younger boys managed to sign up (by falsifying their age) and fight in the trenches. By 1915 boys had been withdrawn from front-line duties. It is estimated that 125,000 youths, some as young as 15, had been killed or wounded in action by the end of the war.

Boy Service continued in the 1920s and 1930s and two Boys' Batteries were stationed at Woolwich. The Boys' Band RA was formed at Woolwich in 1937. These were disbanded in 1939, on the outbreak of World-War II. However, Boys' Service resumed in 1941. A new Boys' Battery RA was formed with boys being trained as trumpeters and in other occupations.

In 1949, the Boys' Battery RA moved from Woolwich to Rhyl. In 1952, it moved from Rhyl to Hereford, Bradbury Lines, and a second battery was raised to form the Boys' Regiment RA. This morphed into the Junior Leaders' Regiment, RA in February 1957.

In April 1959, the Junior Leaders' Regiment took over Gamecock Barracks at Bramcote, near Nuneaton in Warwickshire. It remained there until the regiment was disbanded in 1993.

JLRRA was not the only unit that trained boys for RA service. Because of the post-war birth bulge a number of other boys units were formed in 1959 and 1960, including the All Arms Junior Leaders' Regiment at Tonfanau, the Junior Tradesmen's Regiments at Rhyl, and at Troon and the Junior Musicians Troop at Woolwich. At the same time there were Army Apprentice schools training RA boys at Chepstow and Harrogate

Nowadays, Junior Soldiers for all arms are trained at the Army Foundation College in Harrogate. Recently, there have been calls to abandon the concept of Junior Service in the armed forces for good.

The aims of Boy Service were to provide a cadre of trained men to become NCOs, and Warrant Officers in the regular army, by equipping them with:

- **Education**. To provide each junior soldier with the opportunity to study for and pass the Army Certificate of First

Class Education, thus qualifying him eventually to achieve warrant and commissioned rank. junior leaders could also study for GCE "O" levels.

- **Military and Trade Training**. To provide each junior leader with his basic military training, teaching him the skills of drill, weapons handling, shooting and physical training.
- **Weapons**. junior leaders were taught to shoot and drill with an issue rifle, initially the Lee-Enfield, later the L1A1 Self-Loading Rifle and then the L85A1 and, of course, the Ordnance QF 25-pounders.
- **Trade Training**. Junior leaders were also introduced to the main operating trades in their chosen corps.
- **Leadership, Adventure Training and Sports.** Special emphasis was given to leadership, important for future senior NCOs. Exercises included canoeing, sailing, rock climbing, map reading, cooking in the field and survival in arduous conditions. Junior leaders attended military and civilian outward-bound courses in the UK and abroad. A wide variety of sporting activities were available and competitions with military and civilian youth organisations in the UK and abroad were encouraged.

Readers who did not pass through boy service may like to know that the Regiment was modelled on the public-school system. The training batteries took the place of the school houses, while the officers and NCO took the equivalent place of teachers and staff.

Boys were eligible to join the Army from the moment they left school, the age of which was raised from 14 to 15 (in 1944) and from 15 to 16 (in 1972). Boys who joined the service served as boys until 17-and-a-half and were then posted to an adult service unit. Legally, their actual service for which they had enlisted (six or more years) did not begin until they were 18.

Within the Regiment boys mirrored the rank structure of the non-commissioned ranks of the permanent staff up to, and including, warrant-officer-first-class (RSM).

The training programme was divided into roughly three equal parts and into three terms per year. First, each boy went back to school for education; secondly one third was devoted to military training such as gunnery, weapons and foot-drill etc. The last third was for physical training, not only in the gymnasium but also on the sports fields. In the evenings attendance at a hobby activity was compulsory. At the end of each term leave was granted roughly of length equivalent to the state school holidays.

The stories in this book cover the period of boys' service from 1937 to 2009. The following people have contributed, and we are grateful for their permission to share these stories, thoughts, anecdotes and reminiscences.

Johnny Seaton, Boy's Battery, RA, Woolwich, 1937-1938

Jack Williams, Boys' Battery, RA, Rhyl, 1950 - 1952.

Keith Reeve, Junior Leaders' Regiment, RA, Bradbury Lines, Hereford and at Oswestry, 1957 – 1958

The School for Gunners, Soldier Magazine, June 1960

(Now Lt Col) Michael John Nicholson RA. Junior Leaders' Regiment, RA, Bramcote, Nuneaton, 1969

Fran Horton, Junior Leaders' Regiment, RA, Bramcote, 1970 – 1972.

Mike Luscombe, Junior Leaders' Regiment, RA, Bramcote, 1971 – 1973.

Denis Law, Junior Leaders' Regiment, RA, Bramcote, 1971 – 1973.

Andy Lamb, Junior Leaders' Regiment, RA, Bramcote,1973 -1974.

Phil Hatch, Junior Leaders Regiment, RA, Bramcote, 1985 - 1986

Simon Hutt, Junior Leaders' Regiment, RA, Bramcote, 1989 – 1990.

Lt Kidane Cousland, Army Foundation College, Harrogate, 2008 - 2009

The stories presented below have had minimal editing. Where necessary spelling and grammar have been changed, and minor edits made to the texts for the sake of clarity. Other than that, these are some of the stories of the men who served in the Boys' Battery and JLRRA, told by them in their own words.

Section 1 - Drummer Boy – By Johnny Seaton, Boys' Battery, Woolwich, 1937 - 1938

Join the army and see the world! I'll do it.

I followed the soldier into the recruiting office. I want to see the world. I know it's there, I've seen it in the movies.

The corporal looked up at me.

"What do you want, kid?" he asked me in weary voice.
"I want to join the army and see the world!"
"How old are you?"
"Fourteen."

I was sent in to see the other soldier.

"Name?"
"Johnny Seaton, sir."
"School?"
"St Jude's."
"Parent's consent."
"I can get that, sir." My Ma wouldn't have cared if I'd drowned in the river.

The smell of brasso hits my nostrils. Musty papers on the shelves. It stirs the spirit of adventure in my blood.

"Go behind the screen and take your clothes off."
"What?"
"I've got to weigh you."

He weighed me and measured me and then sent me in to see the MO who examined me. He pronounced himself satisfied and wrote on a form. Then he sent me back to the corporal.

"Now listen carefully. Once you have sworn the oath, got your parent's consent and taken the shilling there is no turning back. Do you understand?"

"Yes, sir."

"You are in for sixteen years. You sign on for twelve years but the first four years don't count. That's boys service. Do you understand?"

"Yes, sir. I want to be a soldier."

"Were you any good in school?"

"Not bad. I swim, I box and I'm on the school soccer team."

"Alright. How would you like to go somewhere where they'll teach you riding, swimming, fencing and gymnastics?"

"I would like that, sir."

"It's the Boys' Battery at Woolwich. It's going to be tough for someone with your background."

He gave me a blue form and some exam papers. I ran home and got my Ma to sign them straight away. I sat at the dirty kitchen table and did one of the exams. I ran back to the office on Lord Nelson Street just before it closed at 6-o-clock.

The corporal helped me with one of the other exams. I had to write a list of my sports. Then I had to write a list of my hobbies. The corporal told me not to mention comic books or going to the pictures. I had to say I played chess and read literature and liked singing.

I took the other exam papers away with me and did the sums sitting in the saloon of the ferry-boat. The skipper let me stay there until I finished. I went four times across the Mersey for one penny. He gave me a bar of Cadbury's chocolate.

I went to see my school friend, Eddie and told him all about it. I was so thrilled. He looked a bit sad but wished me good luck. Just as I left him he offered to try to help me find a job, but it was too late. I had made my mind up.

I had to go to Paddie's Market to buy a pair of long trousers. I didn't want those London boys laughing at me in my shorts. I bargained with the bloke and got a pair, off the stall, for a tanner. The bloke called me 'Wack.'

"Here you go, Wack. A pair of kecks for a tanner."

I'm finally on my way, on a train. I'm not scared. Well, maybe a little bit scared. Not really scared. I wonder what it's going to be like. This is my first trip on a train. Eddie's Ma has packed me some home-made cake and sandwiches. Eddie has put a copy of *The Hotspur* in the pack. I wonder if boys in the army read comics.

I got to Woolwich and a soldier dressed in blue and gold, with red stripes beckoned to me.

"What's your name?"
"Johnny Seaton."
"You're the one. Follow me."

He strode off and I followed him. I could hear the sound of thundering hooves. Horses and a gun-carriage. There they were, bright-faced boys in army caps and polished boots with spurs.

We reached the barrack square. A section of marching boys, arms swinging, heads high and chests puffed out. I liked the look of their uniforms. They were wearing riding britches.

Music surged from a line of boys older than me. Bigger boys. Some of them must have been seventeen. They had trumpets and there was a music teacher who was obviously in charge. The rattle of the drumsticks reminded me of the Boy Scouts.

"Rat-a-tat-tat, rat-a-tat-tat." You're in the army now.

There was so much activity going on that I couldn't absorb it all at once. However, they looked carefree and happy. A voice bellowed out and the square suddenly became a wild mass of scrambling boys.

They passed me without a glance. It was supper time and they were hungry. I know I was.

A sergeant fed me, piled me up with army gear and showed me to a bed. It had been very exciting, but apart from the instructions given, no-one had spoken to me in the noisy barrack room. I was glad to get to bed. After all, it had been a long day.

A sweet trumpet filled the air with music and all the lights went out.

I was very lonely in my little cot. All I could think about was Ma and Eddie and all those people I had left behind. I awoke and shouted out.

"What's wrong, kid," asked a friendly voice at my side. "Are you homesick?"
"No. I'm okay. I must have been dreaming."

The simple, noisy routine of barrack room life pleased me. Kids wrestled and had pillow fights. We slept in our shirt-tails. The kid from the next cot asked if I was settling in. I told him I was settling in just fine.

The comic books I had been reading all my life were full of stories about boys who spent their lives in posh public schools. They filled my heart with joy, but they did not cater for the likes of me. They were not part of the real world. Theirs was a world of make-believe. A world of dormitories, high-jinks, house masters, prep schools, cads, bounders, heroes and happy days on the cricket pitches and rugger fields of 'Merrie-England'. Where the hell was that? Did they only think of kids from wealthy families? How about the kids who got a pair of roller-skates for Christmas but couldn't use them because they had no shoes or stockings?

A Mighty hand had sucked me from the stench of Liverpool and all its poverty and set me down in a brand-new world. It was wonderful. All my boyhood dreams had come true. I was in a posh public school right out of the pages of my comic books. But the lessons were much more exciting. Fencing with real swords. Trumpet lessons in an enormous shed. Horse riding on the common. Bright, modern classrooms and excellent teachers from the Army Education Corps.

God knows how many boys there were in the Battery. Men did not exist. It was a boys' battery. True, we had teachers, instructors, bombardiers and sergeants, but they simply trained us by day, scared the life out of us and sent spittle flying onto our cheeks. At four-o-clock they just vanished. Some barrack rooms were supervised by an adult NCO but others were supervised by an older boy. We looked up to them and admired them.

We were roused at 6am, washed, brushed our teeth and got dressed in our horrible denim uniforms.

My first breakfast was fried fish and chips. I couldn't believe it! Fish and chips for breakfast! There was bread, mugs of milk, scalding tea and plenty of everything. If you wanted a second helping, you stood to attention in front of your plate and a cookhouse orderly would rustle-up a second plate. That was it. Big eats!

I loved every second and could hardly believe my ears when I was told we would get paid for it.

"Pay? We get paid?!"

Seven shillings and sixpence a week. Three bob in your hand and the rest in credits. You'll need it when you go on leave.

Who wanted to leave such a wonderland? Not me. Clean beds, no fleas, fresh laundry and warm blankets.

We had playing fields, gymnasiums, football, boxing, hockey and every sport in the world. Ping-pong in the recreation room. What the hell was ping-pong? Darts: I had never seen a game of darts. People in my part of the country did not play darts. Darts wasn't introduced to Liverpool until after the war.

We were real soldiers, subject to the King's Rules and Regulations. Cowardice in the face of the enemy. Death by firing squad. Stealing from a comrade. The boys did not steal. It was unheard of. Smoking was punished by ten strokes of the cane.

The youngest among us were not allowed out of barracks. When the instructors were satisfied with a lad's progress, and providing the boy was well-trained and disciplined, he could go into town. But not alone. Twos or threes. That was the standing order.

Boys came from all over the world. Lads from military families. They sat around and talked in little groups about their lives in far-away places. India, Africa, Malta, Gibraltar, Palestine and the British West Indies.

I had many things to learn, to adjust to my new environment and fit in with the other lads. I met only one boy from Liverpool. A kid named Quigley. A sixteen-year-old who could handle impossible horses. He was a sarcastic big-head, but I admired his ability.

Another boy wore silk pyjamas and spoke like the ex-king Edward. Everyone made fun of him but he ignored them and listened to classical music on the gramophone. He minded his own business. He was a real gentleman. It would take a lot to turn me into a gentleman.

Boxing was part of the training programme. All the kids hated it because it was compulsory. It didn't matter how good you were or how inexperienced or not. You got thrown into the ring with a kid from another section and there was nothing you could do about it. The boxing instructors put kids of equal weight into the ring together and that was the only consideration shown.

They threw me in the ring with another lad with a broken nose and a hostile expression.

"Take a dive!"

"I wanna gum shield!" I shouted.
"We ain't got one!"
"If you want me to box, I want a gumshield!"

"What the hell for?"
"Because I like my teeth!"

They found a gumshield.

The moment the bell sounded, the other kid came at me like an express train. Except I wasn't there. When he turned around I belted him one. He wasn't expecting that. He thought I was another skinny waster. I can tell you, I showed him something.

"Go on Scouse, let the bastard have it!"

He lost his cool and walked into a couple of hay-makers! All his jabs and feints and ducks and professional know-how were all show-off. He must have been watching too many films and won his fights by scaring other kids to death. Anyway, he never laid a glove on me. In the second round, he came at me with a snarl on his face, and his eyes showing hatred, trying to put the frighteners on. I knew all about this approach and with one solid clout brought the claret streaming down.

That meant the end of that round.

The third round would be the end of the fight. Win, lose or draw. I pulled my punches without touching him. He dropped his guard for a second, feeling confused. That was all I needed; two dirty jabs to his solar-plexus brought his head down. I belted him between the eyes and flattened him with a right cross to the jaw.

There was a short silence.

Then the gym erupted. They had all thought I was a softy.

Christmas and the sounds of sleigh-bells from the radio.

The world was white with snow and Christmas carols filled the air. All the kids were excited and ready to go home on Christmas Leave. I stood in front of the big mirror at the entrance to our barracks, admiring myself in my uniform. Tunic, riding britches, puttees, boots, spurs and military cap. My hair had been cut right back, but my cheeks were pink. I thought I looked good. I was a soldier-boy in my dashing uniform.

One of the other boys had invited me home for Christmas. I agreed. If I had gone home my Ma would have pawned my boxing medals. I never wanted to go home again. It was the best time I'd ever had in my life.

The holiday at an end, we returned to the depot to find all the kids milling around in the canteen, seeking the friends they'd been parted from and glad to get back together.

All the boys had some special quality, something going for them that made them stand out. My friend Teddy was a powerful horseman and strived to attain the rough-rider's badge. I shone at athletics and boxing. Some were fine musicians and sought the crossed-trumpets badge. My other mate, Tony, was the son of a vet and had the magic touch with horses. They just became gentle with him. He promised to help me with the scary ones.

One day I got a nasty kick, playing football. I finished up in the military hospital over on the other side of the common. I was fifteen at the time. I missed my mates from the band and the drums and I was feeling a bit sad and lonely.

The night nurse roused me.

"You can get up today, kid. Be careful on that leg."

I had to get dressed in a set of hospital blues, except I couldn't pull the trousers up. One of the other patients helped me. I think he was a corporal in the Cameronians.

He challenged me to a game of snooker. I hobbled along behind him down the corridor to the recreation room. He asked what I was chewing. Bubblegum, I told him.

"Bubblegum?! What kind of soldier are you?"

"I'm a boy soldier. I'm in the Boys' Battery just down the road."

At this moment, I was busy with a giant bubble, but it burst all over my freckled nose.

"Bubblegum soldiers!" he snorted in disgust.

We never did have that game of snooker.

The drums they go with a Rat-a-tat-tat,
The trumpets loudly play.
Fare the well young Polly my dear,
I must be going away.

The stick can beat a rat-a-tat-tat, but if the drum is taught and tightly stretched, even the sound of a raindrop on it can be heard. Pit-a-pat, pit-a-pat.

The band and drums paraded, full dressed, trumpets highly polished, gleaming cymbals, drums laced with white ropes.

Spur-clad, pink-faced boys in britches formed a military square. A powerful voice rang out and carried out across the waters of Southampton Docks. Music, sweet music filled the air. Young chests bursting with pride, filled out shiny-buttoned tunics. Heads held high, gleaming lanyards at their arms, the band boys played a tune.

I tapped my drum, rat-a-tat-tat, and again, rat-a-tat-tat.

One young lad with a gleaming trumpet, military cap upon his hair.
His eyes were blue, his teeth gleamed white and his wonderful face
was shiny bright.

"So long, Johnny, lad. So long kid! See you in hell!"

"Should auld acquaintance be forgot." A-rat-a-tat-tat, a-rat-a-tat-tat.

The troopship sailed away and the band played on. And the rain fell
on my drum. Pit-a-pat, pit-a-pat, pit-a-pat.

"Fall-out the band. Dismiss the picquet line. Get them on the
transport Sergeant Major!"

What did you join the army for?
Why did you join the army?
What did you join the army for?
You must have been bloody-well barmy!

I've been stuck in the saddle four hours and hours,
Stuck it as long as I could.
I stuck it and stuck it until I said f***-it,
My arsehole is not made of wood!

I can hear the thundering of the mounted troop across the common.
And the pit-a-pat of the rain on my drum.

Section 2 - Jack Williams. Memories of Boys' Service. 1950 - 1952

I think the first thing that struck me was feeling disappointed that the everyday apparel was 'denims' and not a proper BD as I was used to seeing my father, a regular BSM, wearing. I soon got over that though, when I saw the SD uniform.

Kinmel Park Camp

Rhyl Railway Station. Collected by Permanent Staff NCOs and loaded onto an army truck. Thinking: "Not many joining up."

Didn't realise that more would be coming throughout the day. What few there were didn't say much, each busy with his own thoughts I suppose. On arrival at the Camp, we were greeted by an Officer, who made a short address on what we were to expect and then taken to Recruits' Troop.

The first lesson: making your bed! Proper 'hospital corners'.

I have always been proud of my hospital corners until some time ago whilst watching an episode of 'Frost,' the detective played by David Jason. He and his sergeant were searching a suspect's bedroom. Frost looked at the bed and said: "Hospital corners! He's either been in the Army, or in jail!"

Recruits arrived in batches and those who arrived early had to pass on the bed-making procedure to the later arrivals. All those different accents and dialects! Brummies, Scots, Welsh, Scousers, Cockneys and Geordies. Southerners who said 'barth' and buck' instead of 'bath' and 'book'. ('A' as in 'cat' and 'oo' as in 'hoot'.) The start of friendships that would last a lifetime.

The all-important 'army number': "Memorise this! We won't keep telling it to you!"

Roger Stephens from Northampton had real problems with keeping it in his head. We became good mates because I was able to keep reminding him. I learned several months later how my accent had baffled him at first, as he had no idea about the potteries' dialect! Strange how the ear becomes attuned so that even the strongest Geordie lingo can be deciphered. It wasn't too long before the different accents seemed to be far less pronounced. Perhaps it was due to a combination of attunement and the fact that people subconsciously modified their accents.

Kit issue. Now this was more like it! We would begin to look the part! SDs tailored to fit. Webbing and leather to be Blancoed and polished.

"No, it isn't issued, you buy it from the NAAFI."

"You keep working the spit and polish in small circles and after a while, it imparts a very 'igh gloss". Sgt Walker said that, 61 years ago, and I can remember it as if it were yesterday. As soon as we were kitted out and had changed to Army issue, all our 'civvy' clothes were parcelled up and sent home.

Having been knocked into shape by Sergeant Walker and Bombardier Garvey, we were transferred to the Troops. Roger Stephens, Dave Flett, Arthur Hyam and I were sent to Milne Troop. We became close friends and looked out for each other all through our time in the Boys' Battery. Dave and I are still in touch via emails and meeting at the reunions. Arthur doesn't seem to like writing, but I have spoken to him on the phone, although not recently! Roger, who we called 'Steve' wrote a few times after we mustered, but we lost touch and I have no idea where he is now.

Jim LeFeuvre was also a particular mate. He used to regale us with tales of 'Jerry-baiting' during the occupation of the Channel Isles. That must have been a terrible time, but he never dwelt on the horrors of it.

Inter-Troop Boxing

We occasionally had to do a bit of boxing as part of physical training. 'Dai' Davies and I were roughly of the same physique, so we were selected to box each other. Being good mates, we made sure we didn't do any damage, but Sergeant Major Kinnaird cottoned on to that and stopped us:

"Right Davies! Put your arms around his neck. Williams, put your arms around his neck. Now give him a kiss!"

Embarrassed giggles, but order disobeyed:

"Well then, get stuck in!"

I made Dai's head ring and he split my lip. We were still mates though. Then came the time of the inter-troop boxing matches. For my first scheduled fight, my opponent was declared unfit, so I had a walkover. For my first actual fight, I was matched with 'Bomber' Brown, who was to my mind a seasoned professional, having been the battery heavyweight champion for some time and who fought in inter-regimental matches. I lasted into round two, because he couldn't catch me in round one!

Marching

Drill, gun drill and rifle drill all seems a blur, but sounding (learning to play a trumpet) with Trumpet-Major Lawrence was quite an experience. Suffice to say, he taught us the calls and the words to go with them! I could recognise most of the calls, because my father was a regular in the artillery and he used to sing them to my brother, sisters and me, though the words he put to them weren't quite the same as those that TM Lawrence taught.

One of the first lessons in marching drill. The instructor was going through the procedure for the 'About Turn'. He demonstrated each phase several times and was particularly emphatic about the 'Swivel round on the ball of your left foot'. His final run-through before we were to attempt the 'About Turn' went well until he got to the swivel bit. The instruction he gave then was, "Swivel round on your left ball"!

Regarding my brother. I was sitting waiting for a bus on Rhyl Bus Station, when he walked around the corner! He had joined up and the first I knew about it was then! It seemed that recruits were expected to find their own way to Kinmel Camp at that time, whereas I, and those that joined with me, were picked up at the railway station. I took Reg back to camp and was saddled with him for the rest of my time with the Boys!

After a few weeks of sounding practice, TM Lawrence deemed me good enough to join the band. What memories I have of the shows we did and the places we went to.

Blackpool

A performance on the promenade on Princess Parade, as part of El Alamein Commemoration Day. I have a newspaper cutting with a photo (much faded) and a report of that.

Another performance, this time in the Tower Ballroom (or was it the Empress Ballroom?), where we had to march very carefully, because the dance floor was like an ice rink. When we played Retreat, the acoustics made it sound beautiful. We were treated to a meal by the Royal Artillery Association and then went to see a variety show performed by a troupe of midgets. I don't think any one of them was above four feet tall. A man billed as the smallest man in the world came on stage in a little cart, pulled by a cat! That was his act! We stayed overnight at a RAF Camp. Proper pillows instead of straw-filled palliasses! Sheer luxury!

We did several shows in London.

The Festival of Remembrance in the Albert Hall in 1951. I still have a photo! Was it the Festival Hall that was managed by Freddie Mills, the ex-light-heavyweight boxer? He came and had a few words with us as we waited to go in to do a
performance.

The Festival of Britain

I would never have had the opportunity to see that, had I not been in the band. Funny thing, all I can remember of the exhibits are the 'Skylon', a boiled-sweet making machine and the Shot Tower, which was a relic of the days when musket balls etc. were made by dropping molten lead from the top of the tower. As it fell, it solidified into balls and, presumably, the calibre was determined by how much lead was dropped. We did a show in the Festival Hall when Montgomery, Eisenhower and Churchill attended an Alamein reunion. Not too many people can claim to have seen them all in the flesh! We were standing in the foyer. Bob Ruffle called us up to attention and gave them a magnificent 'Chuck-up' as they walked through. Winston, puffing on his cigar, left a cloud of smoke in his trail. One lad was highly delighted because he had had a whiff of one of Churchill's cigars.

Horse Guard's Parade

We did several shows on there. On one in particular, we were countermarching with the massed bands of the Brigade of Guards. They towered above most of the Boys, but at that minute we felt as tall as them. We had a mention on the radio from an American celebrity who was being interviewed in a programme called 'In Town Tonight.' She claimed that our marching outclassed that of the Guards. 'Badge' Hunt didn't reckon so. He never did seem to be too happy with our performance and always scolded us to do better.

He really went to town with the fanfare trumpeters though, on one occasion. He had composed a fanfare which he had called 'The Hunter' and had been teaching the trumpeters for a day or two. The opportunity to play it came when he was asked to play the opening fanfare to one of the shows on Horse Guards Parade. At the rehearsal, the trumpeters lined up on the top of a building and Badge Hunt started to conduct. They got halfway through and then the fanfare petered out as one by one they forgot the tune. He was absolutely livid. He vowed that the Boys' Battery would never again be given the honour of performing the opening fanfare on any future shows.

On one occasion we were to perform twice, with tea at Wellington Barracks
between performances. We marched off Horse Guards behind a Scottish pipe band, who played all the way to Wellington Barracks. The march seemed to take hardly any time at all and we were quite sorry when it was over. After tea, we formed up and started to march back to Horse Guards. What a trek that was! We were amazed how far we had gone behind the bagpipes without realising it!

It's a pity that there are no 'Boy' entrants now. Lifting the school-leaving age caused its demise, I suppose. We were proud to wear our uniforms; shiny brassware and polished leather. Nowadays, if ever you see a soldier, he seems to be always wearing camouflage. Even those on recruitment drives you see in the High Street occasionally, they don't wear their best khaki.

Bradbury Lines

Famous for its association with the SAS, who renamed it 'Sterling Lines' but once had a mention in 'Coronation Street'. One of Emily Bishop's lodgers, 'Percy', was talking about his time in the Army and said: "We followed the artillery into Bradbury Lines." Obviously, fiction, because I doubt he was in the SAS. Sadly, a housing estate now! I wonder what's happened to Milne Troop's ghost! Roger Stephens, coming out of the Blanco shed with his webbing draped over his arms, stepped into the corridor and walked right through an apparition. He came running into the barrack room, looking as pale as what he had just seen!

I had a habit of shaving at night to save time in the morning. (My beard didn't get too evident for morning parade and inspection at that time.) One night I was in the Boys' NCOs' washroom and could plainly hear someone splashing about in the bath. I had my shave and was about to leave when I noticed the splashing had stopped. There were two bathrooms in the ablutions and I noticed both doors were open. No-one had passed me to go out yet there was no-one else in there. I checked both baths and they were bone-dry. I was never in there after 'Lights Out' again.

Did it rain in Hereford in 1952? I don't remember it raining. There was a
heatwave and I remember some of us sleeping outside on our groundsheets. Sunbathers were warned that any cases of sunburn would be considered to be self-inflicted wounds.

Monty's visit

This was the second time Monty had visited the Boys' Battery, as it was called then. He came to Kinmel Park for Parents' Day, and in 1952 to Bradbury Lines, again for Parents' Day. I had done something to my back and was unable to march, so was among the spectators at the parade that lined up on the square. Someone had a cine-camera and made a film of the occasion. It was shown on the camp cinema some time later and I remember a great cheer went up when the camera focussed on Bombardier McGoldrick, he of the jovial disposition who was the keeper of the 'McGoldrick Arms,' otherwise known as the 'detention barracks'.

"You horrible little monkey! Do you know what I would do to you? I'd burn you, that's what I'd do, burn you. I'd love to hear you sizzle!"

'Sir' Danny Soper

There were not too many of the Permanent Staff that would be remembered with any feeling of affection, but Bombardier Soper certainly was one. He would occasionally object when someone addressed him as 'Danny', insisting on being called 'Sir'. He would then be addressed as 'Sir Danny'. He had a claim to fame that I won't go into here, but all who knew him will know what I mean.

I learned of his whereabouts some time ago and we exchanged a couple of letters. I sent him some photos that were taken on Parents' Day '52. My mother and one of my sisters came for Parents' Day and brought along as guests my girlfriend and her mother. My girl had a Box Brownie camera and some of the photos that were taken I have reproduced in my computer and sent to Danny and some of the boys who were on them.

There are many memories that come to mind of my time in the Boys'. Proud ones, happy ones, funny ones, some not too cheerful ones, but all in all I would hate to have missed it.

On mustering, in Summer '52, I was posted to the King's Troop. Probably due to shovelling stuff deposited by horses, but more likely due to the jogging on horseback. The problem I had with my back at the time of Monty's visit cropped up again. I was strapped up in plaster of paris for a while, which did no good, so I was medically discharged!

A few weeks later I took the only job I was offered, as a blacksmith's striker! The job occasionally entailed swinging a 14lb sledgehammer and my very first job was to use it to smash up some old railway sleepers that were to be used to feed a furnace. I did it and had no more trouble with my back! Perhaps I should have been put with the farriers in the King's Troop, although I doubt they used 14lb sledgehammers!

Section 3 – Keith H Reeve. My memories of my service in the Junior Leaders' Regiment, Royal Artillery from 02 September 1957 to end December 1958 at Bradbury Lines, Hereford and at Oswestry

Copyright @ Keith H Reeve - March 2017 (reproduced with permission)

Prologue

I've noticed how, in our two Facebook groups (JLRRA and ex-JLRRA & ex-Boys' Regiment), most people's memories start with their arrival at their relevant rail station - Rhyl, Hereford or Nuneaton - which, whilst natural because it was their first day of service, probably leaves their much fuller and much more interesting story left untold.

You'll all know what I mean when I say that it's the stories you told your new colleagues and mates back in your first week or so.

Remember? Remember how great it was talking to and learning about one another? Telling the other new lads about your own city, your town, your village? Why you joined? The joke swapping? The banter? The beginnings of new friendships? Remember the new camaraderie developing between you all? Most likely it's probably receded into the recesses of your mind, but I hope I stimulate you to think about that first night - that first week, and those first several weeks - because that was the beginning of your comradeship – a time-period you ought to revive in your own minds.

Remembering (and Forgetting) Names and Faces

I've realised that the forgetting of names and faces has happened to most lads who were in the JLRRA and Boys' Regiment. I suppose it was inevitable... but I find it very sad that most lads can't recall most of the lads they served with all those years ago. I can still recall most things and events we experienced, but my own ability to remember names and faces has mostly gone. I've noticed in most posts on our two Facebook groups that it's become a common problem. The saddest part for me was when I joined the Facebook groups of the JLRRA and the ex-JLRRA and ex-Boys' Regiment around August 2016, and announced myself in a posting and when and where I had served, publishing two photographs of myself from 1957/58. Nobody, but nobody, remembered me! It's a strange old world... but I confess that I find it very sad... disappointing at least. In fact, I found it rather alarming that nobody could remember me at all.

I can only recall just a few names and their faces from my days. Teddy McKenzie (yes, he was 'Teddy' back then), Jack Pothecary, Thommo Thomson from 'Bott'm o' Town, Brighouse, Yorkshire', Kes (Keith) from Yorkshire (nicknamed after the hawk from the film), Keith 'Little' from Doncaster. I remembered the name of Tom Rutherford from Ironside Troop. Tom joined the JLRRA just over two months after myself, but until he sent me his photo from those days I had forgotten his face.

I remember Herbert Slaughter from Norwich, who joined in 1958. Elsewhere, I have written a posting about his commendable charity efforts for the RAA. Herbert served for about 30 years. He's known to large numbers of you.

I recall a lad called Keith Rance from Oxford, who was in Ironside Troop. I remember him because he was such a good footballer. He was a bit of a loner. He actually joined my next Regiment (3 RHA) from Germany when I was serving in the Aden Protectorate. Strangely, he couldn't remember me.

Oh, but just as sadly, my memory won't allow me to forget the names of some of the Permanent Staff NCOs who were supposed to look after the lads, but who cowardly turned their backs on us and protected bullying Borstal boys instead. Those permanent members of staff are probably all dead now. But my thoughts about what they allowed to happen to the lads under their protection are 'may they rot in hell'. Nasty? Well, read my thoughts about them and the Borstal boys and you may remember and understand.

I'll remind you that I detested bullies - and still do to this day!

So, in writing from my memory about most of the events which occurred when I served, I'm hoping that this will stimulate all of you into not only remembering events which occurred whilst you served, but hopefully might just bring to mind a few names and faces, and remind you of your lives before you joined Boys' Service.

Inclusion of Fox Troop as part of my JLRRA Memories

I've included my 12 weeks in Fox Troop at Oswestry, Shropshire as part of my time as a Junior Leader because, in my view, although I had mustered from the JLRRA, I seriously believe that my time as a Junior Leader had simply been extended to include the more arduous and rigorous 12-week programme in Fox Troop, training which was designed to bring out further leadership qualities. I appreciate that there are differing opinions amongst you as to what stage or which age we fully mustered, but for me, it was when I fully mustered from Boys' Service at the end of my 12 weeks of the Junior Leaders' Continuation Troop, known as Fox Troop. I was then destined to join a special artillery regiment – namely the 3rd Regiment, Royal Horse Artillery.

My Trip Down Memory Lane

My own trip down memory lane, about my time in JLRRA at Hereford, starts with the reasons why I joined the Junior Leaders' Regiment, Royal Artillery. It covers a period of my life from 5-and-a-half years old onward, because what happened back then had a big impact on what I subsequently did in the Junior Leaders' Regiment, RA, so I have felt it necessary to start there. My reasons are explained below.

The Beginning of My Hatred of Bullies

The beginning of my hatred or detestation of bullies started in the Thomas Anguish Children's Home in Norwich where I had been placed at the age of 5 years and 6 months old. I was a little, skinny boy - timid as hell - with no self-confidence, shy and nervous as hell. A boy aged 8 years, named Frank Cooper, bullied all the other 60 boys and girls. One day, when he started beating up a very small boy aged about 4-and-a-half, I found I couldn't stand for it any more. It went against all principles I had acquired in my few short years. I ran up to him, shouting and screaming at him to stop. Bam! I got whacked - then kicked. Infuriated (and now bloody and hurt) I tore into him with everything I had.

That day I think I must have invented Victor Meldrew's phrase: "I really don't believe it" - because I recall actually saying those words back in 1946 when the bully sank to the ground - crying his head off!

All the watching children called me a hero for taking on and beating the bully. I actually felt guilty for causing hurt to the bully and I felt embarrassment for showing up my timid self and putting myself in the limelight of attention. But this feeling went away very quickly when he got up and pounded my back, yelling that I had only beaten him because, he alleged, I had put stones in my hands to make my punches hurt him. His lies made me so angry that he ended up on the ground again - defeated for not just a second time, but for the remainder of his time in the Thomas Anguish Children's Home.

I have written about this incident, because, although I didn't realise it at the time, from thereon it played an important part in my life. In April 1952, the Thomas Anguish Children's Home closed. Us kids were all put into different Children's Homes. The former bully went to a different Home to me. I was sent to the Woodlands Children's Home, where there were mixed ages, but several were older and bigger than me, up to the age of 15 years.

Thankfully, I didn't get bullied, but only because I discovered my older brother was in this Home. I had completely forgotten I had a brother (and a sister and parents) whilst in the first Home, so it was great, albeit strange, having an older brother at this stage of my life. He was different to me and took savage delight in viciously fighting anyone who tried to bully me.

A year later I was fostered out with a Mr and Mrs Carn. Just over 2-and-a-half years later they emigrated to Australia. I was then in my fourth year of school. Being put back into a Children's Home again seriously impacted on my schooling. At age 15, I had to leave the Children's Home and was placed with a foster woman aged about 65 to 70 years old. This didn't help my schooling at all, and because of the difference in our ages we didn't really communicate. But, of course, I wasn't on my own, although I remained under the care of the Norwich Children's Department.

I've written about this childhood incident because it was to have a profound effect on me in later life. Even at my young age of 5-and-a-half to 6 years old it moulded two principles into my whole being - these being that I detested bullies from that moment on, and that I detested liars. In telling you about my early life in the Children's Homes and with foster parents I am not seeking sympathy, because I came to realise much later in life that I probably had a much better life than many of the lads who joined the Junior Leaders. So, I am truly grateful for that.

Later, within my memories of my service in the JLRRA, you will read how I became a one-man crusade against bullies in the Junior Leaders' Regiment, putting not only my career severely in jeopardy, but also my physical welfare. I've devoted a lot of words to all of this, and I hope you will read all of it below.

Norfolk Army Cadet Force, Royal Artillery

Immediately prior to joining the Army, I was in the Norfolk Army Cadet Force, Royal Artillery. Thought I was the 'bees-knees'. I thought I was the smartest dressed, best Gunner on the 25-pounder artillery piece, could fire a decent .303 rifle, and I thought I was the best sounder of the cavalry-trumpet and bugle. I had even been picked to sound the bugle at the Odeon Cinema in Norwich before the start of the war film 'A Hill in Korea'. Our band had performed at the Royal Tournament at Earl's Court in the same year. Only when the stadium was filling up but - boy, oh boy, was I proud? Proud - but not big-headed.

At a tender age, I had learned prior to this that nobody should become big-headed - only proud. I had learned that big-headed people often became a type of bully. I discovered very early in my life that I detested bullies with a passion from the very young age of just under 6 years old.

School - Bullied by School Teachers

Despite having been institutionalised by my time in Children's Homes, spread over 11 years, with a 2-and-a-half year period plus a 1-and-a-half year period of being fostered by two lots of foster parents within those years, I was fortunate that I had attended a school which had a fifth year, which enabled us to learn and take the GCE – the General Certificate of Education. Unfortunately, two factors worked against me achieving what I needed to achieve. The first, the disruption to my life and education caused by my first foster parents emigrating to Australia when I was 14-and-a-half years old – which threw me back into a Children's Home. The second was the attitude of two of the teachers, who looked down on me because of my background in Children's Homes and with foster parents. They also looked down on another lad who had no father. They treated us very unfairly, which to me is itself is a form of bullying.

One was Mr. Denham, the English teacher. The other was Mr. Fitch, the history teacher, who was particularly nasty. Mr. Fitch just happened to also be the careers teacher, who was supposed to help every pupil with their future career in an office, insurance or banking job, or similar, provided enough GCEs were passed. In early 1957, he sneeringly told me at interview what types of office jobs I would have to do, but implied that I would fail my exams in any case because of my background. He said he saw me as a failure in life. He said that I would end up working in one of the noisy, smelly shoe factories in Norwich.

Rebellion Against the Bullying School Teacher

I rebelled against his words, manner and attitude. Out of the blue, I told him straight that I was going to join the Army. In saying those words, in my mind's eye, I was picturing the Royal Fusiliers Recruiting Sergeant who used to come to our Norfolk Army Cadet Force Royal Artillery meetings to try to persuade cadets to join the Royal Fusiliers.

The Fusiliers Sergeant was always dressed in full dress uniform, with its chain mail, and looked a very fine 'fart-smeller' (smart-fella) indeed. The careers teacher snarled back at me that I would be wasting my education and that I had to do what I was told by him. That did it. Boy - did that do it.

I snarled back: "You're nothing but a bully. You're supposed to help me but all you want to do is demean me and put me down. You're a disgrace and now you've caused me to decide that I'm going into the Army. Just wait until the Head Teacher hears about your bigoted, bullying manner towards me!"

My Decision to Join the Royal Artillery

The very next day I told the Children's Authorities that I wanted to join the Army - the Royal Artillery - when I left school in July 1957, irrespective of my exam results. They contacted my waster of a father who had dumped me and my brother in two different children's homes, seeking his signature to agree to my joining the Army.

Apparently, he gave it like a shot, so I'm told, although I didn't learn about this, or how he had treated me, until 2008 when I researched the Children's Home and Children's Department records to find out about my record in the Children's Homes.
So, ultimately it was a bully - a supposedly mature, grown-up person - who caused my destiny to be the JLRRA. Bullying in the Children's Homes, and at school by two teachers, a love of the Army in the Norfolk Army Cadet Force, Royal Artillery, and the image of a Royal Fusiliers Recruiting Sergeant, were the main factors behind my decision.

Being institutionalised by the Children's Home system helped enormously in causing me to think I could be better off amongst other people of the same age groups, was another factor. I was institutionalised to the point when you can still feel alone within a crowd of about 60 other kids who were the same as yourself. I was institutionalised to the point that I had completely forgotten that I had parents and two siblings. Perhaps the fact that I felt alone in my life helped me make my decision to want to join the Royal Artillery, and catapulted me into the Junior Leaders' Regiment, Royal Artillery.

I am actually grateful to those factors, and to those people, who caused me to have a wonderful time in the JLRRA… but... was it all really so wonderful in JLRRA? Well, you'll all remember there were good times, and not-so-good times, and some bad times. There were hard times, soul-defeating times, soul-destroying times, unpleasant times, proud times and some wonderful times. Memories I hope to share with you and also revive some of your own.

My Journey from Norwich to Hereford

I left my fine city of Norwich early on 2nd September 1957. The school holidays, which would officially end my school term, just wouldn't go fast enough, because I was longing for my first day of Army service to arrive. I was driven to Norwich Thorpe Station in the Children's Authorities' car.

Arriving at the station I experienced getting on a steam train for the very first time and, as it started to pull out of Norwich Station, the thrill and strangeness of it caused all sorts of emotions to arise - trepidation, excitement, wonder at the clanking sounds of the pistons and wheels, the smoke and steam from the engine, the piercing whistle as we entered the first tunnel. Apprehension of the new world I was heading for. Being alone! Had I made a major mistake? If so, there was nothing I could do to reverse it, because I had been firmly told that there was no facility to buy myself out until I was into my six years in the regular army, called the Colours. What would the west country be like? I'd been told that it was warmer than my own fine county of Norfolk which suffered from the extremes of the east wind and the north wind.

I was really looking forward to seeing the Colchester and London areas of countryside because, hundreds of years beforehand, in 60

A.D., the Norfolk Queen - Boudicea or Boudicca - had marched down to those areas with the Iceni tribes of Norfolk and North Suffolk to take on the Romans. Queen Boudicea and the Iceni tribes inflicted heavy defeats on the Romans - so much so that a huge gathering of Roman troops was then collected from other parts of the country and marched to the London and Colchester areas. Boudicea and the Iceni tribes were battered and overcome.

I let myself imagine that I could see ghostly figures of our Iceni tribes battling with Roman soldiers, hearing the battle cries and seeing people dying in valiant effort, and my mind jumped ahead, envisaging that by joining the Army I could be called upon to fight. I actually shuddered at this thought because, apart from taking on a bully at the tender age of about 6, I wasn't somebody who wanted to physically fight. I shrugged aside that particular thought and told myself that if the Army was going to make a man of me, then I would just have to be brave about whatever was thrown at me - because I was going to Hereford… to be a soldier.

My train from Norwich arrived at London Liverpool Station after a two-hour 20-minutes journey. I knew that I had to get across to Paddington Station on the London Underground, to catch my next train to Hereford. I was disappointed to realise that by travelling on the London Underground I wouldn't be able to see the statues of two Norfolk heroes – namely the Queen Boudicca statue on the Victoria Embankment and the Admiral Lord Horatio Nelson, in Trafalgar Square.
The London Underground seemed a maze of train routes to me. I panicked a bit. Fortunately for me, back in those days, people in London talked to other people, and a kindly person helped me find the right tube train to the main Paddington Station.

At Paddington Station, I boarded another British Rail steam train to Hereford for my second leg of my long journey from Norwich in the east of the country. Through the rolling countryside of central England, the train headed towards what I had been told was the 'sleepy' but lovely county of Herefordshire in the west of the country.

Arrival at Hereford

My train arrived at Hereford Station, having given off a long piercing whistle whilst still about a mile away, and then a shorter 'toot' as it drew into the station, emitting a whoosh of steam and clouds of smoke from its funnel, a screeching of brakes and banging of pistons.

Dismounting, I looked for the telephone on which I would have to call for transport to Bradbury Lines. However, a truck was already there waiting for me and two other lads who'd been on the same train. I tried to remember the route to the camp but soon gave up. I didn't particularly enjoy the journey in the bouncing truck, but it didn't take long.

Spider Blocks

We arrived at the barrier across the road entrance to Bradbury Lines Camp and had to dismount to sign in. We were then driven through the camp to the Recruits' Troop 'spider' building. A 'spider' building was constructed of six barrack rooms, with a central ablutions area. It was made of wood. Half of our building was for the Recruits' Troop, whilst the other half was occupied by Dickson Troop.

Recruits' Troop

What a great experience my first night in the Recruits' Troop of the JLRRA became. Most of the lads in my barrack room had arrived that day, whilst some had arrived the day before.

An NCO of the Permanent Staff had told us that we weren't allowed to go to the NAAFI (which we discovered was the Army name for the shop and canteen) for two weeks, and so we had to appoint one of our number to get things for us if we wanted anything. Most new lads didn't have any money in any case.

Animatedly we started chatting amongst ourselves, then calling across the room to make acquaintance with everyone. Even the shyest amongst us had to join in. It was tremendous - and never to be forgotten. Joke-telling started, with everyone cracking-up at the jokes by a lad called Keith from Yorkshire, who had been quickly been given the nickname 'Kes' after the hawk named 'Kes' in the film of the same name.

There were three lads named 'Keith' in our barrack room, so the other lads called a short lad named Keith from Doncaster by the nickname 'Keith-Little'. He was the shortest of us three, and they gave me the nickname 'Keith-Tich' because I wasn't much bigger in any case, although bigger than Keith-Little. A weird form of logic there.

The only joke I can remember Kes telling us all those years ago, was the one about the gnats' eyelids. The joke was along these lines:

"A boy was sent to a hardware store for a packet of gnats' eyelids. The store man's son searched for these but couldn't find any, so he asked his father.

His father said "Just tell him to clear off – he's having you on. Gnats don't have eyelids".

The boy returned home and was told to go back and buy a packet of moth balls instead. He returned to the store and asked the owner's son for a packet of moth balls.

The store man's son told him, "Now don't mess me about - I'm sure if gnats don't have eyelids, moths don't have balls".

In those days, the joke was hilarious.

Back in the 1950s, most boys joined the Junior Leaders from the age of 15 years and onwards, but I was late in joining at 16 years and 8 months, because I'd had to wait until the school holidays were over after doing a fifth year. I was in effect, a sort of older 'brother', expected to know much more than the younger lads. I think the permanent staff NCOs thought that I should be streets ahead of the younger lads, but this wasn't the case. My institutionalisation in the

Children's Home had made me far less street-wise about life in general, so, if anything, I was more naïve than many of the others.

In the morning, we were awakened early by the banging of pick helves and swagger sticks on the steel lockers. This certainly woke everyone up! First it was the ablutions area to wash and shave (provided you had whiskers or stubble) and to clean teeth. Then we formed up outside in three ranks and were marched at the double over to the cookhouse for breakfast. This was almost calamitous because most lads had no idea of drill, and we're turning the wrong way and bumping into one another. It had us all laughing our heads off at the hilarious situation. At that point, none of us envisaged what masters of drill we would become.

The Make-up of the Junior Leaders' Regiment, Royal Artillery at Bradbury Lines, Hereford – Batteries and Troops

After breakfast, we were sat down and told about the Junior Leaders' at Bradbury Lines, Hereford. We were also told about the history of the Boys' Service RA - from the Boys' Battery, RA at Woolwich, to the Boys' Regiment RA at Rhyl and then its move to Hereford, and then the change of name to the Junior Leaders' Regiment, Royal Artillery, around February/March 1957. We were also told the different ways in which we would be trained, compared to how it had been in the Boys' Regiment, RA.

We were told that the Junior Leaders' Regiment, RA was divided into Troops, within two Batteries. We were to be assigned to one of the Troops – provided we passed out of Recruits, of course.

The two Batteries were: 234 Roberts Battery and 235 Campbell Battery.

In 234 Roberts Battery there were four Troops, namely:
Ironside Troop, Alanbrooke Troop, Milne Troop and Ramsay Troop.

Each Troop wore a coloured identification flash on their sleeve, to distinguish each lad to his own Troop, and from the other Troops, as follows:

Ironside Troop - Purple; Alanbrooke Troop - Blue; Ramsay Troop - Green; Milne Troop - Red.

In 235 Campbell Battery there were also four Troops, namely: Dickson Troop, Borgard Troop, Shrapnel Troop and Gunn Troop.

Again, each Troop wore a coloured identification flash on their sleeve, to distinguish each lad to his own Troop, and from the other Troops, as follows:

Dickson Troop - Orange; Shrapnel Troop - White; Borgard Troop - Yellow; Gunn Troop - Grey

Kitted Out with Uniform

Later, we were double-marched over to the Quartermaster's Stores where we were issued with uniform. This amusingly included a small cloth packet called a 'housewife', which we got told we would need to sew on buttons and darn our socks from now on.

The Permanent Staff Sergeant told us that from that moment on: "You've no longer got a mother to wipe your arse or anything else. I'm your mother now and I'll be kicking your arses if you don't measure up."

Outside he told how we would be shrinking the massive berets we had been issued with, and how we would be 'bulling' our boots so that the toe caps looked like mirrors.

"You're going to be the best Recruits' Troop to have ever joined the Junior Leaders' Regiment, Royal Artillery. You will make me proud of you, or God help you," he threatened. His name was Sergeant Bird - a big man with a stentorian voice.

Haircuts

Then we were doubled over to the barber's shop. We dreaded being given a severe short back and sides, but the haircuts turned out better than anticipated; we were relieved because the era of Rock'n'Roll and the 'Teddy Boy' culture had crept into fashion, and with it the stylish hair.

First Day on the Drill Square

Our second day was pretty bad for us because it involved the drill square. This transpired to be quite a monumental occasion. We were shouted at, screamed at, called all sorts of names and insults by a Permanent Staff Bombardier (the surname 'Roberts' comes to mind) and by Sergeants Bird and Gee. At the end of the first session we felt utter prats – humiliated. We felt that we were all useless.

I came in for a lot of abuse as soon as I mentioned that I had been in the Norfolk Cadet Force, Royal Artillery. Instead of this being found fairly acceptable by the Permanent Staff NCOs, they really put me through the wringer. Bloody bullies. Vindictive bastards. It seemed to me they wanted to destroy me. What sort of sadistic humour did they have? What have I let myself in for? I saw these Permanent Staff NCOs as bullies, but felt impotent against them. In the afternoon, we got another dose of this humiliating, soul-destroying treatment.

During that evening, we talked amongst about the day's demoralisation. We were cowed. Not broken - but we had suffered. None liked how we had been treated but there was an acceptance that our lives had changed – dramatically - forever.

Visits by 'Friendly' Dickson Troop Lads

On our second evening, we were visited by a few lads from Dickson Troop, who occupied the other half of our spider block. They brought with them the makings for coffee and tea, and milk and sugar.

"You'll get hot water down the ablutions," they told us.

Our NCOs had told us that we weren't allowed to the NAAFI for two weeks, but, in any case, most lads didn't have any money to buy things there. The Dickson lads told us it would be free on this first occasion.

The second evening brightened up when the same Dickson Troop lads came to see us again. They brought their tea and coffee etc., but this time saying they would have to make a 'small' charge to help pay for their wares - but payment was deferred until payday.

Friday – First Payday

Friday, and it was payday. We all received 10 shillings and sixpence each in cash out of our 31 shillings and sixpence total pay - the rest being held back for us under a 'Credits A' and 'Debits B' scheme.

Hardly any of the lads had earned money at all in 'Civvy Street', so we kinda thought we were all rich. To put this, 1957, pay into perspective, the 10 shillings and six pence is equivalent to £0.525 in today's money, and the total pay of 31 shillings and 6 pence per week is equivalent to £1.563 in today's money. Yes... we were all very rich, indeed.

Our First Realisation about the Borstal Boys

The Dickson Troop lads again visited us that evening, on pay-day, but this time to collect their money. We couldn't believe it when they tried to charge each one of us who had availed themselves of the Dickson lads' tea and coffee, the sum of two shillings each, which was one-fifth of the money we had just been paid that morning.

The recruits were astounded at this, then angry. We all refused to pay, although we were agreeable to pay a small amount of money – after all they had supplied the makings for tea and coffee – presumably out of their own pockets?

The Dickson lads walked out, their attitude now nasty, with the threat that: "You'll regret it". During the early hours they returned to our room and started to beat the hell out of us as we lay sleeping. They used their hob-nailed boots and sticks to strike us, on our bodies and faces, yelling that there would be more if we didn't pay their demands.

The next morning, on parade, the Permanent Staff NCOs asked about our bleeding faces. On being told, they dismissed it as 'high jinks' and that it was our first lesson in becoming real soldiers. I was angry about their attitude because to me they were covering up the bullying. But I was too timid to act on my own. The other lads in the room were of the opinion 'well, nothing could be done'. This incident made me realise that most people didn't want to tackle the bad things in life, which thus allowed such bullying to go on - and seemingly covered over by what I saw as cowardly Permanent Staff NCOs.

'Spit & Polish' – 'bulling' our kit, and all that jazz

From our fairly meagre pay (we didn't feel so rich after a while) we were told that we had to buy black polish for our boots, Brasso for our brasses and Blanco for our webbing. We also had to each buy a candle and matches. These were for 'bulling' our kit which, we learned, had to be done to an extremely high standard.
I think Sergeant Bird may have shown us the rudiments of this, but we learned mainly from Junior Leaders from the Troops which we were designated to go to after passing out of Recruits Troop.

The purpose of the candle was to heat the back of a spoon which was then applied to the toecaps of the boots, in order to get rid of the pimples and make the leather perfectly smooth for 'mirror' polishing with the black polish and spit, with just a hint of water. The Brasso was used for buffing the brasses on cardboard, to make these really smooth and gleam. The Blanco was used on our webbing.

Hour upon hour, every evening, was spent on making tiny circles on the toecaps of our boots. If you got the combination of polish, spit and water wrong on your toecaps, then you had messed up and had to start the whole process again. Everyone soon conquered this, and boots began to take on a lustre, then a gleam, then a 'mirror' shine. Mind you, it took weeks.

On our brasses, all the imperfections in the surfaces of the brass began to disappear with the buffing, until these were really smooth and shiny. We learned how to Blanco our webbing perfectly as time went by.

We also learned from the experienced Junior Leaders who helped us how to make a 'tailored' beret from the giant 'flying saucers' we had been issued with, using a combination of hot and cold water to shrink these and mould them into a good shape. I can't remember exactly how we did it, but many of you will know that it wasn't the simplest of things. Just a few berets proved almost impossible to shrink. Fortunately, Sergeant Bird didn't want anyone on parade wearing a big beret, so he arranged shrinkable replacements for these.

We asked the friendly experienced Junior Leaders about making our caps look better – like those we had seen on the heads of Junior Leaders in the Troops. They told us that peaks were slit and pushed up to make a better angle, but that 'woe betide us' if we did this whilst in Recruits. They showed how to get away with moulding the back of the cap a little – just enough to not get in trouble.

We learned about putting weights (such as bicycle chains) at the bottom of trousers, to make these trousers hang better and look smarter – but were warned by the other lads not to do it in Recruits Troop or 'all hell would be let loose'.

Assessment for the Band

The following Monday we were doubled to the band room. In the band room we were all assessed on our ability to sound the trumpet and bugle, and also whether we could rattle the drum sticks on the taut skin of the side drum. Having been in the Norfolk Cadet Force Royal Artillery, sounding both trumpet and bugle, I assumed that I would excel.

However, when a couple of JLRRA trumpeters sounded their own trumpets, I realised that I was just making a blaring sound on my instruments, which sounded bloody awful by comparison. Nevertheless, Trumpet Major Frost said he thought I would make a good trumpeter one day, and told me I was selected for sounding practice every week, and might get selected for the JLRRA Band.

Boy, oh boy, was I dead chuffed. Other lads who had made sufficient impression on him with the noises they had made were also selected for sounding practice. Several others were selected by Trumpet Major Timmins for drummer training.

Training

The following days and weeks were a blur of various training - square bashing, map reading training, training on the 25 pounder artillery pieces (guns), rifle training - and Army Education. Some were selected for signals training, whilst others were selected for training as TARAs (Technical Assistant Royal Artillery). I struck lucky and was selected to be a TARA.

The Army Education System

The Army Education System run at Bradbury Lines had three levels. Everyone was placed in a level depending on tests of their ability. It was intended that Junior Leaders were intended to be just that – real leaders at a junior level - with education certificates to pass to prove their competence. Whilst most of the lads moaned about it, because they thought their school days were over, all of them came to realise the importance of this additional education, and most relished the opportunities it presented to them - especially the possible incremental pay increases for passing various training.

Our First Sports Day.

We had already been told which Troop we would be going into when we passed out as recruits. We were told that on our designated sports days we would participate with the lads of the Troop we would be joining. I was designated to be in Ironside Troop.

The first sports day was football. During the match, I received another rude awakening. I wasn't very good but stuck out a leg and foot when a lad from the opposing team came running towards me with the ball. My tackle caused me to come away with the ball, and I hoofed it up the field - quite pleased with myself. A few seconds later I was violently pushed to the ground and kicked, with four snarling boys shouting: "You're not allowed to tackle him or any of us". Then they ran upfield. In the second half, I tackled and won the ball. Again, I was flattened to the ground, kicked viciously, and told very harshly that I had been warned about tackling various boys.

They shouted at me: "Ablutions, after the match!"

I stayed dirty, because I was scared.

Shortly, four of these 'Borstal boys' came and got me and wrestled me down to into the ablutions area. There they gave me a cold bath, with a hard scrubbing-brush and then I was beaten, and given threats not to ever tackle the Borstal boys again.

"What've I done wrong?" I shouted in fright and in pain.

"You've defied the Borstal boys and you don't get away with that. We rule the camp".

I know I was scared. I knew I had been given a real hiding - but I was also angry at the bully boys, although I wasn't sure what, if anything, I could do about it. I vowed to myself that I wouldn't allow myself to be continually bullied. Something would have to be done.

Learning More About the Borstal Boys

Later that evening, some of the lads from Ironside Troop came to our Recruits room, and told us how the 'Borstal boys' ruled the camp and how these lads ganged together, whereas most decent lads didn't gang together. So the camp was in the grip of the Borstal boys, who were in every one of the Troops.

I learned that these so-called 'Borstal khaki porridge boys' were really bad lads who had been sentenced to a spell in a Borstal Institution. I learned that Borstal Institutions were youth detention centres (prisons for young people) which were run by HM Prison

Service and intended to reform seriously delinquent young people who had committed serious crimes, especially crimes of violence - but the ones in the JLRRA had been given the chance to join the JLRRA instead of serving their time in the Borstal Institution, and had taken that option.

I learned much more about the Borstal boys and what they got up to. It seemed that there were members of this 'Borstal khaki porridge army' in every one of the Troops of the JLRRA - and that they did indeed 'rule the camp' - operating all sorts of rackets to get our money - and they had the 'power' to bully and beat the other lads whenever they felt the need to assert their power. A power given to the bullies because, it seemed to me, the Permanent Staff NCOs didn't know, or didn't want to know, or couldn't care less, how to curtail it. More about them later.

Food, Glorious Food – A Bed of Your Own - A Whole New World!

As the days and weeks went past, some of the stories I remember most from a lot of the new Recruits, were their utter amazement at finding out they would get three square meals a day. To say they were 'gob-smacked' is putting it very mildly.
Many talked about living in small terraced houses, and surviving on food such as jam sandwiches, sugar sandwiches, bread and dripping, occasionally a nutritious soup or stew, and very occasionally a cooked dinner.

With learning this, I realised that in the Children's Home I had lived like a king by comparison. I had always had three meals a day in the Home, and couldn't understand why most of the other Recruits didn't have the same type of food, and quality of food, that I had enjoyed. I mean, when I got to the age of 10 years old, I was even allowed supper! It was a cheesy sauce on toast – it gave me nightmares!

I learned from the others about how many of their fathers used to go down the pub, spending their meagre incomes on beer – and fags. Apparently, many would get drunk, so there was very little money to buy food.

I learned that many would take it out on the boys' mothers and the boys themselves, often beating them with their leather belts, or a cane, or even their fists.

To me their world was alien to the one I had lived in, despite the fact that I got disciplined by the House Mothers and the male Superintendent of the Home, and subsequently by foster parents, sometimes beaten with a hard slipper and with a cane on many, many other occasions.

No, to be frank, I had entered a world quite similar to the one I had grown up in, with three square meals a day, a bed of my own like I had in the Home. I slept in a dormitory with other boys, which our new barrack room closely reminded me. But I had entered a world without beatings from those in charge of me, but with the exception of beatings dished out by bullying Borstal boys whenever it suited them.

In the Home, I had lived with about 60 other children of varying ages. About half were boys and half were girls - but, such was the situation of our trauma in being abandoned by parents into the Home, virtually every child usually felt 'alone' within the crowd of other children. There were friendships, but usually most children felt alone – isolated.

Here, in Recruits Troop, everyone discovered new friends. There was a growing camaraderie. I loved it. I learned much more about their previous lives. It was a real eye-opening, and even mind-blowing, learning about their lives. I felt I belonged.

I learned from many of the other lads that they'd had to share a bed with their siblings, several sleeping in a big bed. I learned about the 'dry' end and the 'wet' end – but then I knew all about wet beds because many of the children in the Home wet their beds. The difference was that in the Home there would be dry sheets to change the bed, whereas in the small terraced houses, with their limited facilities, their beds had to stay wet, and only dried out with the heat from their bodies. Many houses didn't have electricity or gas. Many had outside toilets.

I learned that very few of them had ever had a hot bath, which I had enjoyed in the Children's Home and when with the foster parents. I learned that some homes had a galvanised metal bath which took a lot of filling with hot water, which took simply ages to heat on the stove or the fire, and that the whole family took it in turns to have a bath – in the same water. I found this almost too incredible to believe - but was assured that it was so. I learned that there were public baths, but then money was needed for essentials like food and clothes, coal, etc.

Now, in their whole new world of the Junior Leaders at Bradbury Lines, Hereford, they found there were several baths down in the ablutions area, with usually an unlimited amount of hot water – where they could bathe to their hearts content. Many lads took full advantage of this topping up the hot water as it got colder, delighting in this new-found experience.

In writing about the comparison of my life in the Children's Home, and the lives of my fellow Recruits, I am definitely not seeking sympathy for the life I had been made to have. I am trying to write about what I learned about the lives of my fellow Recruits, and endeavouring to show how many had lived quite hard lives and had entered into a whole new world by joining the Junior Leaders.

Much later in life I learned that, way back in the 1950s, there was no such thing as a Family Allowance, or a Child Benefits System, or an Unemployment Benefits System if they couldn't get a job. There was no real system from which people could get extra money to make their lives a bit easier. Men had to graft extremely hard in whatever job they could get, in whatever part of the country they lived. Mothers didn't really get to have a job because they were too busy being housewives and mothers to several children at the same time, and trying to manage on the meagre wages which their husbands brought home – which were usually depleted by their husband drinking and smoking.

I also learned much later in life that there was a system called "Public Assistance" for the worst family cases. Usually when the husband couldn't get work. But men had to plead severe hardship in order just to get a few shillings. There were also voluntary charity schemes.

So, I learned that many of our new recruits had lived a life of virtual poverty before joining the Junior Leaders (or Boys' Regiment, as it used to be called).

Of course, whilst hearing these incredible tales from my new friends in Recruits in 1957, I didn't know about any of what I've written in the above paragraphs. It is only by applying information I had learned much later in life that I am able to put into a kind of perspective, the lives that many of my new-found friends had lived before joining the Junior Leaders' Regiment.

Which is why I just couldn't understand, at that time back in 1957, my life had been so different to theirs. I know that at the time their stories made me feel like I had lived a 'privileged' life compared to most of them, but I also realised that they had had the benefits of living with a mother and father and, for many of them, with siblings, in a close family environment. Whereas I had become institutionalised, living alone despite living in a crowd, forgetting that I had parents and siblings. But, as it turned out for me much later in life, I realised that I had probably been far better off in a lot of ways than many of my new-found friends in the Junior Leaders' Recruits Troop back in 1957.

So, lads, have I taken you back in time? Have I jogged or jolted your memories? Have I managed to take you back from the arduous times you had in your whole new world of the Junior Leaders – to the times before you joined the Army? Sometimes it's good to think back – to those hard times – and then compare it to your life as it is now.

Gun Drill on the 25-Pounders

Not sure when it started, but we began to train on the 25-pounders - learning about the gun sights, calibration, manhandling the guns into position and manoeuvring them onto the circular gun bed. With never having done manual labour, this came quite hard to my delicate, office-type hands. At times our hands got hurt, sometimes trapped, or else it was the sheer manual effort of handling these metal beasts we had signed up to fight the enemies with. I quickly thought that the guns weren't for me, and became determined to pass my TARA training - so that I would be able to use my head rather than the arduous efforts needed on the guns. Later during our training, we had to go to Sennybridge Artillery Range in Wales. Circumstances changed my mind about being on the guns.

Singing in my Sleep

One morning I was told I had been singing in my sleep. Apparently, I had woken up some of the lads. Some had stayed awake and listened whilst others threw hob-nailed boots in my direction. The next evening some of the lads asked me if I would sing to them. Well, whilst I did love to sing when nobody else could hear me, I was a really shy boy – very self-conscious. They managed to overcome my shyness and so I sang. I can't remember which song I sang, but there were three 1957 hits which I knew, namely: 'Young Love' by Tab Hunter; 'A White Sports Coat (and a Pink Carnation')' by Terry Dean; and 'Diana' by Paul Anka.

My singing was applauded by everyone in the room, even those who had thrown boots at me. It soon developed into an occasional thing on many evenings in Recruits. Other lads would join in and we discovered there were others who could also carry a tune. It contributed hugely to our camaraderie in Recruits. I can't recall singing like this when I moved into Ironside Troop. Maybe my new 'fame' hadn't spread or, maybe, because I was the new boy again.

Fisticuffs with Jack Pothecary.

Although I didn't like to fight unless I had to, I launched myself at a lad named Jack Pothecary when he accidentally crashed a steel locker door into my face. I thought he had done it on purpose. I came off worst straightaway because Jack was bigger and stronger. We tussled and wrestled and tried to hit each other. Jack got in a few blows, whereas I was total crap. Other lads pulled us away from each other. Some calmed us down and told us to stop being prats because we could all get punished.

I was glad in a way that I hadn't hurt Jack Pothecary because he had quickly learned how to play a 'sweet' trumpet, almost as good as the established trumpeters in the band. My reasons were selfish, because I was hoping that Jack would show me how to play a melodic, melodious trumpet as well. Jack turned out to be the best trumpeter in the band later, so much so that he was posted to the Kings Troop Royal Horse Artillery at Woolwich, to be the Commanding Officer's Trumpeter.

Barrack Room and Kit Inspections

At least once a week, sometimes every day, our barrack rooms were inspected by the Permanent Staff NCOs in charge of us. It seemed to us that no matter how much effort we had put into making our barrack room tidy, the sadistic Permanent Staff had to rubbish our efforts.

We used to spend hours buffing the floorboards with a 'bumper' polisher. This was an oblong metal polisher with a wooden shaft attached to the base on a swivel, which was swung either side-to-side, or to-and-fro, across the wooden floorboards. It had a polishing pad on the base under which polishing cloths were positioned. We used a yellow coloured polish which, although to me smelled horrible, it did a great job – with lots and lots of effort swinging on the bumper, in getting our floor shiny. But, it was never good enough for our hard, nasty, taskmasters, the Permanent Staff NCOs.

Our bed kit had to be folded immaculately on the mattress, with blankets, sheets, and pillows placed in a particular neat and smart way. More often than not these Permanent Staff NCO bullies used to find fault with several of the lads' bed kits, shoving their canes into the neat pile of bedding, and sweeping it so it went across the floor.

"Bastards", I used to say under my breath.

Then they would turn their attention to the contents of our steel lockers. Inside the lockers all our clothes had to be stacked extremely neatly and uniformly. Our miscellaneous items like shaving gear, mess tins and mugs, etc. had to be arranged neatly also. Our aluminium mess tins had to be highly polished. Inevitably fault was always found with some of the lads' belongings in their steel locker, and the lousy Permanent Staff NCOs would just sweep everything on the floor. Sadistic bastards. How was this supposed to be making men of us? My blood boiled at their unnecessary bullying.

Occasionally an Officer would inspect and usually find fault, but not to the same extent as the Permanent Staff NCOs... but he would demand we correct the faults before a designated time later that day, and come back to inspect again. He wouldn't toss our stuff on the floor like the NCOs, so it didn't take much to put right what he said he had found wrong.

We got to realise, that many of the Officers were just 'making a point' and that by just 'tweaking' things, we usually passed his second inspection. What twerps Officers could be, being fooled by lads of 15, 16 and 17 years old. The accompanying Permanent Staff NCO was just itching to wipe the grins off our faces... but too cowardly to do it in front of an Officer.

Sounding Practice and Acceptance into the Band

'Sounding practice' happened almost daily. Everyone who had been selected for sounding the trumpet and bugle was gradually improving, although many continued to 'blare' the trumpet. However, there were two new lads who had somehow learned to make it sound melodic, melodious, sweet. A spotty-faced lad named Jack Pothecary impressed everyone with the beautiful sound he had started to produce. Another lad named 'Thommo' Thompson, from 'Bottom o' Town, Brighouse in Yorkshire,' wasn't far behind him. The problem for Thommo was that the Trumpet Major wanted him for the bass drum, because he was a big lad. He was dismayed that it was his size which caused him to have this problem, but then he been fooling around wearing and banging the big drum and was caught by Badgie Hunt, the Trumpet Major.

I begged Jack Pothecary to teach me how to sound the trumpet like him. He was unwilling at first because we had fought fisticuffs not long before, but we made up. Jack gave me tips, but advised me to watch his lips very carefully. Gradually I learnt to sound a 'sweet' trumpet... not as good as Jack, but good enough to be told by two Trumpet Majors, Timmins and Hunt, that I was now in the band. Everyone who had been selected into the band sounded what I called a 'sweet' trumpet and bugle.... no more blaring noises... everyone was melodious, melodic, 'sweet'! I had made it into the band! Great........bloomin' great.

I got my brass crossed trumpets to wear on my sleeve. I was so proud. Over the moon.

I wondered at the time why the Trumpet Majors didn't seem to be teaching any of the would-be sounders how to sound their instruments 'sweetly'. It appeared they just wanted to teach us the trumpet and bugle calls and the marches. But it transpired that they wanted everyone to exhaust their own efforts in making their instruments sound sweet, and then step in if necessary. They were determined though that there would be no failures, so in the end they gave their individual attention to anyone not achieving it by their own efforts - provided that the lad still showed potential.

The one thing which baffled me was why they didn't seem to teach the positioning of the head, and the lip and mouth positioning of the instruments when being sounded - before bad habits developed. The head had to be perfectly straight, not tilted forward or backwards or on the side. The trumpet and bugle had to be held perfectly horizontally, neither tilted up nor down, or to the side. The mouthpiece had to be placed perfectly on the lips, in the centre, with no up or down angle. It just wasn't allowed. A few lads put their mouthpiece slightly up or down of centre, but it was not allowed. Any lad who couldn't master these strict rules was OUT... no matter how sweetly he sounded the instruments. Standards were exceptionally high. We were told we were the best Junior Leaders' band in the entire British Army and that we would remain at the No.1 position! Without fail.

I was so, so proud to be a part of this superb band.

Tackling the Borstal Boys – ON MY OWN

Me... just little, quiet, self-conscious, shy, nervous me... made a major decision that somehow, come what may, I was going to try to stop the bullying and extortion rackets, and the fleecing and punishing by the Borstal bully boys. Although many of the lads grumbled, no-one else would do anything about the Borstal boys' nastiness. I became determined that I wasn't going to allow them to intimidate or bully me anymore, or anyone who couldn't stand up for himself. Maybe it was my older age which caused me to take on the bullies. I don't know. Well, at that time, I was a nine-stone weakling, who didn't like to physically fight, although Recruits Troop was gradually giving me more backbone, more determination and confidence to try to take on the impossible. So, taking my life in my hands, I realised that I had to do it by my sheer determination, resoluteness and presence, because I wasn't going to be able to physically beat them. There were too many of them.

I confronted the first group of bullies - the Dickson Troop Borstal boys. I told them bluntly that I was determined that their activities had to cease. They laughed at me. One decked me. I got up, bleeding. I stood resolute and determined and told them that I wasn't going to physically fight them, but I wasn't going to allow any of them to ever hit me again.

"Who the hell do you think you are?" they shouted. "We rule this camp. You're just nothing!"

I replied: "Has anyone ever stood up to you lads before, like I'm doing now?"

"No-one has ever stood up to us. No-one has ever been stupid enough", they replied.

"Well, I'm not stupid", I replied. "I just detest bullies and liars, and if you all don't pack it in you will seriously regret it."

"We'll give you 10 out of 10 for your pluck... now clear off!" they said.

I told them that I was staying put until they agreed to at least curtail their activities. I told them that if they beat me up, it would be reported right up the ladder and that they would find themselves under Army discipline. I told them bluntly that, one way or another, I would ensure that all their ways of extortion, beating weak lads up, etc, were finished. In doing this I was 'shit-scared', absolutely petrified... but somehow kept the strength in my quiet, shy, self-conscious voice. You could have knocked me down with a feather when they agreed to curtail, but obviously not stop, their obnoxious activities.

The next day I approached the Borstal boys in Ironside Troop, the troop I would be joining after Recruits, who had beaten me up on my first sports day with Ironside. I found that the Dickson Borstal boys had already spread the word. The biggest lad didn't give me a chance to speak... he just threw a hard punch at me. I got up and exploded my right fist straight into his nose and mouth, and put him down. I broke his nose. I harshly told the others not to interfere, but that I wasn't there to fight... but if they beat me up I would report it right up the ladder and then they would find themselves under Army discipline.

My tactics worked, and I told these Ironside Borstal bullies bluntly that I wasn't going away, and although it might seem that I was 'a one-man crusade', I would come out on top... somehow... 'Shit or bust'!

The Ironside Borstal bullies said they would reduce, but wouldn't stop, their activities. I was amazed, and asked myself did I really believe them? Did they really mean it?
Word had quickly spread to the Borstal boys in the other Troops, because the next evening I was kidnapped by some of them and taken

to a quiet part of the camp where, instead of getting beaten up like I feared, the 25-30 Borstal boys who were gathered there demanded to know why I was challenging them.

I felt very scared. I told them of the bullying incident in the Children's Home when I was 5-and-a-half years old and how I had tackled that bully, and how it had caused me to detest bullies from that time on, and face up to them when necessary. The ringleaders thought I should be given a good kicking but somehow, petrified, I mouthed off that they would need to kill me because I wasn't going to go away. I must have been convincing because they all told me that they thought I was brave but extremely stupid, but they realised from my determined attitude that I would be a thorn in their sides.

During all this, I found that I had, indeed, got very brave (or stupid) with all these lads, but I also saw that some of their own confidence had waned. They had become uncertain and had started talking amongst themselves. The ringleaders of all these Borstal boys then told me that they would all do a deal with me to curtail their activities, but that that they weren't going to stop these completely. They agreed they wouldn't pick on the weakest lads or beat them up. I told them bluntly that I wanted them to stop beating everyone up, but I had to concede the compromise when they said that most of the other lads should try standing up for themselves like I had.

I couldn't believe my ears when the complete group of Borstal boys agreed the terms. Little, quiet me had triumphed... or had I been led down a 'blind alley'? The actual truth was that many of them had lied, with no intentions of curtailing their activities, and they continued just like they had before - bullying, fleecing, beating up weaker lads - the whole works.

I knew that something drastic would have to happen, because I realised that my own efforts in directly confronting them had taken me as far as they could.

Live Firing of the 25-pounders at Sennybridge Artillery Range

Sennybridge Artillery Range in South Wales was a cold, bleak, windy, wet mountain area. It rained there most of the time. It was our first live firing exercise. The road trip from Hereford wasn't too long, because Hereford bordered Wales. The weather conditions and the mountain ground of the Sennybridge Artillery Range made it extremely difficult to manoeuvre our artillery guns. It was muddy, wet and windy - indescribably so. Trying to wrestle the guns onto their circular gun platforms was almost a nightmare in the atrocious conditions.

At times, I was roped in on the guns, away from my more comfortable TARA position. At that time, I hated being put on the guns. It was too physical for me. I felt then that it wasn't for me. My job as TARA was already made extremely difficult by the conditions. The large plotter board on which we plotted targets, was out in the open. Fierce winds and driving rain made my important task almost impossible - but I realised that this is how we would have had to cope in war.

It was the same for the gun crews. Absolutely terrible conditions - which would be the same if we were at war. But we weren't yet men. We were boys, lads, gradually being trained towards manhood. We would find we had these attributes in abundance, at the end of our training as Junior Leaders, after it had been extended by our service in Fox Troop. Sennybridge - did anyone ever see or experience a dry day – without rain? Did anyone ever experience a dry day, without rain, in South Wales?

During our time there we had dry changes of clothes brought out from the camp several times because we had been thoroughly soaked through, day after day. Although we had been warned to open our mouths when the command 'Fire!' was given to the guns, so that the effects of the intense crack of the guns on the eardrums was relieved, I confess to being caught out in the Command Post, which was behind the guns as they all 'fired for effect' for the first time, and I neglected to open my mouth. Boy, did that bloody well hurt my eardrums!

After the several days of long live firing exercise we returned to Bradbury Lines, Hereford, more experienced, but dreading the next visit because of the atrocious conditions. We were delighted at experiencing our guns live-firing for the first time, and feeling like we had really accomplished something important. Knackered, but knowing we had taken a big step forward. We felt that we had become Gunners.

I reflected on my own experience on the guns themselves. I realised that this was why I had wanted to join the Royal Artillery. I realised that I had to get better, that I had to be a part of what all the other lads were doing. I knew I had to stop being a wimp. I realised that if I wanted to be accepted by all the other lads, I had to stop being a 'toffee-nosed' TARA. I vowed that I wouldn't stop being a TARA, because I loved the work, but that I had to become an all-round complete Gunner and maybe go on to teach my job to others so that they, too, could become more complete. Little did I realise that when I mustered into the 3rd Regiment Royal Horse Artillery that I would be doing just that - teaching my TARA skills to other Gunners in the Strategic Air Reserve.

Our First Outward Bound in the Brecon Beacons

Several weeks into our recruits training we were told we were off to the Brecon Beacons mountain area of Wales for a two-day Outward-Bound course. We set out from Hereford in a three-ton truck into the Brecon Beacons, after being issued with rucksacks containing a bivouac tent, a solid fuel burner, matches, tinned rations and other food items, a compass, a map, water bottles and several other items.

We were going to be dropped off in groups of three and given two days to make our way to a rendezvous point from which, provided we got to it within a certain time, we would be transported back to Hereford.

We had to trek up and down, around and through the mountains, map reading and orienteering as we went, reading the contours on the map and using the compass to help direct us. It was putting our classroom lessons into practice. But what we weren't told about was the extremely arduous nature of these Outward-Bound exercises, and the dreadful weather we would encounter on most days. Fierce, cold winds, thick mists on the mountain top, and even further down the mountain sides, which could prove fatal if these caused you to fall over the edge of precipitous cliff edges... and then there was that bloody, almost incessant, rain.

We hadn't been told about the difficulties of keeping our matches dry either, or how imperative it was to keep these dry in order to be able to light the solid fuel blocks in the small stoves. Such a small thing - but oh so very important, or else we would go hungry or eat cold, uncooked rations. Sod's Law prevailed - all our matches got soaked. It was impossible to light our solid fuel blocks (there were no such things as gas lighters in those days!).

We realised that we had no choice but to eat cold, half-cooked food. In our first ration pack it was Irish stew, which could be fairly acceptable when hot, but which looked decidedly unappetising when cold, greasy looking, partly cooked. We had no choice. Starve or get it into our mouths and down our stomachs. We would need the energy from this uninspiring food on the next day.

Our thoughts moved forward into the next day. How the hell would we dry our matches before the next evening meal? It was a gloomy prospect because the rain was hissing down and already leaking through our two-man tents. Yes, you've guessed it. It was 'mission impossible'. We had to settle for cold food the next evening. My group successfully reached the rendezvous point without any further mishaps. Gradually the other groups of three lads arrived.

Each group complained about the problem of wet matches, and having to eat cold food. We all vowed that before the next time we would learn how to keep our matches dry in atrocious conditions. Despite everything, we went back to Hereford feeling that we had taken another step towards becoming proper soldiers.

The Live Bullet in the Barrack Room Incident

This incident happened in the Recruits Troop, when we recruits were all quite naive. Somehow, one of the lads managed to escape the strict security measures at the rifle range at the end of rifle practice. You'll remember the one in which you all declare "Rifle Clear" etc., and handover any unfired bullets. This lad, whose name I've forgotten, managed to retain a live .303 bullet and take it back to our barrack room.

In the evening, he proudly showed us the bullet. We were all excited that we had a real live bullet in our barrack room. There was a lot of discussion about 'should we try to fire it?' and, if so, 'how should we fire it?'

The general consensus was that we should try to fire it, so the discussion turned to 'how'. It was eventually decided that the bullet had to be held quite firmly in something. It was decided to place it in the 'U'-shaped hole at the foot of a bed rest, and hold it securely in place with the bed frame, with someone sitting on the bed frame to prevent it moving.

Someone searched for, and found, an old nail outside, using a torch. The foot of the bed was raised up in the air. Someone sat on the bed frame, holding onto the foot of the bed frame to hold the bullet in place. One lad volunteered to hold the nail against the firing pin, whilst another lad whacked the nail with a hob-nailed boot. Everyone was standing around watching all this, waiting for the bullet to be fired, not realising the dangers.

Whack – Bang!...

In a split instant, the bullet exploded from its casing and went whizzing dangerously around the room, ricocheting off the metal lockers and metal bed frames. Everyone dropped to the floor in fright until the bullet expended itself by burying itself in the wood wall of the room, thankfully without hitting everyone.

We all realised what utter prats we had been. Other lads rushed into our room to see what the commotion was. Did we tell them? Did we hell! It remained our secret of the day. We were so stupid - one of us could have died.

Seriously Putting My Career in Jeopardy

What to do? What to do? What to do? I just didn't have a clue what more I could do to put an end to the misery of the Borstal boys' reign. But then an incident occurred right in front of me which caused me to take further action, but which put my career as a Junior Leader in severe jeopardy.

We were lined up down a corridor of our spider block, waiting to collect our pay. It was a Friday. Directly in front of me in the queue was a very quiet, shy, timid, self-conscious lad. A Borstal boy came down our corridor, punched him in the kidneys as he went past, but paused to hiss in the lad's ear about the money he had to pay him; his protection money when he got his 10 shillings and sixpence. The quiet lad yelped in pain at the punch.

Sergeant Gee was in charge of us. He was just behind me, but leapt forward and bellowed at the quiet lad for his outburst, Gee did nothing about the bullying Borstal boy. The quiet lad was instantly alarmed - stuttering, stammering and not able to speak because of the fright of Sergeant Gee's verbal attack. The lad started to slump to the floor and there was more shouting from Gee.

Up to then I had mostly respected Sergeant Gee, thinking he wasn't too bad a Permanent Staff member - even though he had covered up previous incidents with Borstal boys.

I shouted at Sergeant Gee that he had allowed a Borstal boy to assault and then threaten extortion on the quiet lad, without tackling the Borstal boy. Then he had wrongly proceeded to bollock and bawl out the innocent victim. Gee told me not to talk to him like that or he would do me for insubordination. I just lost it. I told him he was a fucking coward for allowing Borstal boys to bully and extort the lads under his protection, and not protecting them like he should. He again threatened me with discipline for my insubordination, and then threatened to cease my career in the JLRRA.

"We don't want your type in the Junior Leaders!"

I yelled something like: "Not only are you a yellow-bellied coward, but you are a fucking hypocrite, a tosser and a wanker!"

I didn't stay in the pay queue. I didn't get my pay that day. I was frog-marched to the guardhouse and slung in a cell, with Sergeant Gee's threats that my career was over ringing loudly in my ears. I was scared.

'Up Before the Judge' – Discipline Interview

I spent the night in the cells of the guardhouse. I was roughed up a bit by the Regimental Police because they knew of my insubordination to Sergeant Gee.

The next morning, I was double-quick-marched to an interview room. A lieutenant (pronounced 'Leftenant in the RA) sat behind the table, with the Battery Sergeant Major in attendance. After shouting my number and name, the Lieutenant started to read out the charges against me.

I felt as if I was already pre-judged and that my career in the Junior Leaders' would end that very day. I decided that if I wanted to save my career I was going to have to tell the Army about the Borstal boys and how they 'ruled the camp' and my one-man crusade against their bullying and the cowardly Permanent Staff NCOs who allowed the Borstal boys to operate.

I thought that the Lieutenant would be too close to the problem, so I interrupted him and asked if a captain or a major could take my interview. The Lieutenant refused point blank, so I was insubordinate to him, giving him, a few choice words. I was quick-marched straight back to the guardhouse, where I was physically thrown in a cell.

Second Discipline Interview

That same day, in the afternoon, I was quick-marched to the interview room. A captain sat behind the table. I asked if I could speak to him without the BSM being present, imploring him that this was extremely important. He reluctantly agreed, so there was just he and I in the room. He told me that he had received good reports about me, and found my incidents of insubordination completely out of character.

I asked him if I could trust him, because what I had to tell him would cause absolute ructions throughout Bradbury Lines. I asked him if he could offer me protection against repercussions of what I was about to tell him. He said that it all depended on what I was going to tell him, but that he was an honest person and that if he felt I should be protected he would ensure this would happen.

After he had reminded me that this was a discipline interview, and that I was there to plead my case – probably against dismissal - and advising me of the seriousness of my actions, I decided to open up and tell him everything about the Borstal boys and the cowardly Permanent Staff NCOs.

Opening Up to The Captain
In opening up to the Captain I knew that it would probably be called "grassing" if the other lads got to hear about me spouting off... but, for me, it was 'either shit or bust' I felt I just had to save my career. So, I told the Captain everything I knew. I told him about the tea/coffee scam, and the beatings if lads didn't pay up; the sports day incidents and the beatings; and the Borstal boys' tobacco barons who, through their accumulated wealth from their other rackets, could buy cigarettes, then sell these to the other lads at inflated prices, which gradually increased in price as the week went by until pay was collected on pay day - and the beatings and violence which ensued if lads didn't or couldn't pay up.

I told him how the Borstal boys sometimes submitted lads to barrack room trials, at which varying verdicts were made - mostly to thoroughly beat the offending lad or lads; but how occasionally the verdict would be "hanging". A rope noose would be fashioned and tied over the beam of the spider barrack room, but the rope was actually secured on the beam with cotton. This wasn't revealed to the victim, who was stood on a chair with a bag over his head and the noose around his neck. Then the chair was kicked away. The noose would briefly tighten before the securing cotton broke. The victim was left a quivering wreck on the floor - but then afterwards was beaten. I had been made to witness one of these incidents, to put the 'frighteners' on us so that we would pay them protection money.

I told the Captain about the cowardly Permanent Staff NCOs, naming Sergeant Gee, Sergeant Bird and Bombardier Roberts(?) ... but, also a few more that I knew of... and the way which they just left the Borstal boys to do whatever they wanted and, in their own sad way, they in turn were guilty of bullying and mocking the victims.

The Captain was utterly astounded. He questioned me quite closely, taking copious notes.

I told him about my lone efforts to try to at least curtail their efforts.
   I told him that I thought other lads wouldn't join with me because the Permanent Staff wouldn't give us any protection – that they feared retribution from the Permanent Staff NCOs and how, understandably, they didn't want to endanger their own careers.

The Captain told me that he believed me. He could see how earnest I was. He said he would keep me in the guardhouse for about a week whilst he investigated and took corrective actions. He promised not to reveal me as the source of his information, but he asked me to accept up to a week in the guardhouse to camouflage the whole issue. He said that he would need to involve Regimental Sergeant Major Field because of the involvement of permanent staff.

I was horrified when he said this. I said to him that the RSM must already know about it because of conversations, etc, in the Sergeants Mess, and that he must have condoned or ignored that it was happening.

The Captain said that he had no choice in this, but assured me that he would use Officers and other NCOs who he trusted. Oh God, I thought. What have I done? I could see myself being out on my ear or made a leper for the rest of my time in Junior Leaders if I survived it all.

The Days of Reckoning

The Captain worked swiftly. Apparently, he used some of his trusted Officers and trusted NCOs. But... he also involved RSM Field! Two days later Bombardier Roberts was gone, transferred out. A few other permanent staff NCOs were also transferred out. Sergeant Gee was moved to another Troop.

Why Gee didn't receive a sterner sentence I don't know, but I had said that he had been fair and said that I thought that underneath it all he was reasonably decent - except for his cowardly way of avoiding conflict with the bullying Borstal boys.
Sergeant Bird was allowed to stay with the Recruits Troop until their Passing Out Parade, but then he was transferred to another Troop. I had said that, deep down, he was fairly decent, but his cowardice in not tackling the Borstal boys was itself a form of bullying.

The Captain used his trusted Officers and trusted NCOs to gather all the Borstal boys together and warn them that they were no longer 'in charge' of Bradbury Lines Camp. The Borstal boys were told to cease all their activities forthwith. But, of course, it was like telling birds they could no longer fly. Afterwards some of their antics continued more quietly during a period of relative calm. I didn't hear of any beatings taking place. I was told that some of the worst offenders were either kicked out of the Army or made to serve their sentences in Borstal itself.

Where they belonged.

I was delighted. I only stayed in the guardhouse for three days, then was released - supposedly with a suspended sentence. But I feared

that if my involvement came out that my name would be mud. I
would be vilified.

There were a few puzzled glances from a few of the Permanent Staff
NCOs and a few Junior Leaders. Nobody mentioned anything to me
and, as far as I gathered at the time, the only talk was about the
remaining Borstal boys being 'nicer' to everyone.

The Captain had given me his word that he would protect me if he
discovered that all I had told him was true and if I came out of it in a
bad light. He didn't say how he would protect me... but I trusted him.
I just cannot remember his bloomin' name, though. I wish I could. He
was a good man to have in charge. He told me that my charges had
been expunged from my record and also my stay in the guardhouse.
The only record which was kept, as far as I know, is that which he
made of our discussion and his follow-up actions. He told me that my
name wouldn't come out. Why, then, did I still feel uneasy? Was it
because I didn't trust the involvement of RSM Field?

The Aftermath - What Happened Afterwards

After a few weeks, one of the lads from Ironside Troop came up to
me in the NAAFI.

He said: "Keith Reeve, you're a bloody hero for how you personally
took on the Borstal boys".

I asked him what he meant, filled with trepidation that my part in all
the 'grassing up' had come out. I was almost shitting myself that I
could end up being vilified if the rest of the Junior Leaders had learnt
who had spilled the beans to the Captain. For 'grassing'.

So, I asked him what he actually meant, and he told me that I was 'the
talk of the camp' – a bloody hero. Not only for personally
confronting and standing up to the Borstal boys by myself, but for
also getting our Officers to sort it all out, including sorting out the
cowardly NCOs of the Permanent Staff who had been protecting the
Borstal boys and who had been guilty of bullying lads themselves.

To protect myself, I desperately tried to deny involving our Officers, still thinking it could turn out bad for me. The Ironside lad made it clear that I shouldn't be ashamed at all... but tremendously proud of what I had done. He told me that my name was being praised throughout the camp. He told me that a lot of the lads knew that the quiet, self- conscious lad from Norwich called 'Keith Reeve' was a bloody hero. He told me that my actions had enabled and encouraged other lads to now stand up to the remaining Borstal boys, so that I was no longer on my own. Everywhere I went in the camp, I was given quiet appreciative nods and smiles of recognition from lads in other Troops. Occasionally, in the NAAFI, there were friendly nods of the head from groups of Junior Leaders. These made me feel proud.

I felt vindicated. I felt valued. I felt really good. As time progressed the remaining Borstal boys were reduced to stuff like tipping people out of beds during the night, or tipping their neatly folded kit on the floor. They were reduced to being stupid children. Many more lads from within all the Troops were standing up to the Borstal lads. Their nastier stuff came to an end, I hoped. It seemed their reign of ruling the camp had ended. Good had triumphed.

Our First Recreation Pass into Hereford

I can't remember when we got our first recreation passes into Hereford, but we were still in Recruits Troop. The first occasion we had to be in uniform, and were inspected for smartness and correctness of dress. We had to be extremely smart – totally 'spick and span'.

We were warned severely to be on our best behaviour, and warned not to get drunk because we were under age anyway. So, there we were, on our first release into Hereford, anticipating what we might see and do.

We found Hereford to be a lovely city (or 'town' as many of the lads called it). We soon saw signs for 'scrumpy', which was a rough cider and fairly cheap to buy. Despite the severe warnings given to us at the guardhouse upon leaving the camp, most lads decided to buy a half pint of scrumpy. It was only a half pint because of our limited pay. Well, a half pint of scrumpy was good, but nobody really felt really intoxicated. So, everyone ordered a second half. That was fatal.

We were so wrong to do so. The effects of that second half were that it made all our immature heads drunk, and secondly it caused most of the lads to suffer agonising stomach aches.

On arrival back at the guardhouse after that first visit, we all got confined there for the night, spending the night in crowded cells. The Regimental Police were quite happy to swear like hell at us, and call us all the names under the sun, and treat us like shit. We were too drunk to care, though.

I had an extra problem. My Army ID card stated that the colour of my eyes was 'blue' whereas my irises are hazel-brown (now please, please, don't fall for me, just because I've told you that). So, although I looked exactly like my ID photo, the RPs took great delight in trying to take the piss. It was water off a duck's back because I was pissed in any case. They made me stand outside the camp barrier, saying I must be a spy for Hitler (or even a Russian spy). So, I stood outside the barrier, swaying because of my drunkenness, with stomach pains, and I can hear these so-called comedians taking the piss. They were nice enough to us in the morning when they released us, but told us we would all be on 'fizzers' or 252 charges.

But, we didn't get put on charges. Instead, Sergeant Bird decided to bollock us all, using his most choice phrases. Afterwards, we found out that this happened to all the Recruits Troops on their first recreation passes into Hereford... but woe betide us if it happened again.

Improvement in Square Bashing

Gradually during our time in Recruits, lads from the other Troops would start to tell us that how good we had started to look compared to the shambolic mess we initially looked when we first started square bashing. This was quite encouraging, because our Permanent Staff NCOs were still telling us we were rubbish.

However, their abuse was now less, and we were no longer being screamed at or insulted. Importantly, now and then, we were told "We're proud of you". We had begun to acquire self-esteem, maturity, self-belief, determination and a growth in confidence. Sergeant Bird explained: "It's all about knocking you into shape so that you become Junior Leaders... soldiers... leaving all that soppy civvy street life behind, and becoming men at the end of it all... becoming real soldiers."

It really felt good to be appreciated, especially being told by experienced Junior Leaders that we looked really good. Very sharp.

We had even managed to accomplish the 'JLRRA halt'. No doubt you'll all remember that slight drag of the left leg when coming into the halt, which allowed a very sharp, snappy two-foot halt. Although this wasn't in the drill book, nevertheless it was encouraged within the JLRRA and it made the halt look and sound terrific. Classy. Snappy.

Passing-Out of Recruits Troop

We came to the end of our time in Recruits Troop. It had seemed to go on for ever. We were all declared ready for our Passing Out Parade. We were all gee'd up and ready to be classed as proper Junior Leaders.

Sergeant Bird was still in charge of us. He reminded us all that he wanted us to be the best Recruits Troop to pass out. To my delight, when we marched onto the Parade Ground, I saw the whole JLRRA Band standing in full dress uniform, in formation nearby.

Although I had already been selected into the band, I hadn't yet had the experience of marching to the band when it played.

Sergeant Bird brought us to a halt, then we marched onto the Parade Ground with the band playing us on. For me it was a real thrill. There was instant reaction from the marching Recruits... spines straight, shoulders squared, arms swinging in unison, and we began to swagger to the music of the band. Terrific!

All too soon it ended, and we began the various drill movements required of us. The time came to march past the Commanding Officer. The band struck up again and we all swagger-marched down to where the Commanding Officer and others stood.

"Eyes Right!" to salute the Commanding Officer and then, all too soon, it had ended.

Apparently, just before the March Past, the CO had announced that we had all passed out of Recruits Troop. We were now Junior Leaders. We didn't realise at the time the wealth of further training we would be subjected to when we went to our designated Troops.

I'm not sure which part I was most proud of, marching to the JLRRA Band or being told we had passed out as Recruits. Sergeant Bird told us how proud he was of us and declared that we were the best Recruits Troop ever to pass out. Despite this making us feel very proud, we soon learned from lads in other Troops that this had been said to every Recruits Troop beforehand in the Boys' Regiment and the Junior Leaders, to ensure we did our best.

Further Training

Throughout my time at Bradbury Lines we were constantly being trained, being taught every aspect of being a Junior Leader. Life was fairly hard, but good - now that the soul-destroying period was behind us. There was now encouragement in everything we did - but there were also bollockings if we screwed up.

I continued to be trained as a TARA, passing the B3 test and then qualifying as a B2 TARA. Because of my later entry into the JLRRA at a later age than usual, there wasn't time left to be trained up to B1 level or to qualify for it.

The B1 training and qualification came later after I had joined 3RHA, and involved being trained at Larkhill on Salisbury Plain. I still took part in training on the 25-pounder guns, because that was what being an RA Gunner was all about. I had got physically harder over time in the JLRRA, with my hands getting more used to the rigours of the manual side of things.

I was gradually becoming the complete Gunner.

More Outward Bound in the Brecon Beacons of Wales

Periodically throughout the rest of our time at Bradbury Lines we were despatched into the Brecon Beacons mountain area to do more 'Outward-Bound'. This had happened once whilst in the Recruits Troop, but it continued throughout our service in JLRRA.

We would set out from Hereford in 3-ton trucks, with full rucksacks weighing about 50 lbs, containing rations, a solid fuel burner, bivouac tents, change of clothes, a compass and maps and a whole host of other items.

We would be dropped off somewhere in the Brecon Beacons, in small groups of three, and given a destination to reach in a set time period. We had to trek long distances - up and down, around and through the mountains, map reading and orienteering as we went. Reading the contours on the map and using the compass to help direct us.

We learned more about the extremely arduous nature of these Outward-Bound exercises, and the dreadful weather almost every day. Fierce, cold winds, thick mists on the mountain top and even further down the mountain sides.

We had made sure by now that we had learned to overcome the difficulties of keeping our matches dry in order to be able to light the solid fuel blocks in the small stoves. Such a small thing - but oh so very important, or else we would go hungry or eat cold, uncooked rations.

Occasionally we would chance upon a lone SAS soldier - abandoned to the wilds of the mountains - with no tent, no rations, just a compass and map. Living off the land. Hard men - worthy of their reputation. They were under orders not to speak to anyone, including farmers and other soldiers like us. They had to cover greater distances than ours - without food except that which they could forage or trap.

On odd occasions in our Outward-Bound expeditions one would come to our bivouac, to get a bit of shelter from the appalling, atrocious weather, and we'd chat for a few moments - just long enough for him to mentally recoup. Just a very brief respite, but so welcome. Bloody hell, they needed that - they had to be quite desperate to do it, defying strict orders. One even took time to show us how to trap a rabbit in a snare.

We would fill our water bottles from the sparkling mountain streams, of which there was an abundance. On one occasion, after filling our bottles halfway up a mountain slope, we found a dead sheep laying in the stream further up the mountain further up the stream. Water bottles had to be hastily emptied higher up the stream. We soon learned not to drink water, or fill bottles, until much higher up the mountain.

Sometimes our Outward-Bound expeditions would be for two days, maybe three days and the big ones up to 5 days. In the time allocated we had to mountain trek great distances - usually in atrocious weather. Did we enjoy it? In a weird, perverse way we did - but, boy oh boy, it was very bloody hard... the intention being to build character, endurance, strength of mind and to help us mature towards being top class soldiers... towards being an adult... towards being a man... towards being a proper soldier.

Further Recreational Passes and Visits into Hereford

There were numerous Recreation Passes into Hereford over the rest of my time at Bradbury Lines, and we gradually learned how to enjoy ourselves and relax in the town. A few episodes concerned the RAF lads who were based in nearby RAF Credenhill, especially when they came into the city in uniform when the JLRRA lads were in 'town'. The RAF lads were the same ages as the JLRRA lads. Sometimes some of the Junior Leaders decided that the 'Brylcream' boys (as the RAF were known) shouldn't be in town at the same time as us, and so they 'chased them out of 'town'. I can't remember there being any actual fisticuffs, it was more a 'fronting' up to them. It was quite funny to see. In hindsight, I think the RAF lads had been told that there had to strictly be no trouble in the city. I mean, why else would they have run from the JLRRA lads, even when the RAF lads outnumbered our lads?

Knives and Razors

On one recreation pass, in which we were allowed to wear civvies, we all gradually noticed something happening at one end of the barrack room in Ironside Troop. A short lad from Glasgow was seen sliding a long knife in a scabbard down the leg of his trousers, securing it with a narrow belt around his waist.

When challenged: "What the fuck do you think you are doing?" he told us that this was the normal way to dress when lads went out in Glasgow. Knife or barbers' razors. We all shouted in unison that we weren't going to allow him to go out dressed with that weapon, no matter what he did in Glasgow. We told him that there was no need for it in Hereford. Thankfully he agreed.

Later, the little Jock from Glasgow told us about the razor gangs of Glasgow. He told us how no lad would go out without being tooled up with a knife or razor for fear of being attacked. He fascinated us with tales of the violent Gorbals area of Glasgow, which was a vast area of tenement buildings. He told us about the razor gangs who rampaged through the Gorbals district, street fighting with other gangs... slashing each other with their razors in the main, but also with knives... putting people in hospital badly injured. Some would die... killed by the razors and knives. Some would end up having razor slashes on their faces for the rest of their lives. It was only after he had told us all this that we fully realised why he had been so keen to go out to Hereford with his knife. Thankfully we made him realise that Hereford was a peaceful place.

Retribution by RSM Field

As sure as day follows night, and night follows day, I knew that somehow there would be some form of retribution, from one area or another about my part in the curtailing of the Borstal boys. I was fooling myself to think it wouldn't. It came, as I had anticipated it would, in the form of RSM Field.

RSM Field ordered me to his office later in 1957. "So, you're Reeve, are you?" he said: "Well, I don't know who the fuck you think you are, but I'm in charge of this camp and I'm not having you causing problems for my Permanent Staff NCOs".

"You're either stupid, or very stupid, or a complete fucking idiot – but get it through your head that you're in the Army. You WILL do as you're told. Your personal feelings and thoughts on anything don't matter, they don't come into it whatsoever. If you try anything like what you did ever again, you'll be gone lad! Do you understand? Now get the fuck out of my sight. I'll be keeping a watch on you!".

For the next several months I made sure I kept my nose clean, so that there wouldn't be an excuse to put me on a charge. I was glad when RSM Field left the Regiment in April 1958. I wrongly assumed that things might improve.

More Retribution – this time by RSM Hobday

So, in April 1958, when RSM Field had gone and been replaced by RSM Hobday, I thought things might start looking up for me. I was still regarded as some sort of hero by lots of the lads in the Regiment, still getting the occasional 'well done, mate', but I had become increasingly wary about some of the Permanent Staff NCOs, who seemed to have taken an unhealthy interest in whatever I did.

Perhaps I was being paranoid? No... I wasn't... I was absolutely right to be on my guard. I guessed correctly that RSM Field would tell RSM Hobday about what I had done, and to keep a watch on me. RSM Hobday proved he had it in for me! He proved that I was absolutely right to be wary. A few weeks after he had taken over he summoned me to his office. There, he told me in no uncertain terms that it was he who was in charge of Bradbury Lines Camp, and that I was a 'nobody' - who belonged lock, stock and barrel to the Army and to fuck with any thoughts I had on anything.

"I won't have a piece of shit like you trying to upset my apple cart" he said.

He went on to say most of the same things which his predecessor RSM Field had said, ending with the same words: "Now get out of my sight. I'll be keeping a watch on you". Perhaps it was an RSM saying?

So, I just aimed to not fall foul of him or any of his cronies. I knew (or rather I hoped) I would be mustering in July/August from the JLRRA and would be going to Fox Troop, the Junior Leaders Continuation Troop, at Oswestry. But I was always conscious that there were those Permanent Staff NCOs 'out to get me', so I couldn't relax for the remainder of my time at Bradbury Lines, Hereford.

All this just because I detested bullies.

Top Troop Competition

As the months slipped by, training in every aspect increased. I could feel the change in myself... changing from a lad to almost a man. My self-respect grew as did my determination... our 'backbone' as we began to call it.

We learned there was an annual 'Top Troop' competition, and the competition amongst all the Troops to be 'top dogs' or 'Top Troop' was immense. Apart from Ironside Troop, the other Troops were: Alanbrooke, Ramsey, Milne, Dickson, Borgard, Shrapnel and Gunn.

In Ironside Troop we all thought we were pretty good, even though the lads of Ironside Troop each had different lengths of service and age. Some had joined at 15 years of age, whereas myself, for example joined at the much later age of 16 years and 8 months... so the length of our careers was different, and the amount of training had been different, dependent on these factors.

All the Troops looked impressive - but only one Troop could win. In 1958... Gunn Troop won Top Troop!

But whatever the driving force was, ultimately every boy wanted to improve himself - in every way... driving forward to qualify as a real soldier... as a man... ready to take on the world! I learned that Fox Troop would bring us those finishing touches and, although it sounded quite daunting, I just couldn't wait for that day to arrive... so that Fox Troop, the continuation Troop, could finish the job and turn me into a complete soldier... a Gunner.

Helicopter Flights at Middle Wallop

I can't remember when, but I think it had to have been sometime in 1958, whilst I was in Ironside Troop, that we were taken the Middle Wallop airfield. Middle Wallop airfield had been used for Blenheim Bombers and Spitfires during the Second World War.

Now, in 1958, it was used by the Army Air Corp. Can you remember them? They wore the distinctive light blue berets.

They flew the French Alouette helicopters, which looked like a glass bubble stuck on the front of a meccano-like carriage and tail. To us these looked quite fragile. We were apprehensive about being taken up in the air in them. We were told we would be taken up in the helicopters in small groups – quite high in the air. Apprehension set in. Off went the first group. Then off went a second group in a second Alouette.

Watching from the ground we were wondering what the experience was like when, all of a sudden, one of the Alouettes seemed to drop from the sky – heading for the ground. We uttered cries of alarm – but then it rose up again. The second helicopter did the same thing. "Bloody hell" cried out one of the lads in alarm. After flying around for some time, both helicopters landed safely and our lads dismounted – some quite ashen-faced.

"Watch out" they told us, "the pilot pulls a lever when you're not looking and you drop like a stone – your heart will jump into your mouth – you'll almost shit yourselves" they told us. So, forewarned, but with our hearts beating that little bit faster, it was the turn of my small group to go aloft.

The pilot managed to distract us by getting us to look at something, and then pulled his lever and we dropped from the sky. God, was it frightening or was it just scary? The flights had actually been exhilarating. The pilots took us way out over the countryside, very high in the sky. None of us had been up in the air and, although it was nerve-racking – especially the sky-drop – we had thoroughly enjoyed our experience into the blue – courtesy of the men with the Light Blue Berets – The Army Air Corps.

Religious Studies Course

Whether I looked a naturally religious sort of lad or not, I don't know, but I got selected to attend a week of religious studies at a big house. It may have been near Hereford, or it might have been down in Hampshire at a Chaplains Training Centre. – I'm not sure, but it was full of army chaplains. I may have been selected for the course because my records might have shown that whilst I was in the Children's Home and with the foster parents, I had attended a Methodist church three times on a Sunday and also Bible Study on Wednesday evenings.

It hadn't made me a religious 'nut', but I did have a healthy respect for religion, and it had obviously rubbed off on me a bit. I was regarded as a nice boy (NO – not a 'nice' boy, but a polite, pleasant, quiet boy).

Some of the more knowledgeable lads told me that I should 'keep my back to the wall' and to 'watch my arse' whenever any of the Chaplains came close to me.

I think the purpose of it was to recruit more chaplains. The Chaplains were all quite friendly and, in my naivety, I thought that they were all just good 'fellows' – i.e. good church people. However, it soon became clear to me that some were standing far too close and touching us on the shoulder or the arm, and even the back of the head and neck.

More than one such attempt was made to me, but I objected strongly that I didn't like anyone, whoever it was, physically near to me or touching me. I think I spent the remainder of that week sitting with my back to the wall. This caused a lot of their open friendliness to disappear. If any one of them came near to me I would shoot venomous looks ('daggers' I think it was called) at whoever it was. An adverse report was put in against me to the Junior Leaders' Regiment stating that I "wasn't very friendly or co-operative".

When told about it, I crudely said: "Tough, Sir, but I wasn't going to have my shit poked up my brown-eye", adding "I want the sun to keep shining out of it". This almost got me done for insubordination, but the Officer gave a smile at my attempt to be humorous, but rebuked me. I think the Chaplains failed me their religious course. Without doubt, they failed to convert me to their other strange brand of religion.

The Annual Sounding Contest

I think it was around spring of 1958 that the annual Sounding Contest took place. This was a competition to assess or establish the best sounders in the Band. All sounders who wished to take place in the competition had to give their names to the two Trumpet Majors, Frost or Eric Timmins by a particular date. Trumpet Major Badgie Hunt was in overall charge of the Band.

A draw was made to establish which order the sounders would sound. Each sounder had to sound two designated calls, and then were free to nominate and sound a third call of their choosing. When it came to my turn I asked whether I could sound 'Sunset' on the bugle as my third sounding. The two Trumpet Majors tried to tell me that the competition was for sounding on the trumpet, but I pointed out that the notices didn't stipulate this – just that it was a sounding competition for all sounders. I told the two Trumpet Majors that, in my view, 'Sunset' was the most poignant and most beautiful call out of every call, trumpet or bugle, and that I would like to sound it as my third choice.

TSM Frost reluctantly agreed, but warned me severely that if I 'fluffed' any note, however slightly, or if any note was made without it being the full, round melodic sound, then he would have no hesitation in classifying me at the bottom of the list of sounders. Whilst I was confident in my ability, I just hoped that I wouldn't cry when sounding it, like I did whenever I heard it sounded by the Royal Marines Band.

I sounded the two designated trumpet calls perfectly. Not as sweet as Jack Pothecary, but still quite good. After ensuring my bugle and its mouthpiece had been warmed sufficiently, I launched into 'Sunset'.

I knew as I sounded it that every note was perfect, with a full melodic sound. When I finished, all the other sounders applauded me. Eric Timmins came to my side, with tears streaming down his cheeks.

Gruffly, TSM Frost said: "Well done, Reeve".

Overall, I was placed seventh in the list of sounders, although Eric Timmins told me on the side that I would have finished fifth or sixth, but that I had 'bucked' TSM Frost so he placed me in seventh position instead. Was seventh lucky? I thought it was. Apparently, Frost had said that "my timing had been a bit off."

Teddy McKenzie (yes, Ted was known as Teddy back then) finished quite high in the order of sounders. I remember that he sounded a real sweet trumpet. The winner, of course, was Jack Pothecary who, as I have previously said, sounded the sweetest trumpet you ever could wish to hear. Surprisingly, Thommo Thomson (the base drummer) came second. He was one frustrated sounder, being denied a place as a sounder in the band and having to bang the big, bass drum instead, despite being a superb sounder.

Mustering from the JLRRA

And so it came to August of the summer of 1958. It was time for me to muster from the JLRRA, after which I would go into Fox Troop, which as I said, I believed was a continuation of Boys' Service into an even harder world, which would not only make me a full Junior Leader but bring me to full adulthood as an adult soldier.

As I've said, there will be differing opinions amongst you all of when mustering from JLRRA actually occurred. For me, I still fervently believe that that it was still part of my Boys' Service, still a part of my service as a Junior Leader, although we would be regarded as being part of 17th Training Regiment RA at Oswestry.

Some boys mustered at a different age to me because they had joined Boys' Regiment or JLRRA at 15 years of age and progressively all ages up to age 17. I had joined at 16 years and 8 months, so I had less time to serve in the JLRRA, and, so, I mustered from JLRRA into the JLRRA continuation troop named Fox Troop at a later age.

My Goschen Parade

My Goschen Parade, in August of Summer 1958, was probably the last Goschen Parade to have been held at Bradbury Lines, Hereford. Every lad will proudly remember their own Goschen Parade and how proud they felt - and the historical importance of it, so I am not intending to write about the historical importance, merely to try to jog your own memories of your own Goschen Parade.

There were no cine film recordings made in those days, which is a shame. (I think the earliest cine or video recording of a Goschen Parade was in 1984).

I thought my own Goschen Parade was bloody marvellous, but there's something really odd about it in my memory. Strangely, my memory of it is really, really 'weird'.

I truly don't remember what exactly happened that day, because it's a mixed-up memory. On one hand, my mind tells me that I didn't actually take part in the Goschen Parade, because I can somehow see myself standing, marching, and sounding in the accompanying JLRRA Band – like some kind of out-of-body experience.

Yet, despite somehow seeing myself in the accompanying band, I can also vividly see myself marching down the parade ground with all the other lads who were mustering - marching towards the Commanding Officer and other Officers and Dignitaries, and, on the given order 'Eyes Right' swinging my head and eyes over to the right in salute. Then swinging it to the front on the 'Eyes Front' command. And I can see the band standing in the centre of the Parade Ground, doing its stuff. The mind is a strange thing indeed. It's really weird having both 'memories' in my head. Perhaps I was enthralled at being in the band? – but the fact is I successfully mustered.

Despite the RSM's threats.

The JLRRA Band Experience

For all those lads who weren't fortunate enough to be selected for the band, either sounding the trumpet and the bugle or playing the drums, you really missed out on a great experience. I know that amongst you are those who loved to hear the band playing, or loved to march to the band on Goschen and other parades. I know that amongst you were frustrated sounders who were excellent sounders but who just couldn't position properly within the strict rules applied.

For those like myself, who were selected for the band, it was the best experience I have ever had. Every sounder in the band was truly excellent - melodious, melodic, sweet-sounding... a joy to be with and to play alongside. Every one of the drummers was superb. I also learnt in my head every drum march, every drum call, every drum beat. I knew them all, but I couldn't play the drums for the life of me. But to me the drums were magic. When we trumpeters weren't sounding I used to 'tch, tch, tch' my tongue against the back of my teeth to simulate the beating of the drums, in time to our drummers. Our drummers were as good as the USA Marine Band drummers at the August 1958 Edinburgh Military Tattoo.

The 1958 Edinburgh Military Tattoo – August into September 1958

The 1958 Edinburgh Military Tattoo was the first-time a Junior Leaders Band had been selected to play there. It was a huge honour to perform on the Tattoo. My memory tells me that we were utterly superb - every night. Nobody 'fluffed' a note.
None of the drummers mishit or dropped a drumstick.

The American Marines Band were very slick and polished, as were the
Household Cavalry and the Scottish pipe bands. But we had that something extra. We had our historical, full-dress, Royal Horse Artillery uniforms with gold braid across the front and our black busbies with red flap, a gold band and white plume. We had jingling spurs on our boots

We had our upright, perfect marching skills - perfectly swinging, white-gloved hands, polished black boots with jangling silver spurs. We had the truly majestic sounds of our trumpets and bugles and the superb drumming of our drummers.

We had youth on our side. We were exceptionally proud.

With a capital 'P R O U D'!

The crowds loved us - calling out for more when, each evening, we marched back up the castle esplanade towards the gates of the castle towards the end of our performance.

My favourite memory is of our rendition of the "Waltzing Bugle Boy" sounded on our bugles. We played it at a slightly slower march than the Royal Artillery Slow March... which made it very slow, feet pointed and our bodies swaying in unison. This had the effect of bringing out the haunting, thrilling sound of our bugles. The notes hung in the air, lilting, thrilling making it sound almost magical. We looked and sounded truly magnificent!

Such an experience for the crowd, and indeed for us… because it was us who were creating that beautiful sound.

I can recall being billeted at the barracks of the Black Watch. It was the Redford Barracks near to Edinburgh. The building looked as if it should have been in India. We were told that the plans were those for an Indian Barracks, and that the Black Watch barracks had actually been built in India. True? Don't know. Each morning we could see the Black Watch soldiers on the parade ground – in full kilt order. Their Sergeant would inspect them. They were made to 'Stand at Ease', whilst he put his right foot forward between each soldier's legs. His right boot had a mirror affixed to it, to ensure they were naked under their kilts.

Our juvenile humour caused us to wonder whether the Sergeant could be visualising 'plums' as he ate his breakfast porridge (or porridge) – albeit pairs of somewhat hairy plums. It might have given him an appetite! Would certainly have given him balls!

I think some of our band were billeted at another barracks, at which there were said to be WRACs (female soldiers). I wonder which part of the band had the more entertaining thoughts?

Whilst the Edinburgh Tattoo was our highlight of the band for me, we also performed at several other Tattoos and shows. Wonderful stuff. Wonderful times. Wonderful band. Truly magnificent.

The one disappointing thing resulting from our performance at the Edinburgh Military Tattoo, was that we received our pay in Scottish pound notes. Why was this disappointing? Well, we were all given some leave after the Tattoo so we could go home. When I arrived home in Norwich I discovered that most shops wouldn't take that 'foreign muck' (the Scottish pound notes). So, I had to go to the bank to change it into English currency. Well – what a 'con'! The bank would only pay 19 shillings and sixpence for each of the one pound (20 shillings) Scottish notes. That was a loss of 6 whole pence (old pence) for every pound I had been paid. What a lousy system, depriving me, a young lad, of hard-earned money! I wasn't best pleased.

FOX TROOP at Oswestry - The Continuation of the Junior Leaders Regiment RA Training into Fox Troop RA

Around late September 1958 I moved to Oswestry in Shropshire, into the Junior Leaders Regiment, RA Continuation (or full Mustering) Troop called Fox Troop, for 12 hard weeks of further training. Apparently Fox Troop was supposedly part of 17th Training Regiment, Royal Artillery, which was mainly for National Servicemen.

For me it was simply moving from Hereford to Oswestry. I was just moving to Oswestry as an extended Junior Leader. Other lads will, no doubt, have a differing view to myself on this. My logic is that I signed up for the JLRRA and six years with the Colours, and three years on Reserve. My six years with the Colours were due to begin on my 18th birthday However, it transpired that the band's performance at the Edinburgh Tattoo in August and into the first two weeks of September, followed by one week's leave, then 12 weeks in Fox Troop, followed by 3 weeks leave for Christmas, had delayed my joining my new Regiment until the new year 1959.

The captain of Fox Troop was Captain J.C. Carter who, in the Spring edition 1957 of The Trumpeter stated that "Fox Troop training is said to be probably the toughest and most worthwhile basic training course in the British Army". This really summed up everything we did perfectly

Did he mean we were trained tougher than the SAS or Marines?????

At our first evening meal on our first day at Oswestry we were doubled-marched in three ranks to the cookhouse. We looked and sounded really impressive - because we had been highly drill-trained in Hereford. We doubled-marched right to the front of all the waiting queues of National Servicemen already lined up to go into the cookhouse. We came to a very brisk, snappy halt, complete with our accomplished slight drag of the left leg which made it all the crisper.

"Right turn" was ordered. Our hobnail boots screeched on the tarmac, right knee bent and right foot hitting the ground with a hard, synchronised clumping sound. On being instructed to "Fall out", and "make your way in an orderly fashion into the cookhouse", there were vociferous protests noises from the queues already waiting.

Rehearsed before we had left our barrack rooms, we all turned smartly as one and shouted: "Fox Troop"!

The shouting and protests noises immediately stopped. We heard comments such as: "Bloody hell, that's Fox Troop - they're really hard". It seemed the Fox Troop reputation preceded us. It made life simple for us... being accepted immediately as top dogs.

We continued to be trained in all aspects which had previously been trained on at Hereford, but it got harder and tougher. There was more Outward Bound in Wales, but in the Berwyn mountains in the north of Wales - this time in two-men teams, having to travel greater distances than previously, faster or in shorter times. Almost always the weather was atrocious.

On some our rations were limited, and we had to try to live off the land or friendly farmers. On one occasion, myself and my partner were successful in snaring a rabbit, as taught to us by the friendly SAS guy in the Brecon Beacons. The difficult part was the skinning of the rabbit and the disembowelling. That was nauseating - it stank to high heaven. Nevertheless, we managed to cook it after a fashion, and then ravenously eat what we could. We had no Bisto or Oxo to make gravy with, and no vegetables, so it wasn't very appetising to eat. In hindsight, we should have cut it into smaller pieces. Of course, myxomatosis wasn't rampant in the wild rabbit population back then, and we hadn't heard of it in any case, so we just assumed it was safe to eat. We learned later that myxomatosis had apparently been introduced into the UK around 1953.

Mount Snowdon – Up.... then Terrifyingly Down.

Our trip to Mount Snowdon was really something else. Fox Troop was split into two groups, following two different routes up the mountain carrying full rucksacks of equipment.

We were delighted to find a small café at the top from which we bought hot tea and snacks.

When our break was over we were lined up in three ranks and told that we would be running down Snowdon at full pelt - at breakneck speed. We were told that Fox Troop's record for this, reaching a specified point at the bottom, was 17 minutes.

On a whistle blow, everyone charged off individually. Our charge down Snowdon was exhilarating to say the least. It became frightening as we leapt and bounded from rock to rock... not daring to slip or fall for fear of physically damaging ourselves. It was almost petrifying. It was terrifying at times. Our feet were almost airborne. How could we stop if we wanted to, without injuring ourselves? The answer could only be by falling over and hoping we didn't hit a rock.

Everyone eventually made it to the specified finishing target at the bottom. Another one of our instructors was waiting in position to greet us. He had arrived there by truck.

We anxiously checked our watches. Had we made it in record time? Our time was fractionally over 18 minutes. We couldn't believe that anyone could have previously done the downside run in 17 minutes, or could do it in less than 17 minutes.

After our most exhilarating, frightening run down Snowdon we began to seriously think we had been given an impossible target to aim at... but then it had been great fun and, whilst seriously scared, we had really enjoyed this man-making moment in our lives. We will never know whether anyone in any previous Fox Troop had ever achieved 17 minutes.

Sometimes at Oswestry camp, we would observe National Servicemen being made to run repeatedly around the square, holding dummy 25-pounder shells above their heads. These were usually those who had fouled up in their training. To me they were being bullied, but somehow, I kept myself out of it. I knew that amongst those young men some just had to grow a backbone, or a pair of balls. Hopefully a few did.

Fully Mustering from "Boys Service"- from Fox Troop, the continuation Troop of the JLRRA

At the end of our 12 weeks at Oswestry we fully mustered from Boys' Service - or from Junior Leaders. Now we were men... proud, confident, mature, determined, resolute. The JLRRA and Fox Troop had made us so.

I went back to my fine city of Norwich for three weeks' leave at Christmas time.

I had originally understood that I should actually have joined my designated Regiment on my 18th Birthday on 24th November 1958 - but everything went awry with my original timetable. I think it was either because of the weeks performing at the Edinburgh Military Tattoo, or more probably it was that the timetable for our Fox Troop was already pre-arranged months in advance, and the timetable for Fox Troop didn't fit within my original timetable.

So, it wasn't until the new year 1959 that I joined that special Regiment – the 3rd Regiment, Royal Horse Artillery where I spent the next 6 years.

.

Afterword

I hope you enjoyed reading about my memories of my service in the JLRRA at Bradbury Lines, Hereford and in Fox Troop at Oswestry. I hope that I've managed to jog your own memories, of your time before you joined, of your reasons for joining, and of your own time in Boys' Service - whether this was in the Boys' Regiment or in the Junior Leaders' Regiment. Royal Artillery - and that you have rejuvenated your memories – especially the good ones – and that you can now laugh at any bad ones.

Section 4 – Peter N Wood, Soldier Magazine. The School for Gunners. 1960

This section is the text from an edition of Soldier Magazine from 1960

Reproduced with kind permission of Soldier Magazine

"They catch them young in the Royal Artillery Junior Leaders Regiment. And then they train them to become not only fully-fledged soldiers but outstanding leaders as well."

THE SCHOOL FOR GUNNERS

A keen wind snatches at the young Gunners taking theodolite readings and whistles past other groups as they dash into mock action on their 25-pounder guns. It soughs through the vast hangars where more Gunners march up and down on squad drill and rocks the straw-stuffed sack as the bayonets plunge into it.

It's a keen wind, but these Gunners, just as keen, thoroughly enjoy the outdoor life. They're young and fit, proud to be serving in the Royal Artillery Junior Leaders' Regiment and eager to become fully-fledged Gunners in a man's army.

Their Regiment, housed in the former Royal Naval Air Station at Bramcote, near Nuneaton in Warwickshire, is a miniature Royal Military Academy where the army takes a boy and makes a man out of him.

Gamecock Barracks – a title handed on by the Admiralty and happily appropriate to the role of the Regiment – provide splendid facilities for these future warrant and non-commissioned officers who spend a third of their routine in schooling, military training, sport and physical education.

The Junior Leaders Regiment aims to produce soldiers and leaders, able to hold their own morally, mentally and physically in a modern world and prove themselves loyal servants of the Crown.

Boys join the Regiment at any age between 15 and a half and 17 and a half years and enlist for six or nine years with the colours. They muster for man's service at seventeen and a half and leave the Regiment at the end of that term for further training as wireless operators, drivers, radar operators or gun numbers at a training Regiment.

Unless they have passed two subjects in the General Certificate of Education – many lads come from grammar schools – or Certificate "A" of the Army Cadet Force, recruits must pass a simple enlistment test. For the first six weeks at Gamecock Barracks they serve in the Recruit Troop, gradually earning the privileges of being allowed to salute and to wear a cap badge, and then join one of the 12 troops, all named after famous Gunners, which make up the Regiment's three batteries – 39 (Roberts), 77 (Wardrop) and 44 (Campbell) Battery.

The Regiment is organised as a military college and the boys are squadded on academic attainment. The entry standard varies considerably but within the last year or two has so improved that the `junior certificate – a "must" – is now being taken much earlier. This is followed by intermediate and senior certificates, equivalent to the Army's 2nd and 1st Class Certificates and, in the top classes, by the General Certificate of Education.

A staff of officers and senior non-commissioned officers of the Royal Army Educational Corps, most of them trained teachers, give the boys a good general education to fit them for both military and civilian life.

Reveille at 6.30 a.m. starts a normal day's routine in which the boys first parade and drill in their own troops. Then the whole Regiment assembles in one of the hangars for morning prayers.

Mornings are spent in classrooms, gymnasiums and in practical military training, including gunnery, weapon training, marching and rifle drill. On every afternoon except one the boys are out on the playing fields. Then, as at any other boarding school, it's back to work, with prep, military history or hobbies – from chess and metalwork to ballroom dancing, vehicle maintenance and even campanology. Roller-skating is a current favourite but outdoor hobbies like canoeing and cycling are always popular. The cyclists maintain their club's 98 machines. The canoeists build their own craft and have paddled canoes through France (on an adventure holiday) and the Devizes-Westminster race which the Regiment won last year.

Like all schoolboys the young Gunners enjoy making something to take home on holiday – perhaps a coffee table from the woodwork class or a model plane, musical box or cuckoo clock from the modelling room. Others prefer a more utilitarian (and lucrative) hobby like boot and shoe repairing for the permanent staff and fellow boys – and even for girlfriends.

Drumming and sounding, two military hobbies, link this instructional recreation with the earliest traditions of boys' service when. At the beginning of the 17th century, boys were enlisted in the "Artillery Trayne" as messengers, trumpeters and drummers.

Today, all boys practise sounding on trumpet and bugle for three periods a week during their first few months in the Regiment. The most promising then graduate into the band to continue their training under Trumpet Major A. J. Hunt, who has been with the Regiment and its predecessor, the Boys' Battery, Royal Artillery, for 15 years. The 60 – odd boys in the band wear the full dress of the King's Troop, Royal Horse Artillery. And have often played in public.

Eight selected boys form the Regiment's own sword-guard, a ceremonial guard which also wears the Royal Horse Artillery uniform and turns out to pay compliments to high-ranking visitors.

A company sergeant-major instructor and a staff-sergeant instructor of the Army Physical Training Corps, helped by ten bombardiers, watch over the boys' physical development. Fencing and boxing are taught in the gymnasium hangar where equipment includes a trampoline. Physical training follows the normal syllabus for men, but some boys are given additional individual tuition. When SOLDIER's team visited the Regiment, the instructors were building up the physique of a weakling and teaching boxing to another lad who had never practised the art.

Twelve boys of different ages make up the Regimental physical training team, which is a credit to the tuition of the Army Physical Training Corps. The team has already been booked this season for a number of local parades and carnivals and to appear at the Royal Artillery "At Home" in Woolwich.

Academic, military and physical training are brought together in the Regiment's adventure training schemes which take the boys out on camping and marching expeditions. Under canvass or on manoeuvres, studying indoors, drilling with rifles or on 25 pounders, the Junior Leaders work hard and play hard. Only after the evening meal are they free – until lights out. Some go out of camp to a dance or the Women's Voluntary Service Club at Nuneaton, but most boys stay in the camp to study or visit the NAAFI canteen, library and WVS centre, which is equipped with a lounge, billiards, snooker and table-tennis tables and many other games.

Variety in the boys' make-up. At Gamecock Barracks every boy is treated as an individual – gives the essential impetus to the work of the Regiment's permanent staff of 35 officers and 215 other ranks. A troop Commander who may have sniffed at this posting quickly realises that this job of turning boys into men is intensely interesting and rewarding. He works closely with his boys and is their temporary father and mother. They have access direct to him and to their Battery Commander, one of whose jobs is to deal with the problem boys – and with the boys' home problems.

At any time, a boy can turn to the Regiment's Church of England padre, the Reverend David Ridgeway, who was a troop officer in the 5th Royal Tank Regiment, seconded to the Corps of Royal Military Police and an instructor at the Eskdale Outward Bound School.

Today the Junior Leaders are boys, but soon they will be exchanging the peaked service dress cap for the coveted beret of their final term. Tomorrow they will be warrant officers, non-commissioned officers – and officers too – of the Royal Regiment of Artillery.

Section 5 – Michael John Nicholson. Junior Leaders' Regiment, Royal Artillery (JLRRA): The Perspective of a Junior Officer

Introduction

It is assumed that this book will concentrate on the young boys who formed the backbone of the Royal Regiment's Warrant Officers' & Sergeants' Messes; indeed, in that context, I believe over 80% of those ranks had passed through the JLRRA system and that may even be an underestimation. Further, many of them achieved Commissioned Rank as indeed did our Battery Sergeant Major whose progression from newly joined Gunner from JLRRA to Officer I had the privilege to witness. In my view therefore, the young men who passed through the JLRRA process amounted to an elite within an elite – that is to say they were the cream atop high quality milk.

All this being so any reader of this contribution needs to be aware that, as a Junior Officer, my contribution to the JLRRA was personally minimal. In a wider sense too, credit for the quality of training rests with the Warrant Officers and Sergeants; the Officer Corps can take marginal credit for setting the framework and keeping a light hand on the tiller.

All About Me

To put this contribution into some context, if only to assess its validity, it might be helpful to the reader to be aware of my credentials.

Back in 1969 as my tour in 14 Regiment drew to a close, it was necessary to consider my next move. In making such consideration it would be inappropriate to dignify the process by describing it as of *career planning,* since that was an age when the Army was a way of life rather than a long-term project; we enjoyed the moment and rarely looked to the future. A number of factors changed that dynamic including: The continuing contraction of the Army, notably boosted by the implementation of Denis Healey's East of Suez Defence Review; the introduction of the military salary, which obliged us to think about money and its attendant stress inducing responsibilities; and the introduction of the Junior Division of the Staff College which lowered the 'threshold of earnesty' through the curious concept of obliging Young Officers to be able to read and write before the age of 30 years.

Some onward movement options were considered. First, the thought of attending the Gunnery Staff Course seemed rather attractive but, despite help from a Royal Military College of Science (RMCS) Graduate, my score of 8% in the mathematics examination drew that possibility to an early close. Second, flying helicopters seemed a good wheeze but when the Battery Commander (BC) of Blazers heard about my application he called me for an interview (incidentally I was the Gun Position Officer in 5 Battery, so it really was none of his business). During the course of this advisory chat he made it absolutely clear that flying helicopters would not be a smart career move, whereas serving in the Royal Horse Artillery (RHA) would be (as an aside the RHA might also be an example of an elite within in an elite but not a very convincing one!). And so, I joined 1 RHA in the Spring of 1969.

As my tour in 1 RHA drew to a natural conclusion, the CO told me of my next posting – JLRRA. Perhaps such news should have been cause for depression, in that the move from the much lauded RHA to a Training Regiment could hardly be described as 'career enhancing'. However, the Postings Branch always found it a challenge to find a suitable posting for a third tour Young Officer who was neither ADC material nor competent enough to be a Junior Staff Officer (a judgment later confirmed by a JDSC report that stated: "Under no circumstances should this officer ever hold a Grade 3 Staff Appointment). So, without any particular dismay and certainly without much knowledge of training, I arrived at Gamecock Barracks in an old Opel Rekord in the Summer of 1972, to be told that Battery Captain (BK) 39 (Roberts) Battery would be my next challenge. Of course, such an appointment had little to do with training and required minimal contact with the young soldiers, so my opinions are likely to be very shallow in certain areas.

At That Time

Soon after my arrival the Government introduced the Raising of School Leaving Age (ROSLA) on 1 September 1972, raising the age from 15 to 16. Thus, I witnessed the departure of the last of the two-year soldiers as well as the enforced restructuring of the training programme. At the risk of digressing, I feel that ROSLA was a national tragedy that also degraded the value of the Junior Leader concept. Many youths, then as now, did not like school, under-performed and too often, in consequence, became malcontents. The abiding strength of JLRRA had been that it accepted many of these malcontents and 'sorted them out'. Those young men grasped the concepts of teamwork, discipline and many other attributes as well as garnering their Army Certificate of Education to a level that would see them into the Warrant Officers & Sergeants and in many cases beyond that level. In other words, the JLRRA product had been freed to focus on soldiering.

At the local level of Bramcote, the immediate response seemed to be to cram the old two-year programme into a year, the thinking being that all the modules were absolutely essential and that nothing should go. This thinking pervaded such extra mural activities as the PT Display Team and the Band, both of which continued apace while miraculously maintaining a very high standard. So, while the framework setters looked with pride at the revised programme, the Junior Leaders were a lot busier than used to be the case.

Work

As Battery Captain of 39 Battery my daily efforts, such as they were, focused on running the Battery Account and pretending to show an interest in the battery Quartermaster Sergeant's (BQMS's) Store. The latter proved to be particularly undemanding since we were blessed with a very imaginative BQMS who, I am convinced, was nothing more than a likeable rogue engaged in all sorts of illegal activities. It would seem however, that my suspicions were groundless since he left the Army to become a bailiff which, I assume, requires an unimpeachable character.

The only serious interruptions to this undemanding lifestyle proved to be running the Gunnery Practice Camp and supervising any extraneous gun-related activities, such as the annual commitment to fire the Royal Salute at York for Prince Philip. As far as the latter is concerned, it has to be said that the Junior Leaders always put on a magnificent show and, thank heavens, a hang-fire never occurred.

Battery Commanders (BCs) were even more remote from the coal face than I was, but that is not necessarily a bad situation from the perspective of both parties, as Arthur Ladd the Quartermaster of 1 RHA once pointed out. He recalled that when in Boys' Service at Bordon before WW2 they saw their BC one day a week. Every Wednesday the BC would arrive on his charger and inspect the front rank before turning to the Battery Sergeant Major (BSM) and saying: "Have you anything for me this week?" – this week! The BSM, keen to be left alone to get on with running the Battery, would always reply: "No Sir" and the BC would ride off. Arthur said: "We thought he was God". Today the entrails of leaders are laid bare which brings no particular advantage to anybody.

My first Battery Commander, fortunately, had a laid-back style, leaving the rest of the team to muddle through. His conferences tended to last too long, partly because he suffered from a slight speech impediment. I soon discovered that he did not react well if one offered the word for which it was felt he was groping; indeed, such well-intentioned interventions merely angered him.

His successor made many new broom claims on arrival, none of which really changed the flow of Battery life. The poor man suffered from diabetes and during one BC's conference he fell into a coma. During that trance, he talked noticeably arrant nonsense, but I lacked the moral fibre to take any appropriate action and the meeting lasted over three hours before he came out of the coma.

In general, the Army's philosophy had been to ensure that, not only were training units to be fully established, but also to be manned by high quality Officers and Warrant Officers and Sergeants. For those in direct contact with Junior Leaders, such as Troop Officers and Sergeants, that aim was broadly achieved but the rest of us, arguably, covered a wide spectrum of abilities and personalities.

The Battery Commander of our neighbouring Battery, Tom Gibson, might best be described as a forerunner to Paul Gascoigne's mate Jimmy 'Five Bellies'. He owned a matching dachshund that needed to be carried from place-to-place. A genuinely nice man who never said an ill-word of others, Tom had been deployed to India before WW2 and did not return until after it ended, thereby depriving him of what might have been the best years of his life. His office door ajar, anyone passing down the corridor could see Tom sleeping through the day. If one of his tipless cigarettes was still smouldering, that indicated he had only recently fallen asleep. The smoking and sleeping habits also took place in the Officers' Mess and it fell to the bar ladies – *Big D* and Vera (see below) - to check his room at regular intervals less the building burnt down; this was a necessary measure since his sheets and pillows were peppered with cigarette burns. It is highly doubtful that dear old Tom had either taken or passed a Basic Fitness Test (BFT) since 1946.

The Administrative Officer had also been selected to serve in the Indian Army. I use the word 'selected' deliberately since only the top 10% of Officer Cadets passing out from Sandhurst were eligible for such selection. So, they were a quality product and were treated very badly on their return to the British Army.

Unusual characters were not the preserve of the Officer Corps. It seemed to be common knowledge that the Regimental Police Sergeant could neither read nor write. He overcame this liability with such clever wheezes as standing behind a group reading Part 1 Orders and declaring: "I've forgotten my glasses can someone read out the orders".

Our neighbouring battery was in possession of an annoyingly loquaciously loud BSM who eschewed boots for favour of gym shoes. The writ of his sickness exemption certificate from wearing boots continued unabated throughout my time in 39 Battery. Not unnaturally the Junior Leaders probably took the view that the BSM's real purpose was to be able to sneak up on them undetected.

During my second year, the need to sit the Staff Promotion Examination arose. With long leaves and precious little work to do, one could not have asked for a better posting to allow time for studying. Superimposed on that, much time off to attend courses on International Affairs and War Studies all over Wales – from Aberystwyth to Cardiff and places in between. Each course lasted a week, they were hugely enjoyable but not necessarily either intellectually stimulating or demanding; rather they offered a boozy break from the Bramcote coal face. Focusing on the subjects already mentioned, I neglected the third element 'Administration and Morale' which embraced Military Law. During the summer leave, I rectified this by undertaking a single module correspondence course and was rewarded with a mark of 8%, with the attendant comment from the assessor: "What a pity you left it so late to turn your attention to this subject". On the day, the highest scoring question of this module proved to be checking an error strewn imaginary Charge Sheet, which simply required a comparison with the example in the Manual of Military Law.

To suggest that universal surprise at my passing the Staff Examination pervaded, would be an underestimation – incredulity or shock might be a more accurate description. The Commanding Officer (CO) exercised his surprise in his congratulatory letter by ending it with: "Of course, you will never get a nomination for Staff College". Well I did, and the doors were now opened for many months of unalloyed irresponsibility, since the next stage of my so-called career had been sorted.

As luck would have it, the Officer who had just assumed command of Recruits Battery unexpectedly gained a nomination to Staff College. He had to 'move now' which clearly nonplussed the Postings Branch and the CO decided to appoint me as BC Recruits Battery. So, I packed my bags and moved across the Square to take up an appointment that attracted Pay Of Higher Rank (POHR).

In this case POHR was totally unwarranted, but complaining about good fortune is never a sensible option. For an Intake of 32 Junior Leaders, which we whittled down to some 25, I benefitted from the following staff:

Troop Commander
Battery Captain (BK)
Battery Sergeant Major (BSM)
Civilian Personal Assistant (PA)
Troop Sergeant
Battery Quartermaster Sergeant (BQMS)
Bombardiers - three
Civilian Storeman

A huge cast for so few Junior Leaders, who were dispersed after Farren Parade to other batteries. There being no intake for the second half of the term prior to the spring block leave, this bloated workforce was free to pursue its own interests for many weeks.

All good fortune comes to an end, and after block leave Major David Bray assumed command of Recruits Battery and I slipped back into the role of BK on a lower rate of pay. I regard David as an exceptional officer who remained calm and measured in all situations. Having been promoted from Warrant Officer rank, David's chances of commanding a regiment were zero, which was a tragic systemic quirk of the Army in those days. I have absolutely no doubt he would have made a very effective CO.

Snippets

Perforce, the snippets of my fast withering memory now focus on the Permanent Staff. As a BK I was not required to be either Regimental Duty Officer or Duty Field Officer, which allowed for plenty of observational time, although I am not sure that it was put to any good use. So, I guess many memories will focus on the Officers' Mess. There is however, one notable exception – the Boys Saturday Night Disco.

The CO had decided that the boys needed some in-barracks entertainment, and the idea of a disco night was born. Whether this reflected a genuine desire for the Junior Leaders to have some fun, or a cynical attempt to keep them in the barracks, I know not. The task to organise these events fell to me, of which the most onerous element was writing the orders. These were to include such matters as dress, start and finish times, duties of the duty NCOs *et al.* My consequential endeavours resulted in a fifteen-page document which was fed into the Adjutant for approval, or otherwise. When I got the document back, he had made one amendment and that was on the last page where he deleted "at the end of the evening", replacing it with "at the termination of the evening". The lesson is, of course, why use a short word when a long one will do.

Under the tutelage of Hore-Belisha, Secretary State for War, many well designed Messes were constructed on, for the most part, airfields; Bramcote was but one example. Since the Regiment inherited it from the Fleet Air Arm – HMS Gamecock – the Mess was blessed with all-black mock leather chairs and sofas which looked much more dignified than the Army's brown leather variant. The building had a homely aura with large ante rooms and an imposing dining room, and the living-in Officers' quarters were as good as those on offer anywhere.

The bar inevitably provided the focal point for day-to-day life. Doris and Vera took turn and turnabout manning the bar. Both not only undertook many tasks beyond the call of duty (for example checking Tom Gibson's safety), but also suffered banter that young officers considered hugely amusing that, in truth, were probably merely puerile. Of solid build, Doris attracted the soubriquet *Big D,* partly in homage to the packets of peanuts on sale. As a 'treating' Mess, all purchases were logged in each Officer's bar book, from where they found their way onto their Mess Bill. Most Officers' consumption meant that a second or even third book was required during a tour. However, one Officer came and went after a full tour having never got beyond Page One. His *modus operandi* was to move to a group of drinkers whose glasses were nearly empty and accept a drink from the next person in the chair. In this way, he worked the room and never paid for a drink.

The YOs took great pride in being first to the bar but, after a while, were disconcerted to discover that the Dental Officer had got there first. As he was a Lieutenant Colonel it took a while for the YOs to pluck up the courage to ask how he consistently managed to be first in the queue. In response he told us that the Dental Centre had been established to treat 600 Junior Leaders and that after the initial examination the results were:

200 had teeth that required no treatment
200 required treatment
200 had teeth in such decay that the only course of action was to issue them with a rail warrant to go to Woolwich Military Hospital to have all their teeth extracted.

Ergo he only had to treat a third of his patients. To me this was a thoroughly depressing revelation and I am not sure how much of the policy had been dictated by a cynical Army.

The Mess inherited the Mess Manager, who had served in the Royal Navy. Competent and likeable, he ran a happy ship. However, he did occasionally like a drop of booze and on one memorable occasion, as he held the kitchen door open, a waiter accidently nudged him and he staggered across the dining room.
The waitress cum general hand called Ying was the other notable contributor to the comfort of our daily lives. As a Chinese, she did however struggle with English and caused huge amusement in handling, or not, a telephone call from Captain Dumas. The Captain had been trying for many hours to get through to the Officers' Mess while on holiday in Europe, and when Ying answered the phone the conversation went something like this:

"It's Captain Dumas here", to which Ying replied "Captain Dumas? Him on leave" and put the receiver down.

Ying also delivered our morning cup of tea (gosh were we spoilt!). One weekend she came into my room and after filling up my cup she suddenly noticed my girlfriend lying beside me. Unfazed she said: "So sorry I get another cup". She duly did.

Ladies Dinner Nights offered potential for 'events'. One of the more memorable ones involved the General Officer Commanding (GOC), who was adept at using his steely good looks to his own advantage. On this particular night, a disco followed the meal, a treat which soon palled for the General, who told his ADC to let it be known that he was leaving. In turn, we were all instructed to repair to the hall to say farewell to the GOC. As we all arrayed in the hall to say goodbye the General's eyes fell on the CO's wife, and in a flash, he said: "I want to dance". The disco machine being in the 'night club' required the Entertainments Member to race down the corridor, wheel it back to the hall, plug it in and put on a record. The assembled crowd then witnessed the General grope the CO's wife in the slowest of dances. Rank has its privileges!

Soon after my arrival in the Regiment, an older Officer had told me that a tape recorder had been hidden in the ladies' loo. The day after the Ladies' Dinner Night the tape playback revealed this to be one of the comments: "There must be eighteen feet of prick in there and I can't even get six inches of it". It's not for me to comment on the validity of such a tale.

Mess occasions did not always require a uniform to be worn and black-tie nights often took place. Sometimes Officers failed to read the convening orders and some will recall the night the Paymaster and QM (Tech) - Geoff Davidson – simultaneously debouched from their respective MQ with one sporting Mess kit the other in a DJ. Each assumed the other was correct and went back in to change. This must have been a bummer for the one who was correct in the first place.

Goschen and Farren Pass Out Parades on the one hand involved much hard work for the Junior Leaders, while on the other, offered a framework for a Mess jolly for most of us. Such events attracted a General or a Brigadier but during my time the most distinguished guest was the Chief of the General Staff (CGS) – Field Marshal Sir Geoffrey Harding Baker, GCB CMG CBE MC. A distinguished and charming officer who had secured the top job in the teeth of competition of the Cavalry and Infantry who had, more often than not, filled the vacancy on a sort of *Buggins Turn* principle.

Nuneaton would, I am sure, never claim to be a leading the cultural or entertaining places in the UK; indeed, it was once described as "the largest place that nobody has ever been to". After a cursory visit to George Eliot's house, the cinema offered the only other attraction. One memorable cinematic event was seeing *Towering Inferno*. After a succession of surprise deaths of famous actors, one of the stars jumped from a great height, at which point the audience, as one, cried out in shock. When he landed on an inflated mega cushion the whole audience stood up and applauded. Maybe I underestimated Nuneaton's cultural heritage.

Even as a single man, owning a dog was perfectly practical. Having decided that a dog would be a good addition to my life, I made my way to Coventry and bought a semi-trained English Setter bitch. Sad to say the 'semi' status never developed. Every morning we would walk outside for her morning constitution and she would merely sit down and look up at me. She would then be returned to my room while my face was being filled at the breakfast table. On returning to the room I would witness that she had relieved herself all over the room. This behaviour peaked when I had persuaded a young lady to 'see my room' only to discover that the dog had pooed everywhere. After that incident, the dog had to go and a civilian instructor – Bill Rogan - took her on. He eventually managed to train her by rotating his children through the night in the kitchen. They slept on camp beds and took her out when nature was seen to be calling.

Not long after the departure of the dog, strolling around the barracks one Saturday morning I bumped into a morose JNCO from the Medical Centre. He told me that he had been told the day before that he had to take up a posting in Germany on the following Monday. In consequence, he felt he had no choice but to have his dog put down. On hearing this I immediately said I would take the dog. She was a bitch and her name was Cindy, which was not a name that appealed to me and she was re-named Shindy, and she became my loyal companion for 16 years. When I took command of my Battery some years later, the BSM introduced Shindy and me to the full complement with the words that "Officers have dogs on the basis that two heads are better than one." That BSM – Les Burgess – was an exemplar of the JLRRA.

Education

The Royal Artillery Education Centre (RAEC) fulfilled the crucial function of educating Junior Leaders to a level that would qualify them for promotion to WO level. Most of the instructors had served as Warrant Officers in the RAEC – sadly a rank that has long since ceased to exist. The boss of the Centre was a RAEC Major who on posting to Shrivenham decided to leave his cat at Bramcote – incredibly that animal found its way to the new address.

The other important function of one of the Education Centre's staff was to offer a home to my Opel Rekord. Unearthing metric spares parts in our imperial measurement environment had proved to be too great a challenge, and the car passed to Frank Morgan for the princely sum of £17.

Sport

The cup of sport overflowed; indeed, Bramcote offered me the only opportunity to play serious cricket in my entire service. The nine-hole golf course made for a pleasant diversion as long as the club head did not dig too deep into the runway wire that lay underneath the grass.

A squash court lay behind the Officers' Mess and it offered the potential for a healthy stop gap between work and the opening of the Mess Bar. The Padré – Paddy Craig – was a canny player.

In terms of competitive success Hockey proved to be the apogee. The Permanent Staff team performed well in a number of Army-wide competitions.

Medical

The workings of the Dental Centre have been touched on but not so the Medical Centre. The latter was initially run by Colonel George Harman who had also served in the Indian Army. On retirement, he was relieved by Lieutenant Colonel John Whitfield. I discovered for myself the latter demonstrated all the qualities of an intuitive medic when I reported sick with back pain soon after a BC had tragically died from cancer of the spine. Whitfield issued me with a single bar electric heater and the pain disappeared before it had even been turned on!

Reporting sick on that one and only occasion merits a description. I arrived at the Medical Centre to be confronted by wall-to-wall Junior Leaders waiting to see the doctor. Standing by the entrance when Whitfield arrived, he immediately invited me in to his office. Once in there he took off his jacket and replaced it with a white coat, after which he said: "I'm sorry, I can't start work until I've had a cigarette". He sat down in a chair beside the basin and pulled a Guards cigarette out of the packet. After a stem of ash had developed on the tip of the cigarette, he flicked it into the basin and flushed it away by operating the long-handled tap; he repeated this process until the fag had performed its duties.

The tale of how I became the 'Poster-Boy' of the Junior Leaders' Regiment, Royal Artillery.

It was the day the new recruits' intake arrived, and I had been attached to Wardrop Section as the Junior Lance Bombardier (LBdr). I had been instructed by Sergeant Hatto to go down on the bus and round up any strays who looked like they didn't belong there.

On my return, it was my task to march a squad of Recruits' Battery down to 'George-the-Barber' to have their haircuts seen to. There was a civvy photographer there. He asked if he could take a photo of me and this little 'hairy' kid to feature in the local newspaper. We duly obliged and when he came out he had a pretty severe short-back-and-sides. The photographer took another picture, so he had a 'before' and 'after'.

You can imagine my surprise when the 'before' picture then featured on the JLRRA brochure. In later life, I looked through all Nuneaton newspapers from that time but never found it. It was only a couple of years ago, when I reached the ripe old age of 60, that I was looking through some photos of JLRRA on Facebook where, lo and behold, it popped up. I couldn't believe it, to be honest. I right welled up and spilt a tear or two. That photo is now my pride and joy. Since then, I have found other photos of myself from when we marched around Nuneaton after the Freedom of the Borough ceremony in May 1972. So that's the tale of being a 'Poster-Boy'. It's something I never forgot. Strange how things like that stop with us.

Nicholson Troop – The Sports "Champions" (not!)

I'll tell you a story about Nicholson Troop. They were the 'In' troop for sports. They were always winning everything put in front of them. In my fourth term, Mansergh Troop had a cracking football team which I had the honour of being in. As you will remember, Wednesday afternoon was sports afternoon. Anyway, that afternoon Mansergh Troop played Nicholson troop at football, hockey and basketball, and beat them at all three. This had never happened before! They had never lost all three on the same day. So, the following day their TC made them wear black armbands for the rest of the week. How sad. Never mind, eh.

Defending the Honour of the Regiment

In my mustering term, 40 Battery went on Summer Camp to Tenby in Wales. Three of us had the opportunity to go down town where we got into an altercation with some of the local lads. Despite the fact there were five of them, you can believe me when I tell you they came off much the worse.

It got reported back and we were hauled up in front of the Battery Commander, Major Gibson. He was furious. Not just because we had been fighting, but also because we weren't going to back down. In the end, he sent us back to Bramcote under escort.

Anyway, we all ended up with Provo. Joe in his little hotel. We had to fetch all our gear on the RP's barrow and got locked up.

The next day they sent me and Ossie out on cleaning detail with one of the RPs. When we got out to here we were going Ossie says: "F*ck-this." He dropped what he was carrying and legged-it. Guess who followed him? Yeah, me.

Our escort, this RP, could no-way catch us. He weighed about 20 stone. We ended up hiding in the wind breaks wondering what do we do next. After some time, we could hear that help had arrived for the RP, but they didn't have a clue where we were. We decided we would wait till dark then escape. Where to, I have no idea, but that was the plan. To our dismay several trucks turned up with nice, bright light. That put paid to our plans.

We stayed in those windbreaks for twenty-four hours, until hunger drove us out and back into Joe's loving arms. The next day we were on CO's orders, after getting our nuts chewed by the RSM.

I think someone was looking down on us that day. We just got a savage bollocking for doing a runner. For the offence of the altercation with the Welsh lads, we said we were fighting for the honour of the Regiment. We were duly sent back to Tenby where Major Gibson confined us to barracks.

At the time, I was a Junior Bombardier. To this day, I could never understand how I kept my stripes.

Section 7 – Mike Luscombe. The way I remember it. 1971 - 1973

The way I remember it

The summer of '71 was a new experience. This is where my future lay, in what capacity, I had no idea. One thing for sure was I had decided never to go back to the austere environment of boarding school several hundred miles away from my family.

The problem I now faced was I only had a few weeks to convince my parents not to send me back there. I really do not know what I was thinking as I walked through the door of the Army Careers Office in Torquay. It could have been curiosity. It may have been due to the fact that my Head Teacher was adamant how unsuitable I would be for a career in the military. Whatever it was, I was compelled to look inside. I was greeted by a very friendly uniformed sergeant who put me at ease within seconds. He really was an excellent ambassador to put on show for the Armed Forces.

Possibly in his mid-twenties, clean-shaven and square-jawed. He must have been at least six-foot-three. His biceps were only just contained in his heavily starched, short sleeved shirt. He excused himself as he invited me to look at the literature on display while he momentarily serviced the needs of two young women, giggling in the corner by some concertinaed display boards.

Covertly I watched the girls as they eyed the soldier up and down, taking in every inch of his body. One girl licked her lips as the other played with strands of her hair nervously as they were invited to sit a short, handwritten test in an adjoining room. They giggled and whispered in each other's ears before accepting his invitation.

He was every inch a real man. The type of image of a man I would aspire to become one day. He came back over to where I stood and pointing at some pictures near to me said, "See those Royal Marines carrying those logs, I guarantee we would have you looking just like one of them within a few months. The girls will be all over you."

Standing there with my twenty-eight-inch waist and nine stone build, the prospect of looking like that in just a few months did sound very appealing.

He placed his hand on my shoulder and said: "Tell you what, I am just about to give those girls a little written test to see if they're up to it. What about you having a bash at it too? No strings attached. I will then be able to tell you what kind of jobs you would be suitable for. What do you say?"

"All right then," is what I heard myself saying.

Having completed the test within the allotted time, which was more than ample, the girls and I were asked to wait in the main display area for our results. We did not have to wait too long before he called us into his office one at a time. As the second of the two girls left the office he accompanied them both to the door:

"Never mind girls, you can always give it another go next year."

I gathered from that comment they had been unsuccessful. Anxious to know if my unsuitability had surfaced in the written test, I asked: "And how did I do?"

He looked down at my exam paper and reading my name from it replied: "Well, Michael, they don't come much better than you. You can do more or less whatever you choose. You have a very high SSG rating, so I suggest you have a close look at what we have to offer. You can take your pick. Have you had any thoughts of what you would like to do?"

I smiled at him with a thought in mind and said: "I really fancy being a helicopter pilot. What about that?"

He stood up and collected some papers from a filing cabinet beside his desk and said: "Yes, you can be a pilot. However, as you are only 16 you would have to become a junior leader first of all. Then when you reach 18 you can put in a request to join the Army Air Corps and train to be a pilot."

A junior leader? Now that sounded good. This had to where my future lay. If I said yes to becoming a 'junior leader' my parents could not send me back to that horrible boarding school. Not only that, but if I joined the Royal Artillery junior leaders, it was bound to stir up patriotic emotions within my old man, as he would surely understand my urge to follow in his footsteps.

"Yes, yes, yes!" I said: "When do I start?" Somebody had finally seen I had potential for doing something with my life.

Within a few weeks I received an invitation to attend the Army Careers Information Office in Exeter where I was to formally enlist in the Army. The invitation was entitled REPORTING NOTICE and written on an Army Form B2531 (Revised). A rail warrant was also enclosed with additional information informing me that I would be joining my unit, The Junior Leaders' Regiment of the Royal Artillery, on the 14th of September 1971 at Gamecock Barracks, Bramcote, Warwickshire.

I duly attended Exeter, swore my allegiance and accepted the Queen's shilling. I then waited for the big day to arrive. My parents took the news extremely well. As a matter of fact, they were very supportive. Dad was repeating his war-time stories over and over and insisting I was going to love the experience. Mum was proudly saying how this would make a man of me. When the day finally arrived, mum had prepared a few sandwiches for my long journey and dad had placed a carton of two hundred 'No.6' cigarettes in my bag. I said my goodbyes at Torquay Railway Station. Phase one of my life had ended and phase two had just begun.

The train journey had been a long one involving several changes. The closer I got to my destination, the more anxious I became. I noticed other boys of similar age were also filling up the carriages on the last leg. They appeared apprehensive and said very little to each other. I tried speaking to a boy sitting near to me. He confirmed he was going to the same place as me, but his mind appeared to be far away. So, I let him be.

We alighted from the carriage together and were herded outside the local station by two adult soldiers in uniform.

"Come on lads. Over here, this way!"

They appeared friendly enough as they led us all onto a number of coaches.

I do not recall much conversation on the coach. Most of us just sat staring out at the countryside in trepidation of what was to happen next. It was not too long before the convoy drove through the large swing barriers of Gamecock Barracks. The stark contrast between the natural beauty of nature on the outside of the high perimeter fence and the totally organised setting within was apparent immediately. The fresh white paint of the guardroom building gave the impression of an impeccable sense of order.

A young boy dressed in dark green overalls stood on the guardroom veranda, fully committing himself to the polishing of a large brass ceremonial bell. The convoy continued along the road passing numerous building, both modern and pre-war, finally coming to a stop alongside a large hangar where we were ordered to de-bus. We followed like sheep inside where there were several rows of trestle tables. These were divided into four sections, each laden with different colour tracksuits.

As we all grouped together, close to the doors of the building, a voice commanded:

"Come on in and listen in. I shall call out your names followed by a number. You will remember your number for the remainder of your lives. You will then collect a tracksuit from the table I direct you to. Do you all understand?"

There being no questions to follow such precise instructions, he began spouting names, numbers and colours with a melodic rhythm. I was listening intensely for my name in dread that I would miss the opportunity to hear my number clearly. I did not want to be the only one to break his rhythm with a "Pardon?"

Then it came, I was prepared: "Michael Luscombe, number two-four-two-three-two-seven-five-eight. Green!"

My brain grappled with the complexity of the eight-digit sequence. Over and over I repeated it, as did the others around me - ALOUD. It was a cacophonous din.

I was handed a green tracksuit, presumably one to fit me. I then awaited further instruction with the others carrying similar green packages. I saw four distinct groups had formed in the hangar. The other three carried either black, blue or red packages.

Each of the groups was then joined by a young uniformed boy soldier. The one accompanying my group wore a red 'V' shaped stripe on his sleeve signifying his rank. He introduced himself, "Right lads, I am Lance Bombardier Morgan. I want you to arrange yourselves into three lines as quickly as you can!"

He was about 17, slim, with straight black hair, and spoke with a strong Welsh accent. We quickly formed three lines and followed his lead out of the building. We ambled along. Nothing like marching. Those days were to come. I was close to the back so I couldn't actually hear what the Lance-Bombardier was saying but was content to take in the surroundings, whilst still reciting the eight-digit number.

We were led into a modern two floor billet block where we were told to find our 'pits'.

Unfamiliar with accents different to my own, my learning curve was about to embark on a steep upward trend as I was introduced to a collage of colloquialisms. I located my pit on the ground floor in a partitioned room with 15 others. The ends of eight grey metal bunks abutted the walls, four on either side of the room. Between each stood a tall grey metal wardrobe.

The floors were wooden, and gleaming with a depth to the shine as to reflect one's image like a mirror. The reek of floor polish hung in the air. There was a clinical disinfected coldness about the place. No pictures, no plants, no feeling. A duplicate room abutted ours, separated only by a partition wall. The same layout was both upstairs and also on the opposite wing of the building.

Morgan entered the room and spoke officiously: "This is your home for the next 14 weeks. After that you will join your troop and another bunch of recruits will take your place. You will look after this room and leave it in an even better condition than it is now. Do you all understand?"

We nodded and grunted affirmatively.

He continued: "You will not smoke during this 14-week period. If you have brought any cigarettes with you, they will be stored away with your other belongings."

We were then given a list of priorities including a visit to the bedding store, clothing store and barber shop. Upon completion of the three tasks we were to get something to eat from the canteen. We would find a KFS and mug in our metal cabinets. We must take these whenever we ate, and we were ordered to attend all meals.

'KFS'? What the hell is a KFS?

It soon became obvious when we saw there were only several items inside the cabinet. Amongst them, a knife, fork and spoon cleverly clipped together with a swivel clasp. At the bedding store, I was provided with a mattress, sheets and blankets.

At the clothing store, having declared neck size, shoe size, hat size and waist size, I moved along a well-rehearsed human conveyor belt system with a row of adult men handing me that season's entire range of soldiering attire.

Having deposited my new acquisitions in my pit I joined a very long queue for the barbers. Needless to say, we all left with the same regulation length haircut ensuring the cold September wind would bite at our rediscovered ears.

The way I remember it - part 2

Having endured the experience of 'George-the-barber' (I think that was his name), I followed a group of other recruits to the canteen building. A large two-floor building with sufficient seating for 500 diners at a time. I did not eat much that day. My appetite was not that good at the best of times. My physique showed that. I looked like someone from a concentration camp, with my ribs clearly showing.

Returning to the billet, Lance Bombardier Morgan provided some instruction, in a minimalist way, regarding the proceedings planned for the following day.

We were told to make up our beds, mark all of our kit with the last four digits of our military number, put it away neatly and settle down as early as possible. He then departed. It didn't take me long before I was sick of the numbers two, five, seven, eight. Someone finally broke the monotony by parading in the green underwear referred to as 'Drawers Drac'.

We fell about laughing at the realisation even our underwear was subject to control from this moment forward. We introduced ourselves further than we had done previously, taking turns to explain why we chose to join the junior leaders. I really did not have the faintest idea why.

However, many years later, a psychotherapist suggested 90% of recruits come from unsettled backgrounds. The military is considered to be a 'Cold Parenting' structure providing food, clothing, education and sibling-camaradery otherwise lacking in a traditional, loving home environment. Maybe that was true in my case. I digress, before long we all settled down for the night.

Without warning the room was illuminated by the bright strip lighting in the centre of the ceiling and Lance-Bombardier Morgan banged furiously on the side of a metal cabinet with a wooden stick.

He shouted coarsely: "Hands off cocks, on with socks. Good morning lads. Get up as quick as you can. You have five minutes to get washed, shaved and into your tracksuits. Then line up in three ranks outside in the road. MOVE. "

I checked my watch to see it was only 5.50am. I had never been up so early in my life. One moment I had been in the deepest of sleeps, totally oblivious to my new surroundings, and the next, I had entered a world of confusion. I struggled to move at the speed necessary. Fortunately, I succeeded in leaving the building within the allotted five minutes and ran to join my peers on the road. Outside it was dark and cold.

It was as if we had been woken in the dead of night. We stood in silence awaiting our next instruction. The lighting inside other billets was being switched on followed by the din of banging and shouting. A few minutes later and I could hear the crisp sound of metal boot studs on the road heading our way. The sound was unearthly. The footsteps echoed with authority as they increased in volume.

Then into view emerged a uniformed man in his late twenties. Slim but not skinny. Standing six feet tall with sharp facial features and what appeared to be a crooked nose, as if it had been broken a long time ago. He wore an official-looking hat with a black, polished, semi-circular peak coming down over his forehead and resting on the bridge of his nose, effectively obscuring part of his eyes. He wore the rank of Sergeant and carried a small bamboo cane in his left armpit, holding it parallel to the ground with one end 'twixt his left thumb and index finger.

I recall a smile broke across his face as he observed us all standing before him.

Then he spoke: "I am Sergeant Hatto. It is my task to turn you all into soldiers. I am a very fair person. You do as I tell you and we will get on like a house on fire. When I say 'jump', you jump. If I say 'sit', you sit. If you have any problems at all you go to Junior Lance Bombardier Morgan or, if you prefer, me. You do not go to anyone else. You will always follow a chain of command. Is that clear?"

Nobody answered, I suspect with fear they would be the only one to make a sound.

Sergeant Hatto raised his voice slightly: "When I ask a question you will answer, 'YES SERGEANT' - Is that clear?"

In unison we replied: "YES SERGEANT!"

He asked again even louder: "I can´t hear you. I said 'Is that clear?'"

We shouted: "YES SERGEANT!"

He continued: "On the notice board in your barrack room I shall pin up a timetable and any other notices that are relevant. Make sure you read all the information on that board regularly. This morning, after breakfast the Recruits' Battery will parade on the Regimental Parade Square. I shall march you down. The Junior Lance-Bombardier will tell you what to wear and how to wear it. Do you understand?"

"YES SERGEANT!"

We had got the hang of that pretty quickly.

He then continued: "When I say 'FALL OUT', I want you to bring your heels together, turn smartly to your right and walk three paces before heading back to your block."

He paused for several seconds before raising his voice:

"SQUAD... FAWWWLLL... OUT!"

I thought the sound of 30 pairs of pumps coming together in unison sounded pretty good. It was a shame that not everybody knew their left from their right.

Sergeant Hatto turned and walked off shouting: "GOD HELP ME!"

After a hearty breakfast, we returned to the billet and were given instruction by Taffy Morgan (a name we had adopted out of his earshot) on the correct method of wearing shirt, trousers, boots, gaiters, belt, jumper and beret, not forgetting to place little black ringlets of material on our epaulettes to signify our membership of the Recruits' Battery. He also introduced us to the standard way we were expected to make our beds in the morning.

Once a week throughout our military service, we would be able to change our bottom sheet for a clean one. The old top sheet would then become the bottom sheet for the following week and so on. Having stripped the bed completely, one blanket would cover the mattress. We were instructed in the art of 'Hospital corners'.

The remaining sheets and blankets were to be folded in a particular regulation style so as to create a square sandwich of bedding with the remaining blanket encasing it. This was known as a 'Bed-Block' and all were to be the same size and positioned uniformly on all beds. In fact, even the contents of our cabinets were to be uniform. All clothing folded in a particular fashion, with an A4 piece of paper acting as guide to the width of all folded garments.

On each shelf throughout the barracks, one's mess tins would be located at point 'A' and toothpaste at point 'B'. One's rolled up socks would be positioned at point 'C' and so on. All procedures involved a plan that everybody had to adhere to.

Not long after, we were paraded back on the road outside of the billet block. This time we were dressed like soldiers. Except for the berets, which made us look more like French onion sellers, as their shape required moulding to our heads. We were later given instruction on the finer points of shrinking it in hot water whilst still wearing it.

Once again, we stood in our three ranks and awaited the arrival of Sergeant Hatto.

On his arrival he commanded: "When I say 'MOVE' I want to see a line facing me with the shortest on the left, tallest on the right. MOVE - come on, as quick as you can!"

For the next couple of minutes, we ran around like headless chickens. Some were obviously suffering from height delusions as they found it hard to accept the person alongside them was either taller or shorter.

Sergeant Hatto waited for the movement to settle down and then said, "We are going to have to do much better than that if we are to get along!"

He then moved along the line and physically placed each of us in order of height. Through a series of commands that followed involving the identification of each of us as either 'Front', 'Centre' or 'Rear', he formed us into three ranks. This had the effect of creating a squad of boys with the tallest on the outsides and the shortest in the middle.

"Make a mental note of those standing around you because that is where I want you to stand every time you form up. Is that understood?"

"YES SERGEANT!" we remembered to reply.

He then marched us, as best as he was able under the circumstances, to the Regimental Parade Square.

The way I remember it. Part 3

We arrived on the square with several other squads of recruits, each of their sergeants shouting simple commands. We were then instructed to listen and wait for the commands of one of the other sergeants who had the onerous task of calling all of the recruits to attention as an officer and a sergeant major appeared on the square.

"RECRUITS
BATTERRRAAAAYYY..........ATTERRRN.........SHUN!"

A rolling thunderous sound followed as many pairs of new boots
came together. The Sergeant Major addressed us all in a very loud
voice, without the need to shout.

"Welcome to Bramcote. I am Battery Sergeant Major Walls." (I am
not too sure now if that was his name, or if I made it up to keep
the story flowing) "Today your training begins. Many of you have
never been away from home before. Some of you will be feeling
homesick. Do not worry about it, it will pass. You all come from
different walks of life. Some of you think you are hard men. I can
assure you, you are not. Do as you are told, and you will enjoy your
stay with us. Break the rules and we will come down on you like a
ton of bricks. Run away and the police will bring you back. You will
then be punished."

"Yesterday approximately 300 recruits arrived. You are not the only
ones living here. The rest of the Regiment return from their leave
today. Many of them are chuffed they are no longer recruits. They
may take the mickey out of you. Ignore them. We will not tolerate
fighting or bullying. If you have any problems see your sergeant. For
the next fourteen weeks, your sergeant will take the place of your
mum and your dad. Do exactly what he tells you and you won't go
wrong!"

He then addressed the sergeants: "Section sergeants, carry-on!"

His speech completed, he and the officer left the square. Sergeant
Hatto then began to teach us how to 'Stand at Attention'. How to
'Stand at Ease'. How to 'Stand Easy', and then how to brace oneself
having heard the command, 'SQUAD'. How to come to 'Stand at
Attention' from being 'At Ease' and so on.

It wasn't long before I was gasping for a cigarette (which was
prohibited for the first seven weeks) - I was experiencing withdrawal

symptoms at 16.

Learning how to 'drill' became an integral part of everyday life in Junior Leaders. The procedure took many weeks to perfect. It was all 'drilled' into us using numbers. A command would be given, and each recruit would shout aloud the number sequence to perfect uniform timing. "ONE... TWO THREE... ONE!" That way, the rolling thunder of 300 pairs of boots became one crisp earthmoving 'CRACK', as all boots hit the ground together.

We would all be expected to shout out numbers with every drill movement we performed over the next 14 weeks. After that, we would think them instead. We were instructed to march everywhere we went. Even to the canteen, we had to march as a squad carrying our green plastic mug and KFS in our left hand, tucked away in the small of our back, whilst swinging the other arm perpendicular to the body, both front and back.

When we finally returned to the billet we saw the timetable planned for the next seven weeks. The majority of time was set aside for either drill, uniform inspections or sport. There were a few anomalies in there such as 'Confidence Course', 'Inoculations', 'Sparring', and a daily event called 'Hygiene' which was scheduled for the end of each day. The entire day was planned from 'Reveille' to 'Lights-out'.

The events to follow were soon to be made crystal clear. On the timetable the Recruits' Battery was identified as Term Three of 1971. This suggested immediately that the programme of training would last for six terms, each being about 14 weeks in length. This also meant there was possibly close to a thousand boys in the Regiment, all between 15 and almost 18 years of age.

After the first seven-week period there would be a three-day holiday. After a further seven weeks there would be a three-week break. This would continue for two years. I had been anxious, but now I became panicky.

The end of Day One arrived soon enough. I was worn out, as were the others. We heard shouts in the distance informing us 'Lights-

Out' was in ten minutes. We all rushed to shower and ready ourselves for bed.

Then came the order: "STAND BY YOUR BEDS!"

Taffy Morgan entered the room reminding us that at the end of each day was 'Hygiene Inspection'. We would stand at attention at the end of our bunks wearing nothing but a towel about our midriffs. The order was that we would sleep naked anyway. That being regarded as the most hygienic way to sleep. (I am now 62 and have never been able to sleep wearing pyjamas from that day forward.) The cleanliness of our hands, neck and feet would be checked. If ordered to do so, we would let our towels drop to the floor so our genitals could also be inspected. This was degrading and indeed dehumanising, but in retrospect I realise now it was all planned to strip us of everything we had. We were told of the horrific ways a dirty soldier would be dealt with throughout our service in the military. Both boys and men, would be restrained in a bath of cold water and scrubbed with hard bristled brooms, effectively removing skin as well as dirt.

At the end of Day One I had made up my mind.

I had made a big mistake. This was not for me. The first opportunity I would telephone home and ask my parents to sign the necessary release forms to get me out. The big problem that followed was finding the time to go and search for a telephone box. It was the end of Day Three by the time I was able to sneak off and find a box within the camp. The queue for it was horrendous, but, with perseverance, it was finally my turn.

My dad answered the phone and was delighted to hear from me, but said he couldn't talk as he was busy at work. He placed the phone to one side as I waited for mum to come on. I pretended to talk into the mouthpiece as those waiting their turn were becoming impatient. I even pretended to be happy.

My mother finally answered at a time when the queue outside were indicating I'd had long enough and to give someone else a turn. I forced myself to hold back tears as I desperately tried to explain to mum that I was giving up and needed her permission to leave. I begged her to contact the Commanding Officer the following day and secure my release. She said she would talk to dad first.

I prayed long and hard for them to get me out of there. The following day came and went, as did the day after that and the next. Then I received a handwritten letter from my mother.

It was the first letter I had ever received from her and so I knew it was of great importance. In it, she wrote of her deep regret that she had raised a son that did not have the guts to see something as important as this through to the end. She said I would never become a man, and I was therefore no son of hers. She finished by writing, if I did not complete the training, she wanted nothing more to do with me.

I was devastated.

I spent much of that day in a state of shock. I was scared. That evening, whilst lying in bed in the darkness, I tried to calm myself. I started to join in with the chatter of my room-mates. There was Alistair Stevens, with his strong west country accent. We all decided to nickname him 'Pear Drop' on account of his head being pear-shaped.

Then there was Floyd, a lad from Lancashire who we nicknamed 'Pinky' because of his size. He was very small for his age but ended up as one of the tallest in the regiment by the time he reached 18. There was 'Scouse' Carr, and 'Scouse' Kay, obviously coming from Liverpool. In fact, there were a lot of Scousers and Jocks.

There was Rod Laird, a tall blond-haired lad who wasn't nicknamed, on account of nobody risking upsetting him as he declared himself as a junior ABA boxing champion. I was nicknamed 'Pokey' because of the length of my nose. Apparently, they thought I resembled a cartoon character of that time. Fortunately, that did not last long. Then there were others that we could not decide on a nickname for, like Mackins, a heavily built character but warm and extremely enthusiastic about becoming a soldier. There were so many others. However, their names have long since faded away.

The first seven weeks took a long time to complete. Endless inspections, numerous needles stuck in our arms, countless hours spent marching back and forth learning how to turn right, left, about turn, slow march, marching at the double, saluting to the left, saluting to the right, right wheel, left wheel, left incline etcetera, etcetera. All for the princely sum of fifty pence a week.

We were paid more, but that was paid into an account that could only be drawn when on leave. I travelled home at the end of seven weeks with a free rail warrant and several pounds to spend. We all travelled in full uniform and returned in full uniform.

Much of my three days leave was spent pleading with my parents again, but it fell on deaf ears. They took great delight in showing me off to everybody, which made it impossible to convince them this was not my future. Before long, I was back on the train making the return journey to Gamecock Barracks.

The way I remember it. Part 4

The second half of the term was worse than the first for me. This included the boxing tournament where 300 of us would engage in gladiatorial combat in a ring before the officers and their ladies.

The sparring sessions had become more regular, and Sergeant Hatto would pair each member of the squad against another. It was all pretty tame stuff. Nobody was permitted to do any damage. Well, not until the actual event anyway.

The boxing ring had been set up in the gymnasium in preparation for the two-day event. The Physical Training Instructors would provide us with a little instruction as they also, paired each of us off against another squad. To give us some experience of what was to come, they would insist on us having trial bouts of three, one-minute rounds.

Each of us had a couple of sparring fights. I recall being punched senseless on both occasions. I am not even sure if I had managed to land any punches on my opponents. I am no fighter. I had no fighting spirit. I was also the skinniest boy there. The main thing was, I left the ring conscious. No broken bones and no blood pouring from any orifice, although my pride had suffered terribly.

When that first day of the pugilistic event finally arrived, I was terrified. The ring-master was the Regimental Sergeant Major. The gymnasium was packed with the officers and their ladies sitting ringside. The three hundred recruits filled the remaining space.

The order of fights was published on the walls. My fight was listed for the second day. I had plenty of time to wait and contemplate the potential injuries I would most likely receive. The bouts had increased to three, three-minute rounds. The referee would ensure both boxers put their all into it, to offer good sport to the audience.

As the RSM called the number of the next fight, two boys would clamber through the ropes on either side of the ring, aided by their Squad Sergeant. The boys, all wearing red baggy T-shirts and knee length dark blue shorts, would have a coloured sash tied around their waists.

When ready, their names would be announced identifying the colour of the corner where they were standing. The boy would come to attention when his name was called and complete the military movement of 'About Turn'.

We would then shout: "We who are about to die salute you" (Just joking - that's what I felt like shouting anyway).

The referee would invite them both to the centre where they touched gloves. This coincided with the command: "BOX". Everybody would shout their support for either the blue or red corner. The noise could be heard several hundred yards away. Both boys, pressured by the PTI referee would be punching blindly at each other.

Occasionally, a fist would find its target and blood would spray across the ring. The referee appeared to be permitting the fighters to use their knees and heads in an effort to injure their opponent. For me, it was barbaric. I desperately tried to block out the thought of my inevitable slaughter in front of such a baying crowd.

Minutes before my calling I visited the toilet as nerves had got the better of me. As I entered the toilet block I could not fail to miss the blood-soaked floor. The discarded blood-soaked paper towels strewn all over the wash basins. My insides knotted as I stood transfixed with fear. I felt a hand on my shoulder and I understood someone saying I was on next.

I was led to ringside where Sergeant Hatto smiled, placing both hands on my shoulders. Someone else tied the sash about my midriff. I saw the Sergeant's lips moving but could hear nothing. It was all happening as if in slow motion. I was assisted into the ring, hearing volleys of cheers echoing in my head. My eyes became fixed on my opponent standing in the opposite corner. He stood there, staring back, pummelling his gloves together.

I heard someone shout: "YOU'RE GONNA KILL THE SKINNY-TWAT!"

The next word was: "BOX!"

For three long-drawn-out minutes, I kept my head down and swung wildly at a blurred target. I did not feel many punches strike me. I was very much aware of the audience on the outside of the combat zone, spinning around and around. I tasted blood in my mouth against my teeth. I was absolutely shattered by the time the bell rang.

Sitting on a stool in the corner I felt like I wanted to throw up. I gulped for air as Sergeant Hatto lifted my T-shirt and rubbed my chest with a wet sponge.

"You are doing okay, just keep it up. Keep your guard up and go for his head. You have him worried. You almost floored him a couple of times."

The bell rang, and the nightmare continued.

"BOX".

How I made it to the end of the second round I will never know. My skinny legs were beginning to buckle with exhaustion. I knew I had to keep lifting my arms to defend myself, but I felt I was completely outmatched. I knew I had no chance of winning the fight.

The referee had stopped my opponent's onslaught on a couple of occasions and asked how many fingers he was holding up. I should have lied.

Then: "BOX", and my torture carried on.

Sitting in my corner at the end of that second round, I noticed the skin on my arms was flushed red with some severe looking rope burns. They did not appear to hurt either, which surprised me at the time. What Sergeant Hatto said to me during that brief respite was insignificant. I did not hear, but then again, I wasn't really listening. I focused all of my concentration on surviving those final three minutes. I did not care that my opponent was going to win or that I was going to lose badly. I just had to aim for that bell. To keep standing against all odds.

The bell sounded, "BOX" and the battering began again.

This time the onslaught was not as heavy as in the second round. It crossed my mind that I was wearing my opponent out. He had put so much effort into that second round, he was now beginning to buckle at the knees too. It would have been a great ending if could have found the strength to discharge a good punch at that stage. Instead I found my arms were 'rigor-mortised' in a facially protective mode. I was just so pleased it was over when the final bell tolled.

Needless to say, I had lost. I did not have to box again after that day. That privilege went to those who had the capabilities of holding the honour of the Regiment against challengers from other Junior Leader units. Although, we always had to be at the ringside to offer our support to them.

The following day that experience had been put behind me. I had done it and had survived with my big nose intact, coupled with the evidence of rope burns reminding me of my battle.

From then on, I would appreciate just how much energy is expended in the male dominated world of barbaric pugilism. Besides, believe it or not, that was not my worst of dreads. That honour would have to go to 'The Confidence Course'.

The way I remember it. (Part 5)

A quick reminder before I continue, when I joined the Junior Leaders Regiment, I was a very frail child. I had been abandoned by my parents to a public boarding school, hundreds of miles away from home.

No doubt they thought it was in my best interest.

So, from an austere environment of regular caning for misspelling a word and regular elocution lessons to set me apart from the accent I was raised with, I had entered another all-boy austere world of reconditioning. I was terrified, but knew not to show it.

We were introduced to the 'Confidence Course' early on in our training. It had some elements of what is more commonly known as an 'assault course', to which we were extremely familiar. It also included 'dare devil' equipment fastened to the trees, high off the ground.

There were Burma bridges and cat walks and terrifying horizontal ladders thirty feet up in the canopy. No safety nets to protect your fall. The idea being, if you obeyed your sergeant you would not get hurt.

Remember the 'If I say Jump, you will jump' bit? Well, this tested it to the limit. Ropes, scramble nets, platforms, ladders and death slides were positioned in the small woods.

As a squad, we would be led around the course, venturing higher and higher as more and more confidence was lost. The plan was obviously to give us total confidence in our abilities; however, that was going to take the whole two years to accomplish - in my case anyway.

There were always a few expected casualties on each visit. I prayed I would not become a future quoted statistic.

"You are quite safe, lads, if you obey my commands. In all these years, we have only had one death".

Up until then, they had just quoted the one unfortunate boy who broke his pelvis in the long fall down from the trees. I was not inspired by that. In the early days, there would be that moment when one of the boys froze and refused to go any further. This would block the way forwards for everyone else. I would be eternally grateful to that individual who was brave enough to refuse.

This stalled the inevitable gain in height for a little longer.

As time went by, one realised that the journey ever upward was more comfortable than the wrath of the demi-god who wore the stripes. One thing for sure, we always returned to our 'pits' exhausted. Then, we cleaned, ironed and polished for the remainder of our day, before hygiene inspection and lights-out. We would ceremoniously 'bumper' the floors with plenty of polish to retain the depth of the shine. Then, we would lay blankets down, to preserve its gleam till morning, ready for the routine room and kit inspection.

'Bumpering' was an unusual task as it involved the swinging back-and-forth a heavily weighted metal floor pad, secured to a broom handle. Much later in my service these were replaced by electric floor polishers.

It was at the end of such a day, having 'bumpered' the floor of the barrack room, I went to the drying room, where one would customarily hang clothes to dry, and I discovered a pair of my blue PE shorts were missing. Convincing myself that someone had taken them in error, I had to face up to the possible consequence of severe castigation if I was found to be down an item of equipment.

There was only one way I could get out of this mess, and that was to replace the item as quickly as possible. I was not a thief; however, it was likely a thief had taken mine and it was the only option open to me.

Listening carefully for any sign of approaching danger, and my heart pumping pure adrenalin, I selected my target, shoved them up my jumper, and made a dash for my pit.

Karma struck within seconds. As I entered the room, I lost my balance on one of the floor blankets. I slide one way and my left leg went the other. The weakest joint on that limb took the strain and indicated as much to everybody in the vicinity with a sickening, 'CRACK'.

The pain shot up through the length of my leg. Silence fell about the room as everyone watched me writhing on the floor.

I did not release a whimper. All of the air in my lungs was trapped as I consciously held it in, as if to control my agonising discomfort. When the air was finally expelled it was accompanied by a blaspheming.

I was one of the very few who did not use 'industrial language' on a regular basis. Some found it necessary to use several four-letter expletives in every sentence, but it had been brutally caned into me as uncouth and degrading.

At that moment however, I could think of no better way of expressing my feelings and I felt no regret in using those words. It seemed a fitting expression under the circumstances.

I was still writhing on the floor, when Sergeant Hatto was by my side. To my surprise he was calming and supportive. Immediately taking control of my ankle, he commanded one of the lads to run to the medical centre to inform them of our imminent arrival. He then gathered me up in his arms, directing me to hold onto him around his neck so as to steady any movement. He then carried me at least a quarter of a mile, joking all the way.

He gained my total trust and respect that day. From then on, I would repay him by jumping when I was told to.

I cannot recall exactly how long I was out of commission as I hobbled about on a pair of crutches. The medical staff didn't think I had broken my ankle, just badly sprained the ligaments. An x-ray appeared to be unwarranted.

My foot had turned blue with the toes at least two inches from the ground. It resembled a cow's udder more than a foot. To this day, 46 years on, my ankle still appears swollen and disfigured. I had finally made it into the book of injury statistics.

I did not miss out on too much of the training. Most of it was preparing for a camping exercise in Rhyl. I was temporarily billeted in the guard room awaiting their return, after which we were sent on a three-week period of Christmas leave, having completed Term Three of 1971.

Three glorious weeks and £32 in the bank to spend, the most money I had ever had in my entire life. Things were beginning to look up.

The way I remember it. Part 6

The Christmas break soon ended, and it was time to return to Bramcote. I assured myself things would not be quite as bad as the initial training was over and I would now be joining my troop. For the remainder of my stay I would learn a couple of military trades and, as time went on maybe the homesickness would subside.

The majority of my squad had been assigned to join Mansergh troop of 40 Battery, led by Sergeant Crosby. We referred to him, out of earshot again, as 'Bing'. He appeared older than Sergeant Hatto, and more portly in stature. A good man though, and one who carried the burden of responsibility and authority well. He was always fair to his boys and acted sympathetic when required. Having said that, the requirement for sympathy would not be permitted that often.

The biggest difference between the life in Recruits' Battery and in the Troops was that we were allowed to smoke cigarettes again. In actual fact, it was almost a requirement. Smoke breaks would be called at least every half hour throughout the day. Fortunately, I had returned with another carton of 200 cigarettes for the start of the term, as the previous 200 had been stolen from storage. As had all of the other recruits' cigarettes.

We had questioned the Junior Lance Bombardier who had the responsibility of storage of our personal property, but he just laughed in the knowledge we were powerless to do anything. A very expensive Bush radio, given by my grandfather, had also gone missing. He promised to pay us all back someday, but that never happened. In other words, he was the thief who stole everything under lock and key from storage. Being a rank higher than all of us, it had been drummed into us we could not jump the chain of command. He could steal whatever he wanted without fear of reprisal.

Well, not until term five, when I was privileged to witness Pinky Floyd pay him back with one well-placed punch. I am certain the noise from his exploding nose could be heard on the other side of camp.

Anyway, the remainder of terms were different as we performed as part of the Regiment.

Most of our day's timetable would include the learning of a trade, sport or military training and exercises such as the rifle ranges. Every

Saturday we would rehearse for the big 'End of Term' passing-out parade, when the mustering gunners, having completed their two years, were sent off to join their regiments.

On Sundays, we attended church parade, and all of the evenings, but for one, were ours to do with as we pleased. As long as we did not leave the camp, that is. The exception to the rule was 'hobby' evening. Each of us would be expected to choose a hobby for that term. I recall choosing chess for the first term as that seemed to me as the least physical of all.

By the second term I had been ordered to attend the gymnasium and adopt the hobby of circuit-training with weights because of my weedy stature, coupled with their desire to make me look more like a soldier than a victim of starvation. The amount of times I heard a physical training instructor say to me: "I've seen more fat on a greasy chip", is not worth mentioning.

It wasn't until the final term that I managed to sneak in with the photography class.

Most evenings we would prepare our kit for the next day. Bulling boots, gaiters, belts and bayonet scabbards with black polish and spit. Spraying starch on trousers and shirts so they could stand almost unaided, not forgetting the laborious task of polishing the belt brasses.

In the final term, the one where we would 'pass-out' to our regiments, the routine and uniform would change slightly to include white belts, gaiters and bayonet scabbards. They would be whitened by a thick tar-like substance, I was led to believe this was also used to paint centre white line markings on main roads. As we bulled we could watch some television.

On occasion one of us would be chosen to run to the NAAFI to buy an entire list of essentials. Usually the task was assigned to the youngest in the troop. The correct change would be handed over to the volunteer who would make the onerous journey to purchase the goods.

I remember my first delegated trip very clearly as if it were yesterday. I glanced at the endless list and recognised the obvious items, including a couple of tins of Kiwi shoe polish, three packets of Embassy cigarettes, a couple of dusters, a packet of mints, two biros, some envelopes, a writing pad and other such items. However there were a few other anomalies I required help with.

With total innocence and naiveté, I asked the elderly NAAFI woman for a packet of blow jobs, an extra-long, a seven-inch dildo, and a strawberry flavoured clitoris.

Facing her with a dead-pan expression, she realised I was nominated as that day's patsy as she calmly replied, "I am afraid we do not sell those, young man."

When I returned to share out the items, it was not until I announced those unusual items were not sold in the NAAFI anymore, everyone fell about laughing. I didn't actually understand the joke for a long time. That's how inexperienced I was. It was not the last time I was caught either. I actually waited in the Quartermaster's Store for more than an hour before I realised I was again the butt of humour having been tasked an hour earlier to request a 'long weight'.

Throughout my first term the pay given in hand had been 50 pence a week. This eventually rose to £3 by the time I reached 18.

Every now and then my dad would send me a fiver, which really did help. Particularly with the purchase of cigarettes. Everybody scrounged them. A whole bartering economy had evolved in Junior leaders, and it revolved around cigarettes. So desperate would we become for a 'drag' on a cigarette, our friends would plead to have the filter end before discarding it. At least they would be able to have a couple of 'drags' before burning their fingers. Things would get really silly with friends pleading for the 'cork' as the absolute final puff.

Fortunately, the frequency of sport would, in some small way, help clear our lungs of some of the carcinogenic deposits. There was always a lot of running. Both cross-country and forced route marches with full equipment. Then there was the assault course to negotiate every couple of weeks. Football and rugby were frequent, as well as canoeing, rock climbing, abseiling and orienteering.

There were even 'outward-bound' courses regularly held in the Brecon Beacons. Not only that, we all had to attend the ´RAT´ course, the Regimental Adventure Training week close to Snowdonia. An entire week dedicated to jumping in icy lakes and running up the side of mountains.

For me, the worst of all sporting activities was swimming. I had arrived at Bramcote as a non-swimmer and remained one for quite a while. Back in camp, more often than not, we would be paraded to go swimming before breakfast. I would hide my fear well. I cannot really explain why I had never learned to swim as I had spent my childhood by the sea. The older I got, the greater the fear grew. I was not alone either. There were a few of us.

They tried everything to teach us. Throwing us in at the shallow end, then the deep end. Pushing us off the diving board, then the high board; but all to no avail. I remained one of thirty in the regiment who became a challenge to them.

Then finally, one early morning, they came up with a ground-breaking idea.

The way I remember it. Part 7

This part is a memory only a few of us experienced, but one that reminds me junior leaders did have a sense of humour, at times.

Sergeant Crosby had ordered me to report to the swimming pool for a double lesson at a particular time.

It was when I arrived I recognised all of the Regiment´s non-swimmers were in attendance. A PTI stood us all in a line alongside the pool.

"Listen in", he commanded: "I have arranged a very special treat for you today. A double period of swimming."

"Why is it so special? Because today you Junior Leaders will be trying your absolute best, for once, to impress. An Officer has taken a personal interest in your aquatic short comings and will therefore be taking the period. When the officer enters the poolside area you will obey every command you are given."

"Is that clear?"

"YES SERGEANT", echoed around the pool.

I desperately held my nerve gazing into the very still blue pool, as the stench of chlorinated water filled the air. A couple of nerve-racking minutes went by before a command was given.

"SQUAD - SQUAD SHUN!"

We all stamped our feet together.

An officer coming to teach us to swim? This was a very different tactic. Officers were treated as Gods and would very rarely come into contact with us unless it was for an inspection. They were held in awe as they were so powerful in the military.

It appeared to me that the only one not to be unnerved by their presence was the Regimental Sergeant Major. I had heard him shout at officers on his parade square, albeit in a respectful manner.

Yes, I did say 'HIS' parade square. The RSM was terrifying. I felt sure he had the power to order my execution if he wanted.

Anyway, the PTI left the pool area as we waited at attention a little longer.

'Stand easy gentlemen", said a voice softly, but audible enough in the pool area.

All of our heads turned toward the poolside entrance where the command had been given. It had caught us all off guard as we had never heard the voice of a female officer before. She walked toward us as she adjusted the bra strap on her bikini. I kid you not. I am not making this up. I can't speak for the others, of which some maybe reading this article now, but my eyes had explored all of her body within seconds.

She was gorgeous. I would have guessed she was 19 years old, so very pretty with telescopic legs, (you know, the type that seem to go on for ever) and perfectly formed young firm breasts. Other than the women in the NAAFI, and they were mostly very old, this was the first woman we had seen on camp. She came to stand in front of us and inspecting the line briefly from where she stood.

She said: "I am going to teach you men how to swim. You all look like big strapping lads who can look after yourselves but when it comes to water, you face a fear that nobody else appears to understand. I understand because I was like you and I conquered it. You can too. Are you all willing to trust me?"

I recall one on the rank began to reply alone: "YES SI..." and broke off realising what the rest of us had when she walked in. How do we address her? It was more than obvious she was not a 'SIR'.

She smiled and cleared the confusion for us: "YES MA'AM".

We followed her lead: "YES MA'AM".

She smiled whilst placing her hands over her ears speaking softly: "And please, not so loud eh?"

She arranged us all in the shallow end of the pool, ensuring each of us was out of reach of each other. I am sure the temperature of the water had been raised a few degrees. She then instructed us to participate in the game of 'Simon Says'. I know that sounds very childish, but it did help draw our attention away from her body.

She had us standing on one leg, and then the other. Then getting down on both knees so our faces were just out of it.

"Simon says, pinch your nose and put your entire head beneath the water," and so on.

Of course, we did everything she asked in an effort to impress. She went further with getting us to see who could hold their breath the longest and who could do it with their eyes open. By the end of that double period she had every one of us swimming at least a width of the pool unaided.

The Army had finally taught me how to swim. Sadly, but probably best, given the circumstances, we never saw her in a bikini again. Although I am sure the bed sheets rustled that night.

Alas. She was hidden away in an administration block as the Adjutant's assistant and we would occasionally catch a glimpse of her in the church congregation at church on a Sunday. Not the best of places to encourage erotic thoughts, as it was treated as a serious misdemeanour just to be glancing in the wrong direction, if caught by the RSM.

He would be watching everybody like a hawk.

On occasion, he would even ban us from coughing in church. Can you imagine it?

He would bellow: "THE NEXT PERSON TO COUGH WILL BE MARCHED TO MY GUARD ROOM AND BE PLACED ON EXTRA DUTIES".

Now that's just marvellous isn't it? Prior to the order you wouldn't have any need to cough but as soon as he made it, we would all be turning crimson, trying desperately to trap the tickling irritation inside, praying for the hymns to start so that we could clear the last packet of fags from our lungs.

The only other time we would regularly come into contact with the RSM would be on Saturday morning parades.

The way I remember it. Part 8

A great deal has happened over the last 46 years and my memory is fading. I may not be 100% accurate with all that I write and therefore I ask the reader's forgiveness if I make a few slight errors. I am sure you will correct me if I am way off the track.

The rehearsals for the big 'Passing-Out Parade' would always be on a Saturday morning. Our uniforms would have to be immaculate as the RSM inspected every single one of us. I cannot recall exactly but there must have been close to a thousand junior leaders on parade. Inspecting every one of us took time.

The parade lasted about three hours, most of which was standing perfectly still. Each of us holding SLR rifles by our side, and part way through the ceremony these would be fixed with bayonets.

Prior to the RSM inspecting us, our own sergeants, Battery Sergeant Major and officers would do the rounds. If any one of them criticised you, there would be trouble.

We had all previously been issued with two pairs of DMS boots, of which one pair would be kept for such parades. These boots would be expected to gleam as glass, the result of countless layers of polish worked into them over many hours. Spit and polish was the only way to achieve results.

It would be on such parades that it was made clear of our purpose in life;

"Her Majesty the Queen is your Captain General. You will fight for your Queen and, if necessary, you will give your life for your

Queen."

Now I have to admit, as a 16-year-old boy, that did disturb me.
Would I ever be able to find the courage to give my life for the
Queen?

Not all of the comments fed to us were thought provoking,
some were really positive and encouraged self-esteem. It was a good
feeling when one received praise from the Sergeant stood before.

"That's it, shoulders back, chest out, tummy in. Sartorial
bloody elegance - well done son."

Then he would move on to the next and the next. Rank by rank.
Before long the entire Regiment would be called to attention by the
Junior Regimental Sergeant Major. He was always a boy soldier
selected from the final term.

There was a whole rank structure at the boy's level. You entered as a
junior gunner and could possibly be promoted all the way up to junior
RSM.

Throughout my stay I remained Junior Gunner Luscombe. What I
find amusing to this day, and I apologise now if this person reads
this, but we actually had a boy in the Regiment with the surname
'Rea'. To begin one's service as Gunner-Rea must have taken some
stick. It doesn't require too much imagination to come up
with a nickname for him.

Anyway, the Saturday morning rehearsals were a nightmare.
Standing in the same position for several hours, looking straight to
your front requires an enormous amount of patience and self-control.
After just 30 minutes the inside rim of the flat hat felt like a circular
metal band being slowly tightened around one's head particularly in
the area of the frontal lobe.

Then there was the collar stud from the detachable shirt collar,
sticking into one's Adam's apple. All designed as instruments of

torture.

If it was a hot day, boys would be dropping like flies.

If you were going to faint on parade, the rule was that you were instructed to come to attention first, and then collapse forward. This would maximise any injury and dissuade any potential skivers from using that ploy to evade the remainder of the parade.

Fainting on parade with a bayonet fixed on the end of your rifle could prove fatal. A non-fatal version actually happened to me on one occasion. I had been on parade for a couple of hours standing firm. I could hear a Sergeant Major bellowing at a member of another Battery: "LISTEN-IN. JUST IMAGINE YOUR GRANNY ON THE TOILET HAVING A CRAP. THAT'LL STOP YOU FROM FAINTING."

The thought was disgusting but the image was immediately in my mind. He also mentioned another trick, I was already familiar with. Wiggle your toes inside of your boots and ever-so-slowly rock back and forth effectively, momentarily removing some weight off one's spine. At least that gave me something to do. Then he gave a piece of advice I would not recommend under those circumstances. Well it didn't work for me anyway.

"BREATHE DEEPLY, IN THROUGH YOUR NOSE AND OUT THROUGH
YOUR MOUTH."

I'll give it a try, I thought. I felt myself going. I lost vision immediately. My world began spinning out of control. I managed to come to attention and recall hearing an echoing 'thud' repeating in my brain as I lost consciousness.

That must have been the moment I hit the ground with my face.

It seemed like I was waking from a full eight hours' sleep as two Sergeants had gathered me up and dragged me off the parade. I had only lost consciousness for less than a minute, but I came around totally confused as to my location. It took me a few minutes to get-it-together. I was checked for injuries and found I had only grazed my cheek and bloodied my nose.

Fortunately for me, the bayonet had fallen clear out of my path. I had previously met others in the MRS, the Medical Centre, who had lost their teeth, so I considered myself lucky. Within a few minutes I was sent back to re-join the ranks.

Eventually we would 'shoulder our arms' and march passed the dais with the Commanding Officer taking the salute. The drilling was spectacular. The sound made by a thousand precision trained boys coming to attention, fixing bayonets and presenting arms in a general salute was truly impressive. It was awesome and pride inspiring. On the actual day of the Passing-Out Parade, the ceremony would be supported by the Junior Leaders' band adding to the spectacle.

As for fainting, every time I went on parade after that I struggled with the thought I was going to faint again. Needless to say, that was the only time I ever did.

I began this section with the idea I would write something about the RSM. I cannot recall too much other than he was a stocky bloke with a little moustache and a pace stick with which he would meticulously pace out his steps across 'His-Square'.

Then, with a megaphone of a voice bellow: "RIGHT MARKER! "

Nowadays, he actually reminds me of the actor who played a very similar role, Windsor Davies. I do wonder if the two ever came into contact, whereby Windsor was given a few tips on how to act like an RSM.

He had the eyes of a hawk, and I am quite sure he had a couple on the back of his head too. A glance in your direction had you frozen solid. I swear he was a descendant of Medusa.

I was privileged to see a lighter side of him on the day he retired from the regiment.

He was towed by the Regiment's officers around the barracks on a 25-pounder field gun, to the delight and cheers of the whole unit.

Even today, 46 years on, I can see his face. A career soldier who, I dare say, had seen his fair share of action. I cannot imagine for one moment he would have experienced the intimacy of a woman's love or the embrace of a child's arms around his neck. This is the image I have created for him. I could be totally off-key and incorrect on all counts. He was, as they say, a 'man's man'. The army needed men like him. Much more than they needed the likes of me. He had definitely made an impression on my life.

Thank you RSM Smith for scaring the crap out of me. However, you have my lifelong respect for doing your job perfectly.

When I suggested I felt proud with our achievement in drill, I realise it was as a result of countless hours of repetition. From the very early days at Bramcote, where many boys did not know their left from right and would march like Spotty Dog (a wooden television puppet from the 1950s show 'Woodentops'), we had all been transformed into a real military unit.

As I have mentioned earlier, I had surrendered to the inevitability of having no way out of the situation for a long time to come. I had experienced a sense of pride and overwhelming achievement on other occasions, as well. There was a moment when I won the trophy for 'Best Shot' in the Regiment, and another when I surpassed everyone's expectations on a Cadre course. These happened in the last term I was there, so I expect I will recall those next in Part 9.

The way I remember it. Part 9

I remember visiting the shooting range and spending the day completing a number of firearms exercises. At the end of the session there was a competition to find the Best Shot. We were provided with a set number of rounds each and ordered to advance in line, over several hundred yards, advancing toward our individually numbered

Figure-11 targets.

Every now and again the targets would be raised from the butts. We
would fire, change magazine when necessary, and then move
forward together until the next contact was made. The target did not
fall if hit, so you did not know if you had been successful or not.
They were raised and lowered with pulleys by other Junior Leaders,
keeping well out of sight, immediately below the targets. This
continued until we were ordered to cease firing. The hits on our
individual targets were then totalled up and an outright winner
selected according to who had the most hits.

That was me.

I have to admit, going up on stage to collect the trophy from the
Commanding Officer, in front of all the parents on Passing Out Day,
filled me with a great sense of achievement. It raised me on a
pedestal. Who needed rank to justify their worth as a soldier I
thought? Surely one's ability as a soldier was far more important?

Of course, there's always someone who wants to dampen your
achievement and triumphant moment by declaring the boy shooting
alongside me, usually an excellent shot, had not hit his target once. I
guess you know what was being suggested by that.

Pride was an experience I had previously been unfamiliar with. It felt
good when it arrived. It built up what little self-esteem I had.

I had succeeded in obtaining a couple of military trades during my
stay at Bramcote. the first being the basic of all trades in the Royal
Artillery, the operating of a 25-pounder field gun.

All I can recall about that is the mnemonic: 'E.L.X.L.E', that
provided the only mental sequence stimulating my brain throughout
the process. I felt I was more suited to being a signaller. That
involved the learning and operating a variety of radio equipment.

The VHF-C42, C45 Larkspur radios and a range of A-sets, which
were the back-pack variety. Then there was the C13 High-Frequency

set that involved a bit of maths when working out formulas for the required lengths of horizontal dipole aerials. If I remember correctly, that had such a wattage output that it could illuminate a disconnected strip-light in your hand from several feet away. In other words, they were dangerous.

We also learned how to establish a network of landline telephones running 'Don-Ten' wire over and under an obstacle course and how to strip the ends of the wire with one´s front teeth, so that by your early 40s your front teeth fell out of their own accord. Also learning the phonetic alphabet together with a whole new language relating to the directing of artillery fire onto the target. At least that stimulated my cerebral cortex a little.

Unfortunately for me, having qualified early for my two trades someone, in their wisdom, decided to send me on an NCO´s Cadre course. In my final term.

It was obvious I was there just to make up the numbers and give the others on the course room to shine brighter.

The course was normally set aside to assist those who had achieved junior promotions to gain rapid promotion on entry to our selected regiments. Most of the participants were Junior Sergeants and above, including the Junior RSM.

Very surprisingly I found myself enjoying the course. If I remember correctly, a leader chart was also displayed. I excelled in the academic subjects. English, maths, science, military communication skills, map reading, world affairs and German.

Then there were the other physical aspects requiring an abundance of stamina and endurance. I knew I was going to struggle there as, in the length of time I had been at Bramcote, I still resembled someone suffering from malnutrition.

There was also a political exercise whereby each of us was selected to represent a country in a present day, real life, situation. We were expected to progress the present scenario to a conclusion using 'open' and 'secret' moves. This exercise was called 'CRISIS' and I was one of the representatives from Laos. That was the area of the world chosen, with others, representing Cambodia, Thailand, Vietnam, China and the USA.

We were tasked to research the country's politics and military capabilities, coming together several times a day to discuss open moves under supervision of our mentors, officers from the Education Corps. We would give political speeches from a podium. I scored remarkably well in all of those topics and it was beginning to unsettle the achievers.

Then came the day of reckoning. The day I would lose face and come last. A battle against the 'Self' that, over previous terms I had failed to shine. This one would carry the highest marks as it required a strong element of determination. I personally thought of it as proving who was the most brain dead as it was designed to be brain numbing.

The idea was for each of us to be weighed. Then one third of our individual weight would be measured in sand and placed in a metal framed Bergen rucksack, which we would then carry as quickly as possible over the 12-mile route. On completion of the task, the packs would be weighed again to ensure no cheating. The first mile had to be covered as a team, after which, we could separate and continue the remainder of the journey alone, if we so wished.

The Cadre course participants were divided into five teams and each team released from the start point at five-minute intervals. I found my position as the last man in the last team to set off. That first mile was a purgatorial experience for me. The leader of the group took up the pace as if it was a four-minute mile.

I understand that we each carried a third of our weight in the packs, however some of these lads were muscle-bound. I, on the other hand, had not developed a muscle that had any real definition to it. A strong gust of wind could blow me over. Needless to say, after that first mile, which we covered in about eight minutes, I let the remainder of the group disappear over the horizon. I took the pack off my back as it was hurting my sides, dropped in on the ground and kicked it several times.

I swore at it. I spat at it. I was raging at it.

Throughout the course, I knew how badly I was destined to perform when I arrived at this point. I was so disillusioned with the inevitability of entering the camp alone, long after everyone else had packed up, that I gave in to my depression.

"Oh what the hell, all I can do is walk back. I cannot just give up. I was doing so well on the course, there was even a chance I could have come first. That would really have pissed a lot of people off."

I struggled to get the pack back over my shoulders and set off again. It was painful, but I convinced myself to try at least to enter the camp joint last. That meant catching someone up. There was bound to be one other who would find it difficult and, if I could just muster up sufficient determination to catch him, all may not be lost.

The journey was all on road, uphill and downhill, through villages, over bridges, across junctions and around bends. The destination was clearly signposted. There was no danger of being lost, and no possibility of a short cut. After several miles, I had still not caught sight of the second-to-last runner. It was not only demoralising, but infuriating. At one point, I did see an army Land Rover pass me by and one of the course Sergeants leant briefly through the door window: "KEEP IT UP LUSCOMBE. YOU'LL MAKE IT SON," he shouted.

Unfortunately, he was travelling in the opposite direction or I would have blocked his path and conceded defeat.

Not long after that, I did a repeat performance of kicking the crap out of my Bergen, spitting, hurling abuse at it. I now had blisters on my back. I reached that point of despair where I felt hopelessly inadequate. I was having a battle within myself. I could not give up. Not now, after all I had pushed myself through. It was only 12 miles, but my legs just couldn't carry my weak frame and the pack. I knew I had to carry on.

Okay, if I came in last, so be it. I gave it my best shot. I began again with the thought I would just stroll the remainder of the way.

Then I changed my mind and ran between lamp-posts. Sometimes I carried on for two or more lamp-posts. After what seemed an age, I caught sight of somebody ahead. A very long way ahead, far in the distance on a long stretch of straight road. My heart leaped with joy as I ran and ran and ran. I was so determined to catch him up. There was no way he was going to arrive at camp before I did. The truth of it is, I never caught him. My effort to catch him had all been in vain.

I dragged the rucksack through the gates of Gamecock Barracks by its strap. I walked by the guardroom on my way back to the block when I was stopped in my tracks by the Provost Sergeant.

"GET BACK HERE, AT THE DOUBLE. YOU'VE GOT TO CLOCK IN."

He peered down at a clipboard he was holding: "Name?"

"Junior Gunner Luscombe, Sergeant," I replied wearily.

Looking down at his watch he noted the time alongside my name. I could have sworn there was hardly any writing on his pad.

"Well done son. You may have broken the Regimental record."

He said it in such a 'matter of fact' way that I asked him to repeat what I thought I had heard him say. This was impossible. I had not caught anyone and did not pass anyone.

Still confused, I handed over my Bergen to be weighed. It was later confirmed that I had indeed broken the record. It transpired that the runner I had seen a long way ahead of me was from the first group that had left the start-point. The remainder of the course had remained in their groups and had taken quite long rest breaks, whilst hiding behind walls to evade detection from the roving Sergeants. The final endurance test had won me sufficient points to complete the NCO's Cadre course in first place; I am sure, to the embarrassment of many.

I was congratulated by my course Sergeant and ordered to see my Battery Sergeant Major immediately. I was informed that he had the difficult task of notifying me that it was felt I should be placed second on the course due to the fact that I had deliberately not exerted myself to my full potential throughout my training at Bramcote. The final score had been altered and the first position would be handed to the Junior RSM.

I felt sure there was a lesson for me in the experience I had just endured, but it did not sit comfortably with me at the time. Rank may carry certain privileges, but it can also attract elements of abuse. At the end, I did find it mildly amusing that I had shaken the foundations of their course for their chosen future leaders.

It may seem insignificant to many; however, such experiences gave me a foundation to build on. From then on, I knew I had it in me to achieve what I previously thought impossible. I could also go it alone if necessary.

The way I remember it. Part 10 - The finale

For the remaining few weeks of the final term, the pressure was full on in preparation for our 'Passing Out Parade'. The big day, the finale, when our family would be invited to witness their boys becoming men on entry to the regulars.

We had been told to think carefully about the regiment we wished to be posted to, where we would like to be sent for our adult service. We were to research all possibilities and submit a list of our three choices in order of our preference. Rumour had it that the selections would be made according to the achievement and rank. In other words, if you were the Junior RSM, you would be given your first choice. Likewise, if you were a Junior BSM you would also be given your first choice. If you were a Junior Bombardier it is likely you would get your second choice. The likes of me, a total under-achiever would get the third choice.

With this advanced warning in mind it was obvious I would play the system. I put my first choice as my third and my third choice as my first. Pinky Floyd and Pear-Drop followed suit. That's how we ended up being posted to The Highland Gunners, the Regiment we had placed in first position. My plan had backfired. I am so pleased it did. 19 Field Regiment turned out to be a great unit, as I am sure any of the postings would have been. Within 18 months I had climbed onto the first rung of the promotion ladder.

The day of our Passing Out finally arrived. We were finally ready, after months of preparation. Our uniforms were immaculate, our boots reflecting the light like mirrors. We stood motionless for what seemed an age on the Parade Square, our eyes fixed on the crowd gathering before us. I am sure all of us were searching for our family without, moving a whisker. I did not hear anybody hit the ground that day. We all performed well.

The band played as the Commanding Officer and other high-ranking dignitaries, accompanied by his sword-carrying entourage, marched through the ranks, inspecting each boy.

Finally, the band stopped and there was quiet.

The Junior Regimental Sergeant Major took his position, front-and-centre, facing the Regiment.

"JUNIOR LEADERS' REGIMENT, ROYAL ARTILLERY... REGIMENT... ATTERRRN-SHUN!"

Our families looked on as hundreds of boys impressed them all with precision movements.

The Junior RSM bellowed: "GENERAL SALUTE... PREESSERRRNT... ARMS".

Hundreds of rifles with gleaming bayonets attached, were slammed vertically in front of us with a single 'CRACK'.

Every movement commanded was followed with absolute precision. Two years of training had taken us to this very proud moment. Two years of repetition drill, standing in blistering heat or in freezing cold where one's fingers became frozen to the bone.

This was what that training was all about. The band played, and we marched passed the saluting-dais in both quick and slow time. Our drill was impeccable. Having completed the display, we came to a halt and the band fell silent.

The Junior RSM joined our troop as the Regimental Sergeant Major gave the command we had all dreamt of for two years: "THE MUSTERED GUNNERS WILL MARCH OFF... BY THE LEFT... SLOW... MARCH!"

The feeling was tremendous. We were no longer Junior Gunners, we were the real thing. We were Gunners in the regular army. All with the potential of becoming future leaders. The pride, the self-esteem, the self-respect. It felt so good marching past my family with my head held high. I knew my grandad was watching and recalling his time as a boy soldier, who later went on to serve in the Royal Artillery in The Great War, followed by the Second. And then my father, who also served in the Royal Artillery throughout the Second World War.

It brought a lump to my throat as I marched off that parade square for the final time. We marched out of sight behind a red brick wall and then, as tradition would have it, threw our hats in the air with a rousing cheer.

The experience of Bramcote had been brutal at times. I had been abandoned by my family and then stripped of all my civilian past. Not only did this include my clothing but also any elements of indoctrination of my early surroundings. The army had rebuilt me in an image they created. I saw my peers in their naked state and had been given the chance to create bonds with them, far greater than many would have experienced with their own brothers. We became one as a unit and worked as a team.

I saw us all as equals, with the same bodies, the same fears and the same opportunities. I saw, and experienced, rank for the first time. How some changed once they gained a greater position of authority over others.

I was also made aware of another class, separated from the majority and looked up to by those who could never aspire to such position in life, the Officer Class. These early lessons in life provided the foundation for my future survival and success.

Forty-six years ago, on September the 14th, I entered the gates of Gamecock Barracks. I have never returned but I do hope, one day, I will find that opportunity.

Section 7 - Denis Law. Sports and other Extra Curricular activities

There's not been too much written about the sports teams and other non-military activities that provided some legitimate escape routes out of camp, away from our strict routines encapsulated in formality at Bramcote (I often referred to it as Borstal with pay), so I hope my recollections conjure up some memories for you too.

I've never been overly keen on any games or sports, but I quickly saw that certain pursuits or clubs on camp gave you the chance to enjoy non-soldiering breaks, and trips away from barracks.

I had previously played hockey at school to a reasonable standard before joining up, which was a milestone in itself, being a left-hander, but you adapt. I also played for my school's table-tennis team - and without any false modesty, was quite good at both.

Apart from those specific games, I've never enjoyed all the usual mainstream sporting activities; stuff like football, rugby or athletics, and even less so as a spectator. In fact, to this day, I still can't be arsed with ANY sports at all, not even the big stuff like World Cup finals etc ... yawn ... but please don't slag me off for this, and try to remember that not enjoying it is not the same as can't do it or won't do it.

When we arrived at Bramcote, we were all encouraged from the start of our training in New Intake Gunners, NIGS, to give it our best and to endeavour to excel through sporting achievement - ideally by becoming an accomplished team player, but equally, to remember that it didn't hurt to draw attention and get yourself 'noticed' too.

I did just that, and it didn't take me long to win a regular place on both the Regimental hockey and table tennis teams which, bizarrely, I confess to actually enjoying, especially playing at that level - but more importantly, I also very quickly found out that being a member of these teams bestowed we Junior Gunners with a number of extra privileges and some enviable 'perks' ...... and that's what this article is actually about.

First of all, I managed to get off nearly every Saturday-morning Goshen Parade, because that's when most hockey games took place. This also paid extra dividends for me in particular, because no matter how hard I tried, when I did have to go on these Goshen Parades (no match fixture), I inevitably got picked up for something trivial and would promptly be put on Weekend Restrictions.

Anyway, I digress, enough of my punishments during my time at Bramcote. It really was such bloody good fun being part of the Regimental teams, and on a number of different levels: We enjoyed a lot of camaraderie, and as I mentioned earlier, we also got to meet lots of the other folk serving within the Regiment, from the other Batteries and Permanent Staff too.

Another rare sense of freedom we enjoyed was the informality and relaxed atmosphere at all levels within the team, nurtured by the Hockey Officer and his P.S. assistants. It all became quite chummy and matey with them; they would even sometimes use our first names.

As with all sporting fixtures, we also had 'away' games to play too, so we'd often get to travel all over the country to compete in matches against other Boys' Service Units, sprinkled liberally throughout England and Wales. We even played in Scotland once and also had matches against school teams and other training establishments, like the Police Training College. Those away games always turned into a nice 'jolly' for us - quite literally 'playing away from home'. We didn't even have to wear 'Approved Civilian clothes' to travel in either, and always enjoyed a good scoff afterwards. Then to cap it all off, we were regularly taken out at the end of every term to some quiet 'out of the way' country pub for a wonderful (late pass) celebratory team piss-up, with a few quid waiting in the barrel for us.

The table tennis team provided similar perks, but the matches generally took place mid-week during the evening, either in camp or around the Bramcote area. Sometimes, downtown Nuneaton or occasionally over to Hinckley, once again enjoying not wearing 'Approved Civilian Clothes'.

The main perk associated with this activity, however, was that it excused you from the other, less desirable 'hobbies' we were obliged to take part in up till Term 4. But I suppose the best actual benefit of playing for the table tennis team was, and by far, the refreshments (namely the free scoff) that were always provided by the hosts. That's to say, that each home team would dutifully take on the responsibility of providing a decent freebie buffet with lashings of soft drinks. I have to say that there was always a great spread laid on, and if we played a home game, I always carried our left overs back to my Troop lines afterwards for my mates to finish off in the TV room.

Never being one to forgo any other potential extra-curricular opportunities, I eventually explored other, 'over the fence', legitimate escape routes, and thought the band looked like a good little number. I often overheard band members in my Troop speak about the skirt always chasing them at the summer fairs and events where they played at; let's face it, the uniform did look dead cool, so there must have been some truth buried there underneath all of the bragging.

I had previously tried to master the side drum while at school, and could successfully knock out a few drum beats, but, for the life of me, I could not master a simple bloody drum roll; that element always escaped me, and I just didn't couldn't get it right. I again put it down to being left-handed, and having to hold the sticks the 'wrong way'. Anyway, after a couple of terms under my belt, the band eventually started trawling for new talent beyond just the new recruits' intake, and I was persuaded to go along with a couple of mates from Dickson Troop, who were already members, to give it a go.

After we 'wannabees' arrived, we were split into two groups, potential trumpeters one side and drummers on the other, before being given the appropriate instruments to play with. After a bit of 'tuning up' we were put into a loose band formation and drilled up and down for about five minutes to get used to marching with instruments. We were then introduced to some simple musical exercises, but more advanced than our usual 'sounding' drills. Then they let us loose 'en-masse' on our respective instruments, playing together as an (auditioning) band. It sounded murderous, but that was only to be expected. Slowly but surely however, the Trumpet Majors would select a couple of the boys and pull them out of the formation. These were the ones who were deemed to have demonstrated some 'potential'.

I was disappointed not to be selected, and, after a short while, the rest of us were reformed to be dismissed and thanked for our interest. Just at that point however, my chum, who was already an established bandsman, chipped in, and rather loudly suggested to the TSM that he had overlooked me as someone who he knew and who might have some potential.

So, there I was, stood at attention, front rank, in this motley composite band, and the Trumpet Major bellowed: "Okay Law, march forward and give me some drum rolls."

Well, as I stepped forward, I just couldn't muster a bloody drum roll out of me for tuppence. I was so bloody frustrated knowing I really could do most of the other drum beats (honest), but just not a bloody drum roll.... and that's what he wanted to hear. Thud, thud, clunk, clunk was all the sound my sticks could generate, right in front of my grimacing, giggling peers. I felt humiliated and bloody ashamed to say the least, I just wanted the ground to open and swallow me up. The next thing that was a said was a curt "Thank you" from the TSM, who then told me to fall back in with the rest of the rejects.

I was so disappointed, and embarrassed, but the truth was I just wanted another avenue to give me some more weekend breaks. I'll also confess that I fancied wearing the flash uniform too, it's the peacock in me; but most of all, I wanted to be shagged senseless by all of those military band groupies out there ... but life is cruel, and it sadly wasn't to be.

I clearly managed to console myself with my Regimental team places, and I even got to enjoy a 6-week break on course at the RSA in Larkhill while learning Radar as part of my Met course. Now that 'WAS' a jolly-and-a-half to regale you with, and it came with full NAAFI privileges and a female accommodation block with about a hundred, available, babe-tastic WRAC chicks, most of whom were also hormonal, lustful teenagers, just like me. But that's another story that I might cover one day too.

Section 8 – Andy Lamb. Being a boy in JLRRA. 1973 - 1974

This section is compiled from a series of blogs available at:

https://medium.com/@andylamb_82109

THE ROAD TO BRAMCOTE

If you were to ask me why I so badly wanted to become a Junior Gunner in the Junior Leaders' Regiment, Royal Artillery, I doubt if I could give you a clear answer. It's just that, at age 15-and-a-half, it seemed to be the most desirable thing in the world. I can't explain it. None of my family had army connections.

Actually, if you were to challenge me, I couldn't explain even why the Royal Artillery. What was wrong with all the other options? There were loads of them. Why not the Household Cavalry? Or, the Royal Marines? The Brigade of Guards, even the Royal Pioneer Corps? I don't know, for me it had to be the RA.

In 1972, there were plenty of opportunities for the likes of me in 'Civvy Street'. I could have walked into a job or an apprenticeship. My teachers at school were astonished at my ambition and told me so. They plainly thought I was making a mistake. They thought I ought to go to college.

"There will always be a place for you here if you decide to give it up," they assured me.

When I was interviewed at the Army Careers Office, they asked why I wanted to join JLRRA. I incoherently rambled on about tradition and adventure and all that nonsense. In retrospect, I realise I was probably no more confused than any other young kid would be in the circumstances, so no change there. The officer asked me what I liked to do, my favourite activities. I had a little think and told him that I liked to read, go for walks, and enjoy conversation with my friends.

He gave me a funny look.

I now realise I should have talked about sport and competition, and how it was my ambition to destroy my enemies. Sadly, in those days, I didn't really think like that. Instead, I told him about my favourite authors and how I loved the feeling of the early morning.

For reasons I cannot now begin to understand, I was accepted to go for army selection.

I went down to the Army Selection Centre in Corsham, Wiltshire. I spent a few days down there with a group of other kids. We spent most of the time doing tests. But it was an early introduction into some aspects of army life. I had the novel experience of eating army food in a cookhouse. It was pretty good, but the tea tasted funny, like there was some chemicals in it.

It was the first time I slept in a barrack-room. On that first night, I lay awake listening to other boys boasting about their sexual experiences. I'd never had any sexual experiences worth talking about, so I kept my mouth shut and just listened. It was very interesting.

I wondered how much of it was true.

The tests were lengthy and varied. Numeracy, literacy, abstract reasoning, psychometry, engineering, and other skill areas. They seemed to take almost forever. It had been my ambition to train as a surveyor. I'm not entirely sure why. I didn't know the first thing about surveying or sound-ranging. It just sounded like a good option. I was sure I had the necessary numeracy skills. However, I must have been seriously lacking in other areas. I was pretty handicapped when it came to things like spatial awareness and other reasoning skills.

Instead, I was nominated for a junior apprenticeship as a Clerk, RA, to be trained at Bramcote. This was a bit disappointing. I hadn't really considered this. I asked the sergeant if this was a good option. He assured me it was a great option. Probably better than any others. I believed him.

When I got home, they had sent me a brochure. It was an A4

photocopied booklet about life as a junior leader at Bramcote. It contained photographs of young lads queueing up in the cookhouse and doing other soldier-like things. There was a draft timetable. I didn't know what most of the activities were. It all looked too exciting for words. I read it and re-read it every day.

On the cover there was a photo of a smart young lad in uniform next to a wimpy-looking kid with long hair.

The caption read: "To this – in seven weeks - from this."

I showed it to my sister. She said she preferred the wimpy-looking kid. I couldn't understand that. I wanted to be just like the boy in the uniform.

They sent me to have a medical examination. The doctor did all those uncomfortable things they do in circumstances like this. I did not enjoy that at all.

On the 11th of December 1972, aged 16 years, two-and-a-half weeks, I was attested at St Albans with a couple of other lads from my school. They were going to join the Royal Anglian Regiment. Me, something much more exciting. They were going to be infantrymen. I was going to join the Royal Artillery. The Attesting Officer took my oath of allegiance, gave me a copy of the New Testament and an envelope containing £9.00. I was amazed. My family were quite poor and I had never had that amount of cash to spend before.

NEW INTAKE GUNNER (NIG)

The train journey up from Watford only took an hour-and-a-half. I arrived at Nuneaton Station at 09.53 on the morning of Monday 8th January 1973. I was met by a sergeant in immaculate No. 2 dress uniform. He glanced at the cover of my book. It was 'Lord of the Rings'. He asked me if it was about boxing. I was a bit surprised.

The bus took a couple of us up to Gamecock Barracks. We were the first kids to arrive. I was met by my Section Sergeant, Sgt Davies, and a Junior Lance Bombardier, who would be supervising us during our basic training. They conducted me to my barrack room in the Recruits' Battery.

My bed-space had already been allotted and mattress and bedding had been set out. In addition to that, a load of other items were also laid out. Webbing, green plastic mug, knife fork and spoon set, tin of Kiwi boot polish, tin of Brasso, mess tins, the dreaded button stick, and a few other items I can't remember.

The Junior Lance Bombardier took me over to the Quartermaster's stores where I was measured up and issued with my uniform. I carried it all back and was instructed to get changed.
I laid out my personal possessions in my locker. These consisted of:

Item: 1 x suit of civilian clothes comprising a pair of green cords, a plain grey jacket my mum had got from a jumble sale, an old school shirt, a knitted tie, and a pair of plain black shoes.

Item: 1 x toothbrush.

Item: 3 x books.

Item: 1 x pot of hair gel.

That was it as far as personal possessions went. I also had some spare changes of underwear for normal use rather than the standard army issue shreddies.

My first uniform consisted of: shirt-khaki flannel, jersey-heavy wool, trousers-old-battle dress, socks-olive green, boots-DMS.

The Junior Lance Bombardier asked me how I felt. Itchy, I told him. Very eloquent.

I was still the only kid, or should I now say NIG, to have arrived. The section sergeant stayed in the barrack room while the Junior Lance Bombardier took me down to the cookhouse for lunch. There were already hundreds of Junior Leaders there and we had to queue up for a while. It was my first experience of Bramcote food. It was okay, I guess. Better than school dinners, in any case.

When we returned to Recruits Section some other NIGs were now arriving. We all looked nervous and well-scrubbed.

In all, there were 20 of us in Wardrop Section. We came in a variety of sizes and shapes. Some of them looked like they were only 12 years old.

Almost immediately we were under orders and instructions. We were taught how to 'stand by our beds'. We were instructed how to arrange our kit in our lockers. The day progressed in fits and starts. Finally, we were ordered to have a wash and prepare for bed. The Duty Sergeant inspected us and then it was 'Lights-Out'.

On that first day, everything was new and seemed like a lot of fun. We hardly got any sleep that night. There was a lot more chat until the Battery Orderly NCO (BONCO) came in and told us to be quiet.

One thing that was unexpected: I was the only kid from the south-east. I was born and brought up on a council estate outside Watford. All the other kids were from Yorkshire or Lancashire or Newcastle or Scotland. They were Scousers or Geordies or Jocks or something. I didn't understand more than half of what was being said. This was all very strange and exotic.

DAZED AND CONFUSED

Those first couple of days in Recruits' Battery went by in a confusing blur.

On that initial morning, we were roused at 6am. I was, and still am, a natural early riser, so I wasn't too fussed. But some of the other lads felt this was a bit of an imposition and couldn't stop grumbling about it. Ever. One of my abiding memories of those days was the permanent background whining and whingeing whenever we had to get up early. That was one of the first things that started getting on my nerves. There were many others to come.

We dressed in PT kit, blue shorts, red T-shirt, green socks, black plimsolls, and formed up outside. First off, they showed us how to form a squad. Tallest on the right, shortest on the left. There was a bit of competition for who might be the shortest. When it came down to it, it was a toss-up between Malcy Boyd or Titch Barton.

Nevertheless, they wrangled us more-or-less into a squad formation. First instruction: how to stand to attention. Second instruction: how to stand at ease. Now the hard bit: How to transition from one to the other in a soldier-like manner. My God! That was hard.

Once we had managed to master that, in squad formation, we shambled over to the sports field. Any complicated foot drill would have to wait until after breakfast.
For the next half-hour they had us running around the football field.

Against all the odds, I was actually quite good at running. I had been in the school cross-country team and had competed at county level. Never won any prizes, mind. Still, it wasn't too much of a stretch for me. Sadly, some of the other lads were already struggling. I couldn't really understand it. I knew perfectly well I wasn't the fittest person in the world, but there were lads even un-fitter than me.

Back into squad formation and shamble back to Recruits Section. Next instruction: How to make up our beds and bed-blocks. I did think that was all a bit weird. Why not just make your bed properly? In any event, it took us the best part of an hour before they were satisfied. Get changed into uniform.

Our normal working dress uniform:

shirt-khaki flannel. trousers-khaki denim. jersey-heavy wool. socks-green wool. boots-DMS.

Nobody ever told us what DMS stood for. It was another TLA. It remained a mystery for the whole of my army service.

As brand-new recruits, we weren't issued berets. Instead, for headgear, we had this knitted thing that you folded and it became a wool hat. It was called a 'Cap-Comforter'.

We shambled into squad formation and were then instructed how to do a right-turn (One-two-three. One!). We were then marched down to the cookhouse with our KFS and mugs held in the small of our backs. They tried to get us to march in step, but it was a bit beyond our abilities at this time.

Breakfast was consumed at the double. We were allotted about 10 minutes before we had to form up outside the cookhouse and march back. A couple of NIGs had thought to try out the toast machines without realising how long it would take.

Most disappointing. On the other hand, there was plenty of food. It seemed we would be having the Full-Monty every day. Lucky for me I wasn't on a diet. One thing, the tea tasted funny, like there was some chemical in it.

It seemed, in that first week, there were millions of priorities in our training: drill & turnout, inspections, fitness, block cleaning, hygiene, laundry, bed-blocks, inspections, grease-outs, boot-bulling, locker layout, PT, inspections, running around the football pitch, more inspections.

I hadn't brought the brochure with me, but I was sure the stuff we were doing was nothing like the timetable they had advertised.

One morning we went for swimming assessment. It was one of the things we were going to be graded on. At home, I had been a good swimmer but here I seemed to have forgotten everything I ever knew. When it was my turn, I dived into the pool and sank like a brick. I couldn't understand it. At home, I had been a good swimmer. Here, I was put into the remedial swimming group. That was unfair.

Evenings were spent cleaning. Either we were cleaning the block, cleaning our kit or cleaning ourselves. I won't bother describing how to 'bull' your boots.

We had inspections practically all the time. They inspected

everything. Bed-blocks, locker-layouts, turnout, grovelling-pits, boots, teeth. Everything. There was absolutely no question of let-up.

I was almost permanently confused. I didn't know what standards were acceptable. Having said that, I was obsessively pernickety. My locker-layout was always as perfect as I could make it. My bed-block was always perfect. Unlike others, I never had mine thrown out of the window.

For some reason, my boots were never good enough. I don't know what criteria they were using. As far as I could tell, the standard of my boots was no different from anybody else. Nevertheless, they were my personal failure that came in for stick. Sergeant Davies threw my boots down the room every night. Other lads suffered for other reasons.

The other thing that happened in that first week was the developing friendships and rivalries amongst us. Those of us who stood out in any way started coming in for some stick from the other kids. I became the 'Watford-Wanker'. I can tell you, it was better than what others got.

On the other hand, I started making friends. The lad in the grovelling pit next to mine was a soft-spoken Scots lad whom I shall call Jock Carnoustie. We started getting on quite well together. Same thing with another lad from the West Country; Mick Tarren. The last time I saw him, in 1978, he was in 7 RHA and we were in training together for Op Banner.

Another thing that started in that first week; the sergeant took us on, each individually, for a fight. He would pounce on a lad and a struggle would ensue. I was definitely not used to this. Some lads gave a fair return, but I was far too much of a wimp to fight back. instead I offered a stubborn passive-resistance. I wasn't going to fight him, but I wasn't going to give in either. He threw me down the room. I suppose it made a change from my boots.

One unexpected luxury was that we had a TV in our room. When we had finished hygiene inspection, the Sergeant told us we were allowed to watch TV until Lights-Out. However, after he had left, the BONCO would then tell us we couldn't watch TV. That was how it went for the whole of our recruits training. It was an exquisitely subtle torture. Use of the TV was held tantalisingly out of reach.

That was our first week as junior leaders.

GIVING UP—LACK OF CONFIDENCE AND GAINING CONFIDENCE

We were issued with a scrap of paper. It contained our Number, Rank and Name. It was in lieu of an ID card.

'7433 Junior Gunner Lamb, A.

I lost mine and panicked. The sergeant told me I worried too much. He got me another one from the office.

It is probably fair to say I was a bit of a mess. I was out of my depth. I was not in my comfort-zone. I began to think about asking to leave. In those days (1973) you could leave if you thought it wasn't for you.

Me, I was confused and upset. But, I was also stubborn and determined. I saw those kids who decided to bail-out and I knew I wasn't going to be like that. I was going to stick with it. I was having problems fitting-in, but I gritted my teeth and stuck with it.
There were other kids who were also out of their depth. We were all equally out of our depth together. But we weren't friends. We were barely colleagues or comrades. We shared the same barrack room. That was pretty much it.

We shared the same kind of badgering and discipline. We were chased around equally. We all went on the same 10-mile-bash. We all got the same amount of savage bollockings when we couldn't get our drill right. The difference was that some kids were better able to handle it all.

Sgt Davies was teaching us how to mark slow time. We were on the

173

square doing that bit with the knees parallel to the ground. Without a word, he went away and left us to it. We must have been there, marking slow time, for 15 minutes before he came back.

I was beginning to think I couldn't handle it. I remembered that my teachers had said that I could return to school if this wasn't for me.

I was getting grief from the Sergeant. He called me an 'Educated Idiot'. And then all the other NIGs started calling me that too. I had been singled out. That was pretty upsetting. I didn't know what to do.

Nowadays I get it. They were expecting me to bail-out. They were pushing me to see how much it would take. When was I going to flake-out? They didn't take into account my natural pig-headedness and resilience.

One of the other lads took exception to me.

"If I had a problem like yours, I would see a doctor." he informed me, "That's all I'm saying."

I was left wondering what part of my personality had offended him. You could take your pick. Funnily enough, he was one of the kids who bailed-out.

I stuck it out.

We were introduced to a thing called 'The Confidence Course'.

The Confidence Course was like an adventure playground on steroids. High-wires, ropes, death-slides. All sorts of stuff. Unlike some, I was fine with it. I never had problems with heights or death-defying circumstances. My problems were less dramatic and more subtle.

If I was going to panic, it wasn't going to be about some stupid high rope crossing. Oh no. I was going to panic about having multiple creases in my trousers. I was going to panic about being the last on parade and forgetting how to come to attention (which never happened). I was going to panic about my locker layout or my bed-block, or some random, irrelevant crap.

I was a mess.

We were interviewed by the Sergeant Major Instructor of Gunnery. After all the recruits had been through, he came out of his office and singled me out. He wanted me to study gunnery as my trade. I didn't know what to do. I had been recruited on a Junior Apprenticeship. He wanted me to transfer over.

Thinking about it nowadays, I suppose I should have done. I obviously made sufficient impression on him to single me out. It would have been the making of me. But I was insecure and clung on to the thing I knew. I declined.

We went up to the Lake District for adventure training. For the first time, we dressed in our combat uniforms. 20 young lads in uniforms two sizes too big for us. We didn't care.

Amazingly, I found adventure training was a lot of fun. I suddenly found something that I loved. All the rock-climbing, abseiling, hill-walking. We went up Helvellyn. I loved it all.

The only bit I didn't like was when we were canoeing in the lake. I miss-paddled, turned turtle and fell in. It was bloody freezing.

The Sergeant grabbed hold of my hair and hauled me out. I had to spend the rest of that session shivering in my wet combat uniform. I was not in my comfort-zone. And not for the last time.

Apart from that, I enjoyed it all tremendously. I had a natural talent for adventurous training. Who knew? Not me. I think it was this, more than anything else, that turned me around.

When we got back to Bramcote, I threw myself into the routine with increased enthusiasm and determination. My obsessive tendencies came to the fore when it came time for the block-competition. I was detailed to finesse all the other NIGs locker layouts and bed-blocks. It worked! We won.

I felt very proud of myself.

We had all managed to improve our foot-drill. It was time for our first passing-out parade. For us NIGs, it would be the Farren Day Parade. I have no idea who, or what, Farren was. It was one of those army traditions. You name an event or a unit after someone, who then becomes immortal as a result.

My Dad and my younger brother came up to see the parade. We had been issued with our Royal Artillery cap-badges as a mark that we had all managed to come up to standard. We completed the parade very smartly. I was so proud.

I could not have been happier. I had lost all thought of giving up. I had forgotten all those kids who had given up. I was definitely going to stick with this, whatever it took.

MY FIRST LEAVE—HOW EXCITED AM I?

Following our recruits' passing out parade we were given our first period of leave. We all travelled home in uniform.

I cannot begin to tell you how full-up I was. I was 16-years-old and had been inducted into, what I thought was, the best Regiment in the British Army. I was a junior gunner. I was wearing the uniform of the Royal Artillery.

I was the proudest I could possibly have been.

When I got home, the first thing I did was reverentially hang my uniform up in my wardrobe. I made especially sure it was hanging properly and didn't get any creases. Me and that uniform were going to be doing the rounds.

My Mum smothered me with affection. She had cooked my favourite supper: fish-fingers, chips, peas and ketchup.

My younger brother played it cool. He stuck around to welcome me back and then went out to hang with his friends. My sister and older brother weren't living at home any more so, in the end, it was just me and my parents. They asked me all the obvious questions. How did I like it? Did I have any friends? What was my sergeant like?

After a while they ran out of questions. Dad sat in the kitchen, smoking and listening to the radio, as he always did. Mum sat in the living room, smoking and watching the TV, as she always did. I didn't smoke.

Much as I loved my parents, I didn't think they wanted to hear about all the things I had been doing. I didn't think they would be interested in bed-blocks or locker layouts or having my boots thrown down the room, or me falling in the lake.

I ended up lying on my bed and reading. If you want to know the truth, I felt pretty lonely. Against all the odds, I actually missed being in a barrack room with a load of other kids I had nothing in common with. I missed all the late night banter. All the stories that I now knew were a pack of lies. The boring kid who had been in the scouts and couldn't stop telling us all about it. The other kid who seemed to have had relationships with all the married women in the street where he lived.

I can't say I actually enjoyed any of that. I never joined in myself. I didn't have the imagination to spin those kinds of tall tales. But I now realised that, in some odd way, I missed it. I must be an idiot.

The following morning, I knew the 'prodigal son' welcome was over. No big, bumper, blowout breakfast. Instead, I got a bowl of cornflakes and a mug of weak tea.

Back in Bramcote, breakfast was a serious thing. You got the lot! A plateful of eggs, bacon, sausage, beans, fried bread dripping in oil, tinned tomatoes (Blecch!) and a mug of strong tea that tasted suspiciously of chemicals. You had about five minutes to gobble it down, but it was a real start to a challenging day. It is upsetting to have to say that, for me, a bowl of cornflakes and a mug of weak tea just didn't cut it anymore. I didn't say anything, but I don't think my Mum quite understood some of the changes the army was making in me.

Depressingly, I'd had a growth spurt and most of my civilian clothes didn't fit anymore. Equally upsetting, my No. 2 dress trousers were a bit short for me now. I had planned to go around and visit some of my old school-friends to show off. Now, I was going to look an idiot.

After the weekend, my parents were both at work and my brother back in school. To be honest, I didn't really know quite what to do with myself.

I dressed in my uniform and caught the bus into Watford.

The highlight of that trip was when the concierge of one of the department stores complimented me on how smart I was.

Over the leave period I tried to get in touch with my old school-friends. But they were busy with school stuff. I remember sitting on a bench near the library and a gang of kids I used to hang around with wandered past in conversation. They glanced at me but didn't acknowledge me. I know some of them recognised me, but I was 'out-of-context.'

So, this was going to be my life. I didn't fit in at home anymore and I barely fitted in with Junior Leaders. When you think about it, that is pretty depressing.

I can't tell you how pleased I was, when leave was over, to be going back to Bramcote. That is how much of a measure of an idiot I was when I come to think of it. I thought getting back to Brats was preferable to being alienated from my old school-friends. I was going to be posted to my training battery. 40 Wardrop Battery. My God! I had absolutely no idea.

I was going to be moving up into a training battery. I was quite excited at the prospect.

I AM A MEMBER OF 40 WARDROP BATTERY.

I am in 40 Battery.

"Four-Zero-Wardrop-Battery."

I have no idea what that means.

I'm back from leave. I have been posted to Nicholson Troop, 40 Wardrop Battery. I have no idea who or what Wardrop might be. Out of curiosity I go to the library in the Education Centre to look it up. It turns out that Wardrop was a general in the First World War.

In my third term, in November 1973, I had to write an essay about him. There was only a short encyclopaedia entry which listed his exploits, so I had to read up about them as well. He was Commander, Royal Artillery in 1918 and then Commander of British Forces in Palestine from 1921. Naturally, he did a lot of other things too, but I won't record them here because it all gets a bit complicated and I am sure you would get bored.

At the time, when I wrote the essay, I didn't really understand. And I didn't care very much. As it was, my essay got a good mark.

Anyway, in 1973, I am a junior gunner in Nicholson Troop, 40 Wardrop Battery. And I am a complete mess.

I am doing my usual training; Fitness, small-arms, drill & turnout, Block-jobs, etc. etc. Plus, trade training. I am going to be a Clerk, RA.

Plus, I am now in the band. I play the trumpet and have been fitted with a smart uniform. This is a thing I love.

I'm not good at sports in general, but I am a good runner and represent the Battery at the 1000 metres. I come first. I join the Regimental cycling team and we compete with other Junior Leaders' Regiments doing time-trials. My swimming needs a lot of work, so I spend as much time as possible trying to get up to scratch.

I don't realise it at the time, but these are the three disciplines of the modern triathlon. If I had tried a bit harder I could have become a competitive athlete. As it is, I am content to participate.

There are any amount of sports opportunities in Junior Leaders. All the obvious ones: soccer, rugby, hockey, cricket, judo, boxing, athletics. But also, you can try out for others like: volleyball, table-tennis (ping-pong!), actual tennis, motorcycle display team. It is all there.

Quite a lot of kids opt to try-out for the gymnastic display team. They are often Army champions. The Regiment is very proud of them.

For us younger boys, it is all compulsory.

There are all sorts of other activities. I have already mentioned the band, but there is also a 'music appreciation' club where, once a week, I can enjoy classical music. That would never be tolerated in the Battery. On the Battery lines it is 'Top of the Pops' or death. Shostakovich would never be allowed.

Other kids join the photography club. I join the printing club. There is an off-set litho printing machine and we produce programmes for events. I admit, it is all a bit nerdy, but I also admit to being a nerd.

With all the training, and all the exciting activity going on, why is it that I feel sick-at-heart?

I can't answer that.

It comes out in a lot of ways. There are times when I stop bothering to look after myself or wash, or clean my kit. I get picked up on parade. I am charged and get extra duties. I don't very much care.

Often, I go and sit out in the wind-breaks. No one will come out and give me grief. I can just sit there and let my mind go blank.

One evening I am lying on my bunk. It is the bottom tier of a three-bunk arrangement in our barrack room. My mind is in neutral. The lad on the bunk above me is Jock Carnoustie from my recruit section. We were friends. He rouses me, and I roll over.

Without any warning, he pokes me in the eye.

"What was that all about?" I demand in outrage, rubbing at the pain.

"I just wanted to see what it was like to poke someone in the eye."

I hardly know what to say or think. I suppose any other kid would drag him out of bed and give him a bit of a kicking. I don't.

It doesn't matter. The following day he decides to bail-out and give it all up. He reports to the Troop Sergeant and, almost immediately, is out of the Battery.

Life in the Battery is quite hard. We are predated upon by the mustering gunners. They call it NIG-bashing. Some kids come in for a lot of stick. Me, not so much. But there is one mustering gunner who has me in his sights. From this distance in time I can still picture his face and his voice. I won't tell you his name. He steals my watch. He breaks into my locker when I am in the shower and steals my money. He expects me to bull his boots. I throw them out of the window and he beats me up.

So, I go and sit out in the wind-breaks. No one will come out and give me grief. I can just sit there and let my mind go blank.

SOUNDING LESSONS

As New-Intake-Gunners (NIGs) in January 1973, we were timetabled to take 'Sounding' lessons for half-an-hour every morning. We would march, in our squad, to the band rooms, where the trumpet majors would give us our instructions. There were four of them during my time there. TM Timmins, TM Isedale, TM Cooper and one other whose name I have forgotten.

We were divided between drummers and trumpeters. As I had previously learned French horn at school, I had some natural talent on the trumpet. So, when our basic recruit training was completed, I, along with some other likely candidates, was inducted into the band. I was very happy indeed.

The band of the Junior Leaders Regiment, RA had originally been formed in Woolwich in 1937 as the Boys Royal Artillery Band. It was transferred over and re-named when the Junior Leaders' Regiment was formed in 1957.

For us, in 1973, band training took place in our spare time. In actual fact, us younger Junior Leaders were expected to participate in extra training activities in any event, so it wasn't spare time at all. I didn't care, I loved it.

We had to learn a number of trumpet marches. I can't remember all of their names, but these spring to mind: *Marine, The Gunner, Nuneaton* and half-a-dozen others. I have an obsessive memory, so I managed to pick them up quite quickly.

In addition to the marches, we were expected to memorise a number of trumpet calls. *Last Post, Reveille, Royal Artillery Call, Five Minutes, Parade Call* and some others. I forget.

The drummers had a spectacular drumming display called Drummer's Call.

One of the very pleasing things about being in the band was the uniform. It was based on a version of the Royal Horse Artillery uniform of the late 19th century. We wore blue tunics with yellow frogging, blue trousers with bright red stripes shiny boots with spurs and a busby hat with a red bag and white plume. Being young teenagers, we looked really cute.

Apart from playing for parades in the Regiment, we also travelled around playing at shows and military events. There seemed to be a lot of that sort of thing in those days. Far more than I think we have today. Almost every weekend over the summer we would be out, around the country. Occasionally we might play at a military tattoo somewhere.

One abiding memory was having to learn a new march. It was a German fanfare march by the composer Henrion. It was called '*Fehrbelliner Reitermarsch*'.

The reason we learned this was that we were due to play at a big event at the Royal School of Artillery at Larkhill. We would be playing with the massed bands on the green outside the officer's mess.

We practised our drill and counter-marching and playing until we were as perfect as we could be. When it came to the event, I was the proudest I had ever been in my life. The audience of officers and their guests loved the show. We didn't know it at the time, but we had been acknowledged as the star turn.

Later, that year, the Royal Artillery Band came to the Junior Leaders' Regiment to do a concert. They got a couple of us up on stage to play *Fehrbelliner Reitermarsch* for the Regiment. For some reason, I was shaking in nervousness and stage-fright.

Later, I was selected with six or seven other lads to join the Fanfare Team.
As a team, we picked up even more playing opportunities. I think we played a fanfare when one of the adult regiments was awarded the freedom of Leeds. I can't remember which. Another abiding memory was when we were booked to provide fanfares for the prize winners at a gigantic judo event. There were dozens and dozens of them. TM Isedale was supervising us. As the event progressed he became more and more inventive until we collapsed in on ourselves.

"Bloody Crows!" was his verdict.

As a member of the Fanfare Team, I was one of those selected as a candidate for best trumpeter. Sadly, I was having a long series of 'off-days' and wasn't able to compete with the rest of the team.

STAND BY YOUR BEDS!

Let us now discuss the matter of 'block-inspections' and 'grease-outs'.

In the first week in Recruits' Battery, we were inducted into block-cleaning. For us, there were going to be any amount of block inspections.

This meant, literally, everything. Our bed-blocks, locker layouts, the floor, our uniforms, walls, windows, our personal cleanliness, the ironing room, the drying room, the bogs (*shudder*), the bathroom and showers, plus the corridor and stairs. Nothing would be missed.

When you think about it, the chances of getting everything spot-on were practically 'zero'. It was a case of: 'Set yourself a low standard and then fail to achieve it' (as was included in one of my Annual Reports). They were bound to pick us up on any number of things.

In those early days, it was a joint effort. Collectively, we shifted all the beds and furniture around to clean the floor.

First, we had to scrub all the peculiar stains off. Then, using rags, put the polish down. The polish itself, was a glutinous orange substance. Next come the bumpers. Just in case you can't remember, these were heavily weighted chunks of cast iron, suitably padded, on the end of a long, hinged handle. A boy would have to swing the bumper to bring the polish to a good shine. It was exhausting and often used as a form of punishment.

There was a thing about whether you were then allowed to walk on the polished floor in boots or you had to be in stockinged feet. I had mixed feelings about this. Boots DMS would leave marks on the newly polished surface, whereas boys' sweaty socks would strip the polish. Who knows?

Someone would have to take all the rugs out and sweep them with a bass-broom, to get all the dust and gravel off. I have no idea where it all came from. The dust-and-gravel pixies I suppose.

Next, we would move all the lockers and furniture back into position. It was during one of these manoeuvres that I got my hand mashed against the wall and had to go down to the MRS. When I arrived there, I threw-up on the medic and fainted.

This block-cleaning business was dangerous.

Come the inspection, everything was fair game. Despite it being a joint effort, we would be picked up individually. If your patch of floor wasn't up to scratch, you would be the one to get a savage bollocking, not the kid who had polished it.

Due to being obsessively pernickety, I always made sure my bed-block and locker layout were perfect. But that didn't stop the inspecting officer finding fault. Someone, using permanent marker, had written a stores' number on my locker mirror. I couldn't get it off but still got bollocked for it. Then, the officer took exception to my books and hair-gel. He made some sneering remark about my choice of authors.

In any event, come the Recruits' Battery block competition, my obsessive attention to detail came to the fore and Wardrop section won. I was nominated to select which boy would go up to receive the prize.

When I got to 40 Battery it was a whole other story. We didn't do grease-outs as a collective. It was every boy for himself.

The rooms were not arranged in the same way as in Recruits' Battery. Some of the lads managed to grab the corner spaces and arranged their lockers to form little cordons. In effect, they had created miniature bunks for themselves, while the rest of us were left completely exposed.

Being inventive and naturally lazy, we were always on the lookout for easier ways of doing things. We were so averse to using the bumpers that we found other means of polishing the floor. One favourite was to get a boy in a blanket and two or three other boys would swing him around. I suppose it worked, after a fashion. I can't say it was any better or worse than using a bumper. In any event, it usually ended with the blanket-boy crashing into a wall or getting the bumps.

In addition to maintaining your own personal space, there were dozens of block-jobs to be done. I was almost always nominated to clean the toilets. I don't fully understand why this was. Just lucky, I guess. It became my own personal struggle.

I don't mind telling you, it was pretty horrible. We didn't have any 'Toilet-Duck' or even any bog-brushes for that matter. Instead, I got some toxic detergent and a threadbare cloth. And it wasn't just the toilets themselves. I also had to clean the cubicles. There are some stains that are too stubborn to be removed by toxic detergent. If you get my drift.

HOW ADVENTUROUS

Regimental Adventure Training. RAT.

The Junior Leaders' Regiment, RA is big on 'Adventure Training'. Someone has made them watch *'The Blue Peter'* (the film, not the TV series) and it has given them funny ideas. They think it is the thing to do. Along with everything else, it will give us confidence and help build character.

More character-building. Why can't they give it a rest? I'm happy with my character the way it is. Yet, plainly there are others who aren't.

I have been sent to a shed in North Wales along with a gang of other kids. We do the whole journey in the back of a 3-tonner. By time we arrive my arse is like a sheet of coarse sandpaper.

The only other kid I can remember being on the course is a lad who had failed the previous time and has had to re-take it. His name is Duncan McCall. The latest I heard, he had recently retired as a lieutenant-colonel.

Some people might find it hard to believe but I am actually quite good at this sort of stuff. At age 16, I have a good level of fitness and stamina. I am good at map-reading. I am good at running. My upper-body strength is enough to help me with things like rock-climbing and canoeing.

For me, out of all the opportunities Junior Leaders offers us lads, Adventure Training may be my favourite thing of all. I am good at it, which is just as well, because I am going to be doing lots of this stuff over the next 9 years.

We arrive late. We are allocated bunks in the freezing bothy, stow our kit and go into the cottage for our first session. It is a basic induction
.

If truth be told, anyone can guess what we are in for. Over the next week, we will be pushed beyond our limits and then get shouted at for being useless.

How can I predict this? Because that is the default Junior Leaders' training method. They don't know any other way. They have never read 'The Peter-Principle'. Push your subject beyond their limits and then find exciting ways to humiliate them.

So, the week is planned out. There will be no let-up. We will be hill-walking, orienteering, rock-climbing, canoeing, abseiling, etc., etc. All under pressure and always being assessed and appraised.

Fine. I can live with that.

What I can't live with are the domestic arrangements. The bothy is cold, wet and smells horrible. It stinks like a school gym bag that has been left in a locker over the summer holidays. Every time I go through that door I am physically repulsed.

Also, we have to take turns in various domestic activities. On the first morning, it is my turn to take the bucket up to the noisome cess-pit, septic-tank.

Get this: There are about 20 of us on the course. We are there for seven days, yet I have to do the bucket duty three times. Why is this? With my advanced mathematical skills, I can see that the duty rotation ought to let me off the hook. Yet and all, I am bucket-monitor three times while other kids never get to do it at all. I can't help thinking it is more than a little bit unfair, not to say unreasonable. I suppose they must think I am good at it.

I am working to my strengths.

One thing I am good at, one of my strengths, is planning ahead. I read the schedule and see that we will be doing some long trekking. Accordingly, that morning, I make a packed lunch. Cheese sandwiches and an apple. Okay, a bit basic I admit.

So, there we are, half-way up 'Blue-now-festering-in-the-bog' and we stop for a brew-up. Hexamine-burners are lighted and mess-tins filled with water. I open my Bergen rucksack and take out my sandwiches, wrapped in tin-foil. The rest of the kids are amazed. The Directing Staff are impressed. With this one feat of organisation I am going to pass RAT.

For me, the week has been reasonably successful. On the upside, I got to do lots of activities I enjoyed and excelled at. The weather was generally fine. I managed to keep relatively warm and dry. I didn't screw-up or alienate too many people.

SAIL TRAINING SHIP—CAPTAIN SCOTT

I enjoyed myself. I enjoyed myself so much that, when an opportunity came up the following May to do a month on the training ship 'Captain Scott' I snapped it up. It even meant I would have to give up driver-training. I didn't care. I really wanted to go on this course.

Instead, I would be a trainee crew-member on the three-masted, topsail schooner, 'Captain Scott'.

We would spend a month sailing around the Inner Hebrides. There would be land expeditions, including hill-walking, rock-climbing, orienteering. All the usual stuff I was good at.

Also, I would have to learn lots of nautical skills. I would learn how to dangle off a yard-arm, while the ship was clipping along at an alarming angle and at an alarming rate of knots.

Apart from being permanently sea-sick I loved it. I could manage that stuff with ease. I was even allowed to be a *'Navigator's Yeoman'* and steer the ship through all the rough shores.

I was proud of myself. And sea-sick. Very sea-sick.

What I was not so good at was social skills. I was terrible at getting along with people. I didn't know why that was. Something in my nature, I guess. It has taken a good while for me to learn what that might have been.

As it was, a number of the other trainees were keeping an eye on me to make sure I didn't screw-up or go too far wrong. God bless them. They deserve all my belated thanks.

SMALL-ARMS TRAINING

In June 1973, I go into hospital to have my appendix out. Afterwards I am sent home on sick leave. Then, two things happen.

First, I receive a letter telling me, in future, I will have to travel in civilian clothes. They have raised the security level and don't want us being targeted by terrorists. So, no travelling in uniform.

My immediate problem is that I don't have any civilian clothes worth talking about. We are quite poor, so I don't have many good clothes. Most of what I have is second-hand, from jumble sales. Also, I don't have the first idea about how to dress myself. Ask anyone.

In JLRRA, if you want to leave camp, there is a strict dress-code. None of my civilian clothes are up to scratch, so I seldom leave camp.

I ask my sister and she helps me to buy some stuff that would conform. I can't say I particularly like the result. Boys' fashions in those days were terrible. Flared trousers, huge collars and leery colours.

My sister gets me a pair of purple flares, a check-patterned shirt, a yellow tank-top and a blue jacket.

To be honest, I really don't think the outfit suits me.

The other thing that happens, when I get back to Bramcote, is that my locker has been broken into and a lot of my kit has been pilfered. I am left with two sets of working-dress, boots, beret, overalls and a few other items.

I report to my troop sergeant, but he has other matters on his hands. We are going to Sennybridge in the Brecon Beacons on small-arms training.

In any event, I report to the MRS to have my stitches out and then return to parade to draw my rifle. The BSM demands to know why I'm not in combat-uniform. I try to explain but I don't think I am entirely coherent. I stammer and stutter. I generally do that when I am stressed.

I get charged and have to go in front of the Battery Commander. This time, I manage to explain my problem more clearly. They aren't very sympathetic, but I get off with an admonishment.

It is too late for me to draw a new combat-uniform, not that I could have afforded one, so the rest of the Battery are ordered to wear working-dress for Summer camp. This is in order that we are all in the same uniform. That gets me into trouble with some of the more stroppy kids.

I bet it was one of them who nicked my kit in the first place.

We travel in a convoy of 3-tonners. We sit in the back, with our rifles and all our kit, singing funny songs. I rather enjoy that bit.

On arrival, we are allotted accommodation and are immediately immersed in small-arms training.

Amongst the stuff that has been pilfered are my ear-defenders. Or I lost them. Actually, that last one sounds more likely. Whatever, the sergeant stuffs my ears with grass and calls me a number of rude names which I will not record here. I nearly burst into tears.

This is not going well.

For the next fortnight we are completely immersed in small-arms training. If we are not on the ranges, we are doing rifle drill or stripping-and-assembling and cleaning. In my memory, in my mind, we have our rifles with us at all times. I don't think that can be right, but that's what I remember.

The first day on the ranges our sights are adjusted so that we are working at optimum capacity. From then on, we start practising all sorts of scenarios. I imagine this is what infantrymen do all the time.

We are broken down into small sections to learn about giving support fire. We go on a field exercise. Because I am still recovering from the operation they make me stay and guard the ammunition rather than go running around. That's a bit depressing.

One of the kids has a negligent discharge and gets put in the guardroom. He has fired his rifle unsafely and we are all at risk. He was in my section in Recruits' Battery. I feel sorry for him. He is deeply in trouble.

One of the really important things they are training us about is gun safety. The chances are that we will all end up doing internal security duties in Northern Ireland. Recently there have been problems with lads being too 'gung-ho'. They are determined to minimise any risk of negligent use of arms. So, gun safety is high on the agenda. That kid in the guardroom is deeply in trouble. I feel sorry for him.

Whenever we finish using our rifles, we always have to remove the magazine, cock the rifle three or four times and hold the breech open so the inspecting officer can see there is no round up the spout. But, sometimes this can go wrong. It went wrong for that lad and, really, it is his own fault.

We are being trained to use small-arms and it is our responsibility, even at age 16, to ensure we are doing so responsibly and safely.

He failed and now he is in the guardroom. That's the deal.

By the end of the two weeks my shooting has improved beyond measure. I don't get awarded a marksmanship badge, but I do pass my Annual Personal Weapons Test. I can't begin to tell you how pleased I am.

In the evenings, we are allowed to go to the NAAFI. It is much more basic than the posh one at Bramcote. There aren't any pin-ball games or pool-tables. The dart-board is monopolised by the mustering gunners, so us NIGs get to buy pop and sit out on the step.

Small-arms training for kids. It ends up with a bottle of pop.

I HAVE LOST THE PLOT

When you are a kid, the good times are the best times ever. The bad times are just too terrible to think about. You really have no sense of perspective. Me, I am confused. I am almost permanently confused.

Here's a thing.

In March,1981, I was supposed to be catching the train back to Woolwich. I was a patient on Ward 9 of Queen Elizabeth's Military Hospital. Never mind why. I would rather not talk about it right now.

Let's just say I was a bit ill.

I'd had a day-pass to go into London for an afternoon of mediocre fun and was returning to hospital. I was waiting on the platform at Waterloo-East and was amazed to meet Trumpet-Major Cooper and the Junior-Leaders' Fanfare Team. They all looked good in smart suits. Me, not so much. I think I may have been a bit of a mess. When I was in Brats, in 1974, I had been a member of the Junior Leaders' Fanfare Team. Therefore, I was very pleased to meet up with the new lot. Unfortunately, I got so excited and confused that instead of getting on the train to Woolwich I accidentally caught the train to Sidcup.

I always seem to be messing-up like that.

The thing is, I get confused about stuff. For example, when I was in my Regiment, I was supposed to be sitting a typing test but went to the library instead. The Chief Clerk went nuts.

So, it is not too surprising that, when I am returning to Bramcote from leave in April 1974, I get the wrong train. The journey from Watford Junction to Nuneaton is supposed to be direct and requires no changes. Therefore, (I can't explain why) I am standing on the grey, wet, dreary platform at Crewe. That is nearly 100 miles out of my way.

When you are a kid, and you mess-up, and it all goes wrong, you generally don't have the capacity to articulate what has happened. You can't explain why it has gone wrong. At age 17, you just stand on the unexpected platform, in the drizzle, in your shabby-suit, with your army suitcase, looking a bit lost and feeling a bit miserable. That's me, that is.

That sort of thing seems to happen to me quite a lot. Even now.

In any event, I get back to Bramcote nearly 7 hours late and I can't find ways to explain myself.

It hardly matters. The RPs are going to find fault regardless.

Accordingly, there I am, Junior Gunner Lamb, in my shabby suit, looking a bit lost and feeling a bit miserable and doing circuits of the tiny exercise yard in 'Joe's Hotel,' for reasons I can't explain and don't understand.

Now I am a mustering-gunner. I am supposed to have special privileges, but I don't feel particularly privileged.

I have qualified as a 'Clerk-RA' and I am working in the Battery Office. What I am actually doing is running around. The Battery Clerk doesn't really want me hanging about, so he makes up stuff and I run futile errands. It is all a bit of a waste of time really.

If you want to know the truth, I am depressed. I have given up most things. No more sport activities. No more clubs or hobbies. I tend to spend any free time lying on my bunk and staring at the ceiling.

Once again, I have stopped looking after myself. I have stopped going down the cookhouse. I have stopped washing or doing my laundry.

I am on parade and the new troop sergeant from 1RHA charges me for being scruffy. He's probably right. I get extra duties. I have to mop out the control tower, under supervision.

Then something a bit odd happens. I am in my grovelling-pit bulling my boots. The sergeant is giving grief to one of the other kids. He throws his boots down the room and instructs him to follow my example. He holds up one of my boots and says that is the standard he is looking for.

I look at the other kid and he looks at me. Neither of us know what the sergeant is talking about. My boots aren't of a particularly high standard. We both know it. They never have been. We don't say anything.

I don't quite know what to think. A couple of days earlier I was being charged for slovenliness. Now I'm being complimented on the standard of my turnout.

I don't know.

All I can tell you is that I've lost the plot.

BOXING

When I was a kid at home, when I was about 13 or 14, there were any amount of options open to us. My older brother had guitar lessons and joined the Air-Cadets and did judo. My sister did ballet. My younger brother did rugby.

There was even a local boxing club. Just like in 'Billy Elliot'.

I didn't go to judo or rugby or boxing. Or even ballet for that matter. My parents sent me to speech classes. I attended speech therapy sessions, I learned how to pronounce words clearly and how not to stutter or stammer.

I joined a book club.

I competed in the poetry section in the Watford Festival of Speech and Drama. I came second and got a certificate. I was so nervous I nearly threw-up. My sister had to escort me off stage.

So, you can imagine how I felt when, in week-7 of Junior Leaders, we were paired up in the gym for boxing.

We lined up in the gym, dressed in baggy blue shorts and red t-shirts. The PTI, wearing a white vest with the crossed-swords emblem, paired us up according to size and shape. I was matched with this scary-looking Scouse kid from one of the other recruit sections. In my memory, he had a broken nose, and a Prussian duelling scar! (Bullshit-alert). Anyway, to me, he looked scary.

When it was our turn, we climbed into the ring. I shivered nervously in my corner, while he bounced around on the balls of his feet, shadow-boxing.

The bout started, and I realised I hadn't got a clue.

No amount of poetry or received-pronunciation was going to get me out of this one.

It is probably fair to say he beat me to a bloody pulp. I had never boxed in my life before and I had no idea what was happening to me, or what to do about it.

About a minute into round-2, the PTI stopped the bout. He hoisted me, bonelessly, off the canvas and went through the pantomime of waiting for the judges to come to an agreement.

Obviously, no-one else had seen my opponent beating seven-bells of shit out of me, so we had to wait for the judges' decision.

Amazingly, I didn't win. The other kid was declared the winner. I guess it was predictable enough when you think about it.

I fell out of the ring in a daze and staggered around. They had to get a couple of other kids guide me over to the mats and lay me down to recover.

Now, here's a thing. They plainly valued this sort of stuff. I had to compete in dozens of boxing events and I was so obviously ill-equipped and unsuited for it.

Yet, at no time did my Troop Sergeant or Troop Commander send me off for boxing lessons. They just thrust me into the ring with some Geordie bruiser to see how long it would take him to finish me off. It was like some kind of blood-sport.

If I'd had an ounce of sense, I would have gone to the PTI to see about getting lessons.

Or, perhaps, I could have taken the hint and applied for discharge. I could have done so. No questions asked.

I didn't, and I was scared shitless.

Nowadays I have begun to understand that they were expecting me to bail-out, which would explain why they didn't invest too much energy in my development. That's how I have started seeing things now.

Here's the thing: at the time, if I had applied for a discharge, and I could have got one, I would have had to admit to myself that I had failed and done the wrong thing. And everyone else would have known it.

I could never have done that. Not in a million years.

LIVING IN THE FIELD

The training staff of Junior Leaders RA were very keen to get us used to the idea of living and working in the 'Field'. By this, I suppose, they meant anywhere that was not indoors or warm, dry and cosy.

This is not unreasonable. Let's admit it, if we were ever to swing into action as a group of fighting people, the chances are that it probably wouldn't be in a comfortable hotel. If we needed to set up a firing-position or a command-post, most likely it would be somewhere infested with a large percentage of mud.

We needed to get used to that.

Looking back, I have to say, in JLRRA, they didn't drop us right in it. They gave us a series of gentle introductions to the concept of what constituted the 'Field'.

When I remember how much, as a boy, I enjoyed going to festivals and camping and night barbecues, it surprises me how much I came to hate going on field exercise when I was in the Army. Possibly something to do with the lack of a Prosecco-bar.

Our first experience of the 'Military Field' (rather than a comfortable civilian one containing facilities) was in Recruits' Battery. They got us dressed in combat uniform and jogged out to the windbreaks. We would spend the afternoon cooking our own supper.

We were issued with hexamine burners and 24-hour ration packs that we had to share between four of us. I had previously cooked for myself on short camping expeditions and was familiar with the procedure. That is why I was surprised that half the rest of the squad hadn't got a clue. That is why I was kind-of surprised when it was about an hour-and-a-half before I got a turn on the cooker.

It doesn't take a culinary genius to open a tin of stew, empty it into a mess-tin and put it on the burner.

According to the wisdom of a good friend, it is all part of life's rich tapestry. People have different skills and develop at different rates. Judging by the rate some of these lads were developing, I could be waiting for the next ice-age before I had a chance to cook supper.

That was also my first introduction into how you clean a burnt mess-tin without the aid of hot water, detergent and a scouring-pad.

In any event, I eventually had supper.

During all of our basic training and subsequent training at Bramcote, they managed to filter-in field training exercises at all times. To start off with, I was fine with it. But after a while, I fell out of love with it.

I wasn't happy, sitting in a wet field, with wet underpants climbing up the crack of my arse.

In the summer of 1974 we went on field exercises to some ranges up in Scotland. Somewhere near Dundee, I think. We spent a fortnight in the field in this huge pine forest. We had our small-arms with us at all times. We were armed with blank-rounds and we had those yellow gadgets clamped to the muzzle of the rifles.

During the day, there were all sorts of set-pieces. We would have to break up into small groups and practise assaults on set positions. We would prepare our own meals from ration packs.

At night, I would climb into the basher I shared with another lad, take my boots off, open the tent flap to get rid of the smell, get out of my damp combat uniform and climb into my damp sleeping bag.

You can imagine my annoyance when, at about three in the morning, a rival squad raided our position and stole my tent. I eventually found it in a field about a mile away.

The two kids who were supposed to be on watch were found cowering in a ditch somewhere.

I really started hating the 'Field'.

On another occasion during that same fortnight, our sections were divided up so as to provide protecting cover for assault teams. Our J/NCOs convinced themselves that the assault teams were certain to attack us via a forbidden route and sent all the hard-lads to cover that area. That left a few of us less-aggressive kids to guard the main route.

Sure enough, the assaulting team came via the main route and trampled all over the dregs who were left. I remember some kid belted me in the eye with his rifle butt and I was out for the count.

From these humble beginnings, I learned such a loathing for field-training.

EDUCATION

Nowadays, those young kids at the Army Foundation College at Harrogate have a formal education programme built-in to their recruit-training. Much as we did back in Brats. Apart from all the usual drill, weapons training, fitness, etc. etc. they also have to study Maths, English and IT skills to a level roughly equivalent to GCSE

Levels A*-C. The authorities there expect a success rate of between 86%–100%.

Back in our day, expecting a pass rate like that must have been wildly over-optimistic. It is my guess that quite a lot of kids joined JLRRA as a means to avoid going to school any more. Although, I am sure, for many kids there must have been many other reasons.

For a lot of us Spotty-Herberts it was a shock to discover we were expected to do lessons as well as everything else.

I think, in my memory, we had to attend lessons every day. But I could be mistaken. We studied maths and English. Most kids studied for the Army Certificate of Education. You needed one of them for promotion beyond bombardier.

As a kid, I had a reasonably high standard of education (Swot-Alert!). Except I also had a distressing tendency to panic, and so I bailed out of school before taking any exams. But it seems the education staff at Bramcote must have spotted my potential. Therefore, against all the odds, I studied English and maths for GCE O-level.
On 22nd November 1973, they converted one of the class-rooms into an Examination Centre. I sat in there, on my own, with a Royal Army Education Corps officer invigilating.

Before I went in I had a panic-attack and had to go outside to lean against the wall and be sick.

As it went, I passed easily with impressive scores. I won a prize. I got a book, which pleased me very much. *J Gnr Lamb. GCE Prize.*

In addition to the prescribed education subjects, they also got us to deliver lectures on military subjects. I remember one young lad was quite good at it and they put him on the leadership training course as a result.

I wasn't quite so good at delivering lectures in those days, which is ironic considering what I do for a living now. Anyway, they didn't put me on any leadership courses. I guess I was less of a Junior

Leader and more of a Junior Follower. Ha ha! (Sour joke alert!)

I see, now, that it was a useful tool for identifying talented youngsters. I also see it had some use in identifying those of us who had, what you might call, 'other-strengths'. Me, being a bookish nerd, came in for a bit of stick. I got called an 'Educated Idiot', which was not really motivating.

TRADE TRAINING

The other thing they got us doing in the Education Centre was our clerical trade training. During my selection interviews and tests, I had been nominated to become a Clerk-RA. I had no real idea what that was.

It was here in the Education Centre that I learned what that was. I discovered that I was destined to become a pen-pusher with a gun.

We trainee clerks (shiny-arse alert!) had to learn about army documentation, and how to keep a library of publications, and how to register the mail, and how to keep an office diary, and how to 'flag-up', and how to keep all the files numbered and up to date. We had to learn how to prepare charge-sheets. We had to learn about *The Manual of Military Law*. We had to learn about *Queens Regulations for the Army*. We had to learn about a thing called *JSP 101*. We weren't going to be mere clerical assistants. We were going to be Clerks-RA. Something much more important.

We had to learn to be literate, analytical and have good numeracy skills. We would be working with sergeant-majors and officers. We would be permanently on parade and under minute scrutiny. Any mistake would be noted. There would be nowhere to hide. Always immaculately turned-out. No swearing.

I wish I had known. I would have applied to do gunnery. I am sure you were allowed to swear as much as you liked being a Gunner-RA.

I suppose it might all sound a bit boring, but it was hard work. We had to learn how to conform to a common standard so that you could

201

take over an office and it would be the same anywhere you went. No getting any funny ideas.

We learned typing. Every day we practised on the old-fashioned typewriters. We had to clean them and change the ribbons. Some of us gave our machines names. I called mine Doris. Doris Olivetti.

They had all these typing tests and you had to go through the lot. For Grade-3 level we were aiming for a speed of 30-words-a-minute, with less than three mistakes. I am not all that dextrous and am prone to get confused, so it was a problem.

We had to learn how to operate rotary-duplicating machines so that we could publish Battery Orders. All done to a single standard. And all without getting printing ink all over our uniform.

After a lot of angst, and agony, and repetitive practice I finally managed it and passed my trade-training test. That would have been just before Christmas leave in 1973. Thank God for that!

LESSONS TO BE LEARNED

Despite all my panicky avoidance from when I was at school, at JLRRA I ended up getting some educational qualifications. I got two O-levels, a Grade-B Class-3 army qualification and a book I have never read. Not too bad then you think about it. Especially when you consider all the other stuff that was going on.

You have to agree, that is a bit of a result.

CODA:

I was doing some background research into all this and discovered that Army Education had been initially introduced in 1861 to encourage Victorian soldiers to develop their literacy and numeracy skills. This was one of the outcomes of the debacle of the Crimean War, when all those professional deficiencies were made public in the newspapers. Something had to be done.

This was when Army Education was born. This was when it was developed and linked to soldiers' promotional prospects. Reading the article, it all looked a bit hard for the lads. But it had to be done.

Nowadays, there are all sorts of educational opportunities for serving men and women. I was amazed to see the breath-taking amount of free and subsidised programmes that soldiers are eligible for, today. Professional and academic. I recently read an article, published in a peer-reviewed journal, by a staff-sergeant who is studying for a Masters' degree. That is very impressive compared to the standards we used to work by.

FUN, FUN, FUN!

Of the various surprises waiting for us, one of the most surprising things that happened during our first term in Recruits' Battery, was when our section sergeants arranged a barbecue for us. It put me on the back-foot.

I was amazed. I had gathered, judging by all the shouting and insults, all the contempt they heaped on us, that they hated us. So why would they do something nice like this? I can only imagine someone higher up must have ordered them to do it.

There was a piece of waste-land on the fringes of Bramcote. We spent the afternoon gathering scrap timber and sculpting it into an attractive heap. A group of lads was detailed to report to the stores to collect the compo-rations. These included tins of sausages and burgers. I have to say, I always find the texture of tinned sausages and burgers a bit strange. A bit like spam I suppose. Anyway, we also got baked potatoes.

Drink was provided in the form of bottles of pop.

At dusk the bonfire was lit and the food cooked. Afterwards we all had to sing songs. One of the sections had plainly practised and did a filthy version of 'Old MacDonald's Farm', complete with rude gestures, which had me in stitches. My section sang 'Be kind to your web-footed friends'. I laughed so much that I got the hiccups and snorted lemonade down my nose.

It was fun, and a good time was had by all. Once the fire had gone down we returned to Recruits' Battery billet in a happy frame of mind. They even let us watch TV for a while. Sheer luxury.

Mind you, it wasn't to last. We were roused with shouting and banging and crashing at 5am the following morning for our run. Hey-ho. Everything was back to normal.

When I joined my Regiment, I discovered that the army does this sort of thing really well. I had many happy times around bonfire barbecues. The difference between Junior Leaders and adult regiments would be the choice of accompanying beverage. I remember at the barbecue at battery camp, in Cuxhaven in 1976, I got so drunk I, along with several others, fell backwards off the log.

After Recruits' Section, when we were posted to our training batteries, one enjoyable thing was the chippy-run to Bulkington. The RPs knew what we were up to and sent out patrols. In a way, that thrill of the danger of capture added to the fun. It was always a 'Result' if we evaded the patrols. If we got the parcels of chips, and made it back to the Battery, we were heroes. We had used our 'escape-and-evasion' skills effectively and to good purpose. Except, if you got caught it wasn't much fun at all. You would end up doing circuits of the exercise yard in Joe's Hotel.

There was usually some kind of bean-feast after any inter-regimental sporting event. Something modestly celebratory. Buns and orange juice. Whoopee!

During the summer of 1973, us lads in the band went to Larkhill for a couple of weeks. We were playing at the big artillery show that was going on. It was a big deal and included all the RA bands, the motorcycle display team, the King's Troop, the gymnastic display team, and us. They built a big arena for the displays. It was huge. We worked a lot over the time, but it wasn't relentless. We did get to have a bit of fun. One afternoon they took us boys on a jolly down to the seaside. We got to splash around in the freezing English Channel and did the whole 'seaside' bit. Candy-floss, throwing stones in the water, fish and chips, throwing-up. That was a real laugh. Plus, we got to send the bus driver round the bend with our singing on the return journey. That was definitely fun.

The really big party came at the end of our mustering term. They decided the party for 40 Battery in August 1974, would be held in our billet, rather than going out anywhere. They provided us with loads of snacks and a supply of Watney's Party 7s. It was the first beer I had ever had, so I didn't have anything to compare it with. I suppose it was nice enough, in its way, but it didn't get me drunk. I recently discovered it was only about 2.5% Alcohol-By-Volume. That's not very strong at all!

I was in a gloomy frame of mind at the time but tried to join in with the jollies. The following day was spent clearing out the billet in preparation for departure. We had packed all our kit and handed in our bedding to the stores, so would be sleeping on the floor that night.

One of the lads had stolen a can of Party 7 and offered to share it with me. I thought that was a pretty generous offer and we found a quiet corner to drink it.

Unfortunately, the duty sergeant was peering through the window and caught us in the act. Straight down to Joe's Hotel.

That was no fun at all!

IT'S AN ODD-SORT WHO DOESN'T LIKE SPORT

I sometimes think they probably valued sport above most other activities in the Junior Leaders Regiment. Most afternoons and weekends something was going on. My problem was I was never a hairy athlete.

When I was at school I was one of those kids who preferred cross-country running above other sporting activities.

Why?

Well, I was good at it. Also, probably, because I hated team sports. I was a bit of a loner. I competed as an individual. I was a member of the school cross-country team and competed at county level. So, I competed in a team, but really it was all about the individual.

They would take about five of us in a minibus to some muddy field in some random corner of the county. We would stand, in our baggy shorts and vests, along with three-or-four-dozen other kids, while some adult tried to get the starting pistol to work.

I never won anything.

I can tell you this, I was never any good at soccer. Don't get me wrong, I enjoyed the odd kick-about. I had some modest footballing skills. For example, from a standing start, I could send a football flying off in almost any direction except the one I was aiming at. It was an uncanny knack. Just lucky I guess.

It always made me wonder why they forced me into playing it. They must have seen I had no talent for it.

Same thing happened in junior leaders.

It was so obvious I was crap at soccer, but they insisted I join one of the teams. That was just stupid. I didn't have the necessary spatial-awareness skills to understand how the shape of the team worked. I would be listening to the team-captain explaining some tactical set piece and be completely mystified.

My mind would wander, and I would go off into a bit of a dream. "Hello clouds, hello sky."

I had no idea what 'square-ball' meant. I had always understood balls to be spherical in nature. Mine certainly are.

I had the same problem with hockey. No idea. You could give me a hockey bat today and I wouldn't know which end went where. Although, I am sure there are plenty who would be only too willing to tell me.

I could just-about get away with playing rugby. All you had to do was point me in the right direction. I could happily run up and down the wing, provided there weren't any of those gigantic thugs in the opposition ready to bulldoze me down. Sadly, there always were.

Let's face it, I was a massive physical coward. Still am, come to that.

Whenever I went out onto the rugby pitch, the opposition always looked huge. Like those rugby-league sides from the M62 corridor. Massive stumps of boys with no necks. They would lumber out onto the pitch and the earth would shudder. They all had terrifying names. Names like; Ox and Moose and Mad-Dog and Nigel. Terrifying names for terrifying boys.

Strange, then, that I didn't get smeared across the field as often as I was expecting. Could it be that I had some modest talent for this?

No.

At least, not enough to be considered to join the Battery team. There were plenty better than me.

It was pretty annoying, but the thing that annoyed me most about all this were the officers. Their efforts to motivate us as they strode around in their 'British-Warm' overcoats. They weren't the ones having their faces trodden into the mud. They weren't being humiliated by the opposition thugs. Ruperts, eh? What are you going to do?

What I did join was the regimental cycling team. Somewhere out on the fringes of the barracks was the HQ of the cycling team. We had some great bikes. Real class components. Eddie Meryx stuff. And great cycling kit. Our shirts were pale blue, but with the RA 'stable-belt' colours across the middle. I swear to God, we were the flashiest-dressed cycling team you had ever seen.

Mostly we did time trials. Teams of four. One in the lead, setting the pace with the rest behind. Periodically, the leader would cede position so that another could take over.

We competed against lots of other junior leader teams. The roads around Bramcote were acceptably straight and uninterrupted, so ours was a popular venue for competitions.

We never won anything.

My other big sporting endeavour was swimming. There was a pool behind the education block and we got to use it in our spare time. For some reason I can't explain, I had lost all my swimming prowess and seriously needed to get it back together again. With a lot of practice and hard work I managed. My swimming grade was raised from 'D' to 'B'. I couldn't have been more pleased.

LIES, MYTHS AND LEGENDS—THE NAKED TRUTH!

Did you know, as we were led to believe, it was possible to fit every piece of our uniform and equipment into a mess-tin if it was folded it up properly. That is what we were told. Although, I am guessing, not all at the same time. Otherwise, why would they issue you with a kit-bag?

This would be including your greatcoat.

We had been issued with a greatcoat. I don't quite know why. I don't think I ever wore mine in my life.

The last time I saw one of those greatcoats in action was some years later, in Civvy-Street, worn by a friend of mine. A bit of a 'header' if you get my drift. Geordie Fox by name. A skinny, spotty, shambolic young man with weird habits. The coat was his personal equivalent of Batman's utility-belt. It contained everything he ever needed. It was all in there somewhere. Sandwiches, condoms, tobacco, papers, roaches, matches, other aromatic or repulsive stuff.

"You are supposed to be able to fold up your greatcoat to fit it into a mess-tin."
I don't think so.

One time, in Bramcote, we challenged our Troop Sergeant on this. This particular one was a really nice bloke. He wasn't going to fob us off with some platitudinous pile of bollocks. We assembled the various components, and each had a try.

No luck.

When it was his turn he regarded the issue for a while and then asked if anyone had a cigarette lighter, with a view to reducing the coat to ashes.

Fail.

This was only one of a whole load of lies, myths and legends we fervently believed in JLRRA. There were many others.

MYTHS ON TURNOUT:

You could use soap, as a substitute instead of starch, for your trouser creases. The alleged problem being that if it rained, your trousers would start foaming.

Using 'Duel' liquid floor polish to provide a lustrous sheen to your boot toecaps. The alleged problem being that if it rained they would go milky and you would get picked-up (didn't stop us doing it).

Instead of polishing your brasses in Brasso, you could put them in a dish, pour some Brasso in and set light to it. Yes, that worked brilliantly (no it didn't).

God alone knows where these ones came from. I doubt if anyone ever tested them. Yet, they were firmly believed by us all.

We tried all sorts of dopey things that were supposed to make it easier/quicker/better. The problem was that we weren't disciplined in scientific research. We had no means to make a value-judgement.

We just believed. We blindly believed.

THE MYTH OF THE HAUNTED HANGAR

Gamecock Barracks had previously been an RN air-base, hence the control tower, hangars, airfield, etc.

One of the legends doing the rounds, was that the ghost of a Polish pilot haunted one of the hangars.

A couple of lads, for reasons I can't imagine, ended up spending the night in the 'Haunted Hangar'. By all accounts they crapped themselves. When you think about it that is probably fair enough. Even without the implausible ghost story, if I'd had to spend the night in one of those hangars, on my own, I'm sure I would have been scared enough to soil my breeks.

THE TURNING WORM

One stupid story that stuck with me for many years, was about how us NIGs turned on one of the bullies and gave him a serious beating. According to the story we hurt him so badly that he later died of injuries. We were terrified of the consequences.
There certainly was an incident and we did have to go in front of the BC. I seriously thought it was a big-one. But I don't recall we ever got any fines, or anything else if it comes to that.

Years later I discovered that he hadn't been hurt at all. It turns out he was discharged. "Services No Longer Required".

We had hardly dented him. But in my mind, we had done severe damage. Christ-on-a-bike! What kind of half-wit was I? I seriously believed that I had participated in manslaughter.

THE LONG-LONG WEEKEND

They asked us to make a choice on where we wanted to go for the Battery training weekend.

I had no idea what they were talking about. We had been given an open option. Where would we like to have a 'Training Weekend'.

I thought it would be nice to go to Berwick-upon-Tweed. It's a lovely historical town, with exciting historical architecture and substantial Elizabethan defences. There is a great museum, a good gallery, and also the Russian gun they used to get the bronze for the original VCs back in the 19th century.

When I was a young teenager I used to go there to visit my grandparents. I liked the place very much. I loved the history and the sounds and smells of the North Sea. I loved to walk on the old town walls. The air was bracing, and I felt enervated.

One time, when I was about 14, I went swimming in the sea-pool. It was freezing. My recently-descended testicles shrank back into my body and my muscles seized up. I couldn't move. I panicked.

Luckily, there was a bloke and his girlfriend passing by. They heroically dragged me out of the water and revived me in ways I will never describe.

So, when we were asked where we wanted to go, I put down: Berwick-upon-Tweed. I thought it might be a nice place to spend a Battery Weekend. Better than Watford, in any event.

Of the various things I didn't take into account:

The Battery had a lot of lads from around the Liverpool area.

Nobody would be remotely interested in going to Berwick except me.

This wasn't a real Training Weekend. It was a 'Jolly'.

Berwick-upon-Tweed was 250 miles from Bramcote. Liverpool only 120.

When we paraded in front of the block, I couldn't help noticing how depleted the ranks were. There was no sign of the bloated BC, or any of the other officers if it came to that. The parade was conducted by one of the troop sergeants. No sign of the BSM. Or even the Junior BSM for that matter.

Also, a lot of the other lads had found plausible reasons not to attend. I couldn't understand it. This was a Battery Training Weekend. How was it that so many people weren't going to be involved?

We boarded the bus and headed for Scouse-Land.

All the other kids were pleased and excited. I was just a bit confused. How was this going to be a training weekend if half the Battery was missing?

We arrived at some superannuated barracks in the Wirral and were allocated our rooms. I made myself at home and set-up my bed-space. The rest of them didn't even unpack their bags or make their beds.

Then, the sergeant came in and told us we could all stand-down for the rest of the weekend. In a twinkling, they all picked up their bags and vanished.

I was the only person left. I couldn't understand it.

It was Friday afternoon and I was the only person in camp for the next two-and-a-half days. I hadn't even brought something to read. I thought we were going to be doing 'exercise-stuff'.

What the flip was I going to do?

I got changed into the terrible civilian clothes my sister had bought me, and explored the camp.

I found the cookhouse. They weren't pleased to see me but served up a very nice supper.

I occupied a table at the end of the big dining room. I was the only one there. The corporal-cook asked if I was going to be around for the rest of the weekend. I told him: 'Yes'.

I don't have words to describe the expression on his face. But, fair-play, he made some of the best meals for me that I have ever had in my whole time in the army. I would arrive at the cookhouse, at the appointed hour, and I would feast like a king! That man, despite his obvious loathing of me, created fantastic meals. Breakfast, lunch and supper. In my estimation, that man was a culinary God!

Meanwhile, I had nothing to do with the rest of my time.

The barracks was too far from any centres of excitement for me to go exploring. Plus, in any event, I had hardly any money. So, when I wasn't snoozing in my pit, I was in the NAAFI.

Given the age and status of the barracks, it was no surprise to find that the NAAFI had no facilities.

No pool-table, no pin-ball, no library, no juke-box.

Frankly, nothing.

There was the woman behind the counter, some old bloke, a few vacant tables and me.

They asked if I was going to be around for the whole weekend. I told them: 'Yes'. They didn't look all that pleased, but they didn't look as annoyed as the corporal-cook.

So, that was it. I had a whole barracks to myself for a long weekend.

Friday afternoon until Monday evening.

All on my own and nothing to do.

So, what do you do?

I had many, many showers. I laundered everything I had to within an inch of its life.

I lost the plot again.

Luckily, the corporal-cook, who hated me, loaned me a book. He hated me, but he could see how I was out on a limb. He loaned me a Harry Harrison sci-fi book. The 'Stainless Steel Rat'.

I read it avidly and loved it and forgave him.

That turned me around in a new way. I stopped obsessing about 'Literature'. I started enjoying fun books.

By the Monday morning, all the other lads dribbled back into camp to catch the coach back to Bramcote.

I dressed in my No. 2's and went to say goodbye to the corporal-cook and the NAAFI gang. For me, it was a kind-of nostalgic experience. They complimented me on how smart I was. The cook gave me one of his other books. The NAAFI man gave me his old cap-badge.

I burst into tears.

I thought I had been lonely, but I hadn't.

THE FANFARE TEAM

It is early 1974, I am 17 years and 4 months old. I am a junior gunner in JLRRA and I am a member of the fanfare team.

Those of us who were good trumpeters in the band could be selected to join the fanfare team.

They called us a 'team' but it didn't matter if you were a nerd, or a spod, or a hostile-loner, or any combination thereof. If you could play the trumpet well and looked good in the uniform, you were in.

There were six of us. We were good trumpeters and each roughly the same size and shape. 5 feet 7 inches, or so, and of a lean, cute physique.

Let's face it, we were gorgeous!

Being in the fanfare team was, kind-of, a big deal. We got to represent the Regiment in all sorts of places and at all sorts of events. We were the best-of-the-best when it came to being Junior Leaders' Band-Boys. When we stood out there in our great uniforms, with our silver fanfare trumpets, we were something special.

I had never been anything special in my life before.

And now I was special. I can't really describe it.

We were booked to play a fanfare for an Artillery Regiment in Leeds. They had been honoured with the Freedom of the City.

In those days, that was a 'Big Thing'. You could march through the town, with bayonets on your rifles, with colours flying, drums beating, and bands playing. Except, the Royal Artillery didn't have 'colours' *per se*. Our colours were the Guns. So, it was traditional to have some random piece of ordnance in the parade. Usually a highly-polished 25-pounder hitched to the back of a Land-Rover.

In any event, us members of the fanfare team went up to Leeds to participate in the big wing-ding.

We went up by train a few days early. We were supervised by Trumpet Major Isedale (Also known as: Captain-Grumpy) and an adult bombardier. They would keep us in line. We had to make sure all of our kit was in our suitcase, including our smart busbies.

We weren't used to that.

To tell you the truth, we were actually a complete shambles. I had my busby in a shopping bag and my band uniform was in a bin-liner.

TM Isedale was not impressed.

I don't know what they expected. We were dopey kids. You can't expect us to be all responsible. I could barely tie my bootlaces.

Here's a thing: On a previous event, we returned on the bus and dispersed to our billets. You can imagine my confusion when I discovered I didn't have my busby with me. I did an extensive search of the billet before I realised I had left it on the bus

I really don't know how these things happen to me.

In any event, I had managed to pack my kit and my uniform and my toothbrush. I was good-to-go.

We boarded the train to Leeds.

We spent most of the journey wandering to and fro. The bombardier spent the whole-time snoozing while TM Isedale was getting increasingly annoyed. Eventually he snapped and ordered us all to sit down. If we wanted to go to the toilet or get a drink from the buffet, we would have to ask permission.

On arrival, we were picked up and driven out to some random barracks somewhere. I really have no idea. It was occupied by a battalion of the Green Jackets. There were squads of them doing that 'double-marching' bit everywhere.

Us six boys were billeted in a barrack room designed to hold 30 men. It was a bit scary. The bombardier and the TM were allocated their own bunks.

We were immediately ordered to get into working dress for a drill rehearsal. Fine, I could probably manage that.

That was up to the point I needed clean socks.

I stared into my suitcase in mystification. I had packed no spare socks. I only had the ones I was wearing, and they were already a bit rank, if you get my drift. And we were going to be here for a week.

This was not good.

I looked at the timetable and could see there were no opportunities to go out and buy socks.

I couldn't wear these ones for a whole week. They were already beginning to make their presence felt. I did that first parade sockless.

I needed a plan.

At the first opportunity, I washed them in the sink. Good plan. Now, how do I dry them? I have no idea. I wrung them out and draped them on the end of my bed. That was a bit perilous. Any thieving bastard could nick them. There was only a pair of socks and me, versus five potential sock-thieves. We were outnumbered.

I don't know if you remember that movie *The Treasure of the Sierra Madre*, with Humphrey Bogart, where these American gold prospectors all go mad with paranoia. That's what it was like for me.

Whatever we were doing, all I could think about was my socks.

TM Isedale picked me up for being distracted on so many occasions, but I couldn't help it.

My Socks! My Socks! My Socks!!

Anyway.

Come the day, we boarded a bus with the Royal Artillery Band. Before we departed, one of them asked to make sure we had everything we needed with us. I checked and was pleased to report I had my socks with me. Nicely dried and free from teenage foot-odour. Plus everything else.

When we arrived at the venue, a couple of the kids reported to TM Isedale that they had forgotten their trumpet mouthpieces.

He went completely ballistic. He went doolally. He went utterly nuts! I have never seen a man go quite that far off the end of the pier. I was in awe. My mouth hung open, as it so often does.

He managed to borrow some mouthpieces off the band, so we could do the fanfare. But he was fuming like Vesuvius. This was not going to end-up well.

We played the fanfare and got inspected by the General and the Mayor. They loved us. We were young and cute. We were their pet mascots.

And over there, by the back wall, glowering like Hades, was TM Isedale. This was not going to end-up well.

PASSING OUT—WHICH IS TO SAY, GOSCHEN-DAY PARADE... RATHER THAN ANYTHING ELSE... IF YOU GET MY DRIFT.

The big 'marker' event in our lives at Bramcote was the passing-out parade. 'Goschen-Day'. That was the big parade when we would 'muster-out' and be acknowledged as adults. They held three of them per year, so that each group of mustering-gunners would have their own special day. There would be a General and other dignitaries, and a band. Our parents would come and be proud of us. We would be men.

This was what we had all been working towards.

The Goschen parade was named after Captain John Goschen, MC, RHA, who was killed in action at Tobruk in December 1941. In his memory, the Goschen Prize for the best junior leader of the term was awarded at the bequest of his father, General Goschen.

Fair enough. Someone had to do it.

This event was very much the 'Big-One' when it came to our lives in JLRRA. The RSM would hold practice parades every Saturday morning. The whole Regiment would parade on 'His-Square', to be inspected and rehearse the process of the parade. It would go like this:

The Troops would march on. They would all form-up on the fringes of the parade-ground. The order would be given: "Right… Marker" (pronounced: "Ree-ight-Maakkaar!). The right-marker (usually the tallest lad in the Regiment) would march forward and take position on the Square. The Order would be given: "Get On… Parade!" (I'm not going to keep on doing the pronunciation.) The Troops would march forward for 15 paces and spring to attention in line with the Right-Marker.

"In Open Order! Right-Dress!" The troops would attempt to shuffle into position. On the presumption this had been successfully accomplished, the rest of the parade could now continue.

The RSM (or the Inspecting Officer) would then go through the whole Regiment. This was probably the most nerve-wracking bit for the junior gunners. Any tiny imperfection would be spotted. If you weren't 100% up to scratch you were doomed. With a Regiment of 1000 kids, it could take almost forever. Many kids fainted with the stress.

March-Past in slow and in quick-time. The big problem with this was keeping the ranks in straight lines. There was any amount of opportunities to mess-up. Given the variable abilities of the accumulated participants, this was when it was all going to turn into a shambles.

Me, I never did any of that.

I was a Boy-in-the-Band. Every Saturday morning, us Band-Boys paraded at the band room for practice. We made sure we had polished our trumpets and bugles. We had bulled our boots and ironed our trouser creases. The Trumpet Majors would inspect us.

In many ways, they were harder on us than the RSM would have been. He had to inspect one thousand boys. The TMs only had to inspect 60. We had a higher intensity of inspection.

TM Isedale was particularly pernickety. He could pick a boy up for having the wrong kind of bobbles on his beret.

Yet and all, we probably had it easier than the rest of the Regiment. We practised our tunes and marching and counter-marching. All of the special set-pieces. We made sure we were spot-on. It was our pride to be the best we could be. I don't know about any of the other kids, but this was the biggest thing in my life. I was never going to be sub-par on this. I had to be the best I could be. I was determined to try to be my best.

When it came to it, we participated, along with the Royal Artillery bands, at the Goschen-Day parades. I think I did five of them.

I am only now aware, this was leading to one of my biggest disappointments in JLRRA.

My mustering term was May—August 1974. This was supposed to be my term of privilege. I would be allowed to wear a lanyard and a bayonet-frog. All the NIGs would look up to me. At the end, I would slow-march off the square and throw my hat in the air.

Except the NIGs didn't look up to me and I didn't get to throw my hat in the air.

I spent most of that term scratching my head and wondering what had gone wrong with my life.

I was going through a bad patch and wasn't really together very much. The band were busy. We were out most weekends. Also, I was

in the Fanfare-Team and we were busy. Accordingly, I never got to go on Saturday-Morning Parade and learn rifle drill. I never was in a troop, marching past the dais, slinging an 'Eyes-Right'.
I was definitely not prepared for a Goschen-Day parade.

I suspect the RSM and the Trumpet Majors had had a conflab and decided the best thing was that I should stay in the band for my Passing-Out parade.

I wasn't going to be inspected by a Major-General. I wasn't going to march-past the dais. I wasn't going to march off the parade to the tune of Auld-Lang-Syne.

I wouldn't throw my hat in the air.

I would stand in the band, with my trumpet at my hip, and watch all the others march off and throw their hats in the air.

Then we would march back to the band room. I would change into my working-dress and hand my band-kit in for the last time. Then I would go back to Nicholson troop with a couple of other lads and watch, while the other mustering gunners celebrated.

That was my Goschen-Day Parade.

THE ENTRANCE TO A NEW LIFE.

When I arrived at Bramcote in January 1973, I was a pink-scrubbed, skinny, immature half-wit. As were most of us. In fact, some of my intake were little more than children in uniforms.

Still, there were some boys, at 16-plus, who had matured further than the rest. They were more than halfway to manhood. Those lads would soon grow and mature and become NCOs in the junior leaders' hierarchy. They would have seniority over the rest of us.

Other boys would also mature rapidly during the following 18 months. They would become taller and more muscular and hairier.

They would quickly adjust to being soldiers. They would be good at sports and be able to buy beer without being asked their age.

I wasn't really one of them. It would take me another six years before I could even grow a moustache. Bar staff were forever asking me how old I was; even at age 21.

Yet and all, there came a point, during junior leaders' service, when we were no longer 'boys' and became 'men'.

For most of us, that point was when the mustering-gunners marched off the Square and threw their hats in the air.

I always thought that was a bit unfair and awkward. Why?

Well, some of the lads had done training with 'P'-Company. They had earned their Paratroop wings and had ball-buttons on their No. 2 dress uniforms. They were going to 7RHA and no discussion. That was a damned sight more impressive than most of the Permanent Staff had ever accomplished.

Also, there were those lads who had trained with the Royal Marine Commando and earned their green-beret to serve with 29 Commando, RA.

These were young men who had done a lot. Yet and all, they were still treated as minors.

To me, that didn't seem fair.

I knew perfectly well that I was still a minor. What had I done at age 17 years 8 months? I had played in the band. I had only ever had a couple of pints of Watneys. I was still a virgin. I had never seen a porn movie. I didn't smoke. I still had childish interests.

Yet, when I mustered in August 1974, I was no longer a 'boy'. I was now a 'man'.

I went off on a dismal family holiday and returned a couple of weeks later, lacking any enervation.

I was no longer Junior Gunner Lamb, I was now 'Gunner Lamb'. That was going to take some getting used to. Over the previous 18 months I had been conditioned.

I was now a temporary member of the staff. I had been nominated to go to 94 Regiment in Celle, in Germany. But no-one had sorted anything out. Instead, I would be a member of the JLRRA Permanent Staff.

I didn't really feel like one of the staff. I was 17 years and 8 months old. I still felt like a junior leader. I was posted to Recruits' Battery to help out with the new intake. Until my posting and travel was sorted out I would be assisting the Recruits' Battery.

That new intake in September 1974 was huge. There were hundreds of them. More than I could count. They kept moving around. They wouldn't stand still for long enough. I couldn't cope.

I had to work in the office with the BSM, the Battery Clerk, the BC's Secretary, and some other people I couldn't really identify. They were all senior and important and scary. I didn't quite know what I was supposed to be doing.

I quickly discovered my main task was to sit at my desk and keep my mouth shut. They would tell me when it was time to do some work.

One weird job was to take the 'bail-outs' down to the guardroom. I remembered all those kids in my intake who decided they couldn't hack-it. They were taken down to the guardroom.

I had originally thought that meant a cell in Joe's Hotel. I felt so sorry for them. I would never have risked that. I didn't realise there was an accommodation block around the back. If I had known that I might have considered my own options in a different way.

As it was, if a kid decided it wasn't for him he would have a word with his troop sergeant. He would then be sent for an interview with the BC and then I would march him down to the guardroom and hand him over to Joe Finch.

This was an awkward position for me. I was terrible at it. I wasn't used to giving orders. I couldn't tell left from right. Ask anyone. Still, that's what I had to do.

One perk of the job was that I had a bunk in the Recruits' Battery block. I had a bunk all on my own. This was the first time I'd ever had a bedroom to myself in my whole life. It was a novel experience. At home, I had shared with my brothers. As a Junior Leader, I had lived in a billet with 13 other boys.

Now I had my own room. I wouldn't repeat this experience for another seven years. Even as a Bombardier in 94 Regiment I would be sharing with someone. It was only in 1981, when I spent a couple of months working in the Depot at Woolwich, that I was allocated a single bunk.

The other novel thing was being treated like an adult by the other Permanent Staff. They invited me down the NAAFI. Not the Junior NAAFI, I wasn't to go in there anymore, but the other one around the back.

I could go into the NAAFI bar. They bought me beer even though I was technically under-age. Double-Diamond. Blecch!

I was invited for Sunday lunch with the Battery Clerk and his missus. They were friendly and hospitable.

I was definitely not used to any of this. Frankly, I was still a kid.

I finally got posted out to Germany in October. When I arrived at Taunton Barracks, Celle, BFPO 23, I reported to the guardroom.

"'7433 Junior Gunner Lamb," I announced.

Everyone in the room cringed.

Section 8 - Phil Hatch, Junior Leaders Regiment, RA, Bramcote, 1985 - 1986

I enlisted at the Torquay recruitment office on the 25th of September 1985 with my life long school mate, he was destined for the Junior Parachute Regiment and I was destined for the JLRRA. I was sent a travel warrant and expected to turn up at a place called Bramcote on the 22nd of October 1985.

This was to be my first departure alone, without family or friends accompanying me. I remember the blissful feeling of embarking on the journey, and the nervousness that soon followed as the train slowly pulled away from the platform of my birth town Totnes. Train travel was long back then and I felt alone. Eventually I arrived at Nuneaton station after a change at Birmingham New Street. A coach driver picked us up and whisked us away to Bramcote.

I won't lie, some of the boys on the bus, I took an immediate dislike too and some others, like me, sat silent and observed. We arrived at camp and I thought "This isn't bad". We were escorted, processed and had our basic haircuts in the first few days.

The troop Sgt said, "Get your heads down tonight lads and expect recruit training to start tomorrow morning"

And f**k me it did. 06.00hrs two bin lids being bashed together as a wake-up call. Shouting so loud it was inaudible, lesson after lesson of how things were supposed to be. More lessons about bulling, starching, ironing, cleaning and polishing.

(By the way, "WHICH BLOODY LEFT WAS THAT"?)

Everything continued like that for the next eight weeks, and on and off for the next twelve months. Some cried, some broke, some tried to stop bursting out laughing with a wry smile.

After the initial recruit stage, we had Christmas leave. I remember returning home and looking at my brothers' habits of leaving empty food bowls and glasses by their beds and thinking they were minging? I'd started to change from the boy that got on that train back then and was returning to camp with a different perspective towards life and my self-worth.

I got back and it was all bed-blocks, block-jobs, boots and kit as usual. Nothing seemed to have changed but the changing parades and prolonged yelling at us had subsided to always in the mornings and mainly later in the day. Beds and kit flew out the windows so often we thought they had wings but you knew by then then, it was never gonna be good enough.

Pay parades were always a blast (Did you ever get sent to the back) and KFS inspection, "Ha, don't even go there"

The next stage:

Now was about Army training. We drilled like a bucket of frogs. Many of the lads who had previously attended Army cadets resigned to the fact that it was like trying to teach a dog how to pick up its own doings to start with?

There was a regimental parade which was the biggest cock-up imaginable. The dreaded grease-out of the blocks and lockers ensued, which turned out quite well to everyone's astonishment. There were lumps in this jelly from all corners of the British Isles but finally something started to congeal as a team. There were many more months to go, but that day we felt accomplished. Next week I was appointed room leader. We suffered a week of drill, NBC, field-craft, military studies and preparation for our first exercise, FCC1.

Before we started the exercise, we had a CO's inspection and were allowed out into Nuneaton as a reward. Some of the boys thought it might be a good idea to cause trouble and subsequently we were all confined back to camp (Cheers lads).

The morning took us to Nescliff. There were upright stoves in the glorified nissan huts, which were hard to light. So here goes – field-craft, camp, bugged-out, speed-marched, soup, bed, section battle-drills, section-attacks, bayonets, night-patrolling, NBC, yomping, patrol base, bugged-out, yomping, breakfast, back to Brammers.

Returned to a parade and had so much kit to catch up on after Nescliff. Personally, I had a wobbler and nearly said F**k it!

The following week was full of military studies, orienteering, map reading, bumpering, polishing, changing parades and beastings. On the Saturday, we had a whip round for the TC's and Sgts leaving pressie.

Sunday, we left for Leek (snow everywhere). Leek was about navigation and endurance. The accommodation was quite good, and the food was very good. It was bloody freezing and unforgiving, but no one gave up. We got back and even the regimental parade was on standby due to the drill square being buried in snow.

We passed the time bulling boots, bumpering, polishing, starching, etc. etc., getting ready for CO's inspection. The week was full of MS, hobbies, PT, fkn canal-run and drill. It ended on a high note where I found myself in a cinema at Hinkley, watching Rocky IV on the Saturday. One more week before leave and it was SAA week. Monday 4 mile run with gats. Tuesday Kingsbury ranges with complimentary stew. Wednesday same gig SAA. Rest of the week, lots of drill, lots of runs, rugby, hockey, CO's inspection and then finally leave. But only after we'd picked up our boots and kit for the next phase which was known as "RELT".

Friday 21st March 1985, we all returned to camp.

Block jobs resumed and loads of kit needed to be dohbied, pressed and ready for inspection. Saturday and Sunday was consumed with traffic control drills and all of us strived to press and polish our kit for the Battery parade on Monday morning. Battery parade done, we started L1 for the week which was overshadowed by the ever-increased threat of being put back on recruits with loads of bumper bashing, bulling and block jobs to boot.

Changing parades were no stranger to the lads of Ramsay Troop. As the week went on I was awarded a B grade for L1, which I remember being satisfied with, being the short, shy one of the troop.

Sunday was all about getting our kit/webbing ready for SAA/FCC2. Monday started with the Wolvey run, which I struggle to remember but I'm sure it was quite pleasant. SAA consisted of SMG drills a range safety video, some grenade drills and more SMG. The following day was all about firing the SMG on range (the good stuff).

Friday came fast we packed our exercise kit for FCC2/L2/L3 Proteus, which would involve a lengthy journey in the four tonners where we all realised what the square hole in the canvass covered backs floor was really for.

Sunday saw us preparing for our 48-hour exercise on the Tuesday/Wednesday. Mostly packing kit and watching field-craft videos. Monday was trench digging (we won't say any-more about that) and Bayonet drills with a legendary DSM 'In, twist, out, ARRRRGH'!!! Tuesday up an at 'em! Tabbed out to trench position, filled them in and patrolled tactically to Patrol base, set up bashers and made our tea. Wednesday bugged-out early doors, we were slow and an immediate threat of extending the exercise was thrown in the hat.

We were immediately marched to a new position which we guarded overnight while others did attacks. Early morning saw a second bug-out, which was also a gas attack. We doubled back to camp with full NBC kit, respirator, all our other kit and rifles, it was a hard slog but upon our return we were presented with a jug of ale and humour was restored. Friday took us back to Bramcote, we returned all our FCC2 kit and re-drew the RELT kit. Everyone slept like a log.

Saturday involved travelling to the Brecon Beacons, there was no welcome, we went straight into 'yomp' mode upon arrival. Our troop Commander used this time to teach us how to navigate to a deserted pub, his self-invented version of the fan dance while wind pushed snow in our faces and the issue of live rations, lots of walking for miles and miles. We arrived back at Bramcote on the Friday, leave started on the Saturday, 12:30 but only after our kit and blocks were deemed satisfactory.

Memories of RELT

After a week leave, I made my way back to Bramcote. Upon arrival, it was just like we'd never been away. It was good to catch up with the lads and the familiar routines but we would only be at camp for one night.

The following day saw us set off for Snowdonia. We arrived after a long trip, which seemed to take forever but no sooner had we been allocated our places in the cottage we were ordered to assemble outside for a run and after that we were lined up naked and had to do a press up in a bloody freezing stream!

The following morning this was repeated then onto rope lectures, river crossing test and orienteering. Evening saw us Preparing our kit for "Hill" walking, which turned out to be walking up slopes that anyone else would have described as mountains?

The following day saw us potholing, dark cramped conditions with a smidgen of H2O to keep us alert. We went back to the cottage and prepared all our kit for Snowdon. 1085 mtrs of grit and determination, overcoming difficult conditions with heights unknown to us previously. Bloody hard ascent and testing descent to the campsite that awaited us.

Morning soon came, today we were off to scale Tryfan with its dreaded Adam & Eve leap of faith challenge. I completed it but I don't really remember how? A surprise awaited us the next day, mostly admin and kit organisation followed by a briefing from our new Troop Sgt (initials D. M.). Next day saw us trying our hand at mountain rescue all day but only after we'd completed the old "Run & stream" malarkey again.

Day 9, A trip to Colwyn bay. We hit the arcades then went for a swim in an actual swimming pool.

Monday saw us on a gorge walk, rough terrain and a few decent soakings through to the scats (Very funny). Tuesday saw us canoeing on a lake, something which I'd always enjoyed. But little did I know that later we'd all have to strip off for a swimming test and capsize drills (Bloody freezing). Wednesday we were taken sea Kayaking followed by a womble around Porthmadog, with the familiar brown paper bags, A good day was had by all.

Day 13, a small climb and a small abseil in preparation for tomorrow. Day 14, Massive abseil down an old mine shaft, another leap of faith moment followed by the buzz of touchdown on the smooth slate surface below. We returned to the cottage, gathered our kit and packed for our return to Bramcote.

RELT to me was a test of our self-belief, our fears, our fitness, our friendships and our determination to carry on, it was truly a character building experience and for all its ups and downs (no pun intended), to me it was a brilliant two weeks.

Wednesday 7th May 1986. Last day of leave.

Boring mainly, thinking about camp. Went down the Queens arms for a couple of pints (if your old enough to wear the uniform, you're old enough for a pint of beer) then walked over me mates house and watched Hot Bubblegum and Brewsters millions on video.

Packed and ready for return, I headed back to Bramcote on the Thursday. Didn't get back till 22.00 hrs, unpacked kit, caught up with the lads and sorted kit for the morning. We had a relaxing weekend before troop training, which was to begin on Monday.

Monday came fast we were doubled out to Bramcote mains and put into 4 man blocks, we practised attack drills then set into the main task which was trench digging that started at 16.30 hrs and didn't finish until 08.00 hrs the next day. The trenches were judged then we tabbed to the dreaded assault course which was swiftly followed by a morale crushing run. The exhaustion of us all showed itself in various forms, I just kept my mouth shut, as always.

The afternoon was spent at the ranges, "Couldn't hit a cow's arse with a banjo" springs to mind, then back to the block where the pressure seemed to have been turned up a couple of notches?

Wednesday, we'd sorted all our kit and set off to Kingsbury for a day of SAA. Thursday was leg-jelling drill, we competed in a drill competition which my diary says we may have won? Friday was orienteering and MS with the threat of being put back on recruits was firmly in the air.

The weekend was about kit/block cleaning and polishing, I got dicked to go down Kingsbury to take down a tent on the Sunday. Monday, the threat of recruits has become a reality. Early doors for five inspections/changing parades followed by a day of German MS, drill and PT. Tuesday MS, changing parades, block good, rooms ransacked but evening inspection good. We may come back off recruits tomorrow?

Wednesday, we have done our kit 100%, we've done our block 100%, will we come off the dreaded recruits? (answer NO)?

Thursday started the same but then by some small miracle recruits was ceased.

The evening was all about the WRVS disco, one of the lads entered a break dancing competition and came third. I wasn't interested and went down the NAAFI for some starch then pressed my kit. Friday, we had a German test in MS, I did really well and got elevated to stage 1.

Drill was becoming a big thing in our daily routine, again and again we were marched around the square but we were improving at a steady rate and the instructors knew it. Saturday, TC's inspection, it went well.

Sunday afternoon we did the run for the world (two laps around camp in fancy dress). I thought I'd do it dressed as Darth Vader. What a monumentally stupid idea, it was redders and numb nuts ere ran the whole thing carrying a four-foot strip light tube (my light sabre) while wearing an army blanket as a cape and a respirator to complete the look. I'll never forget that run, nor any step I took on it!

Monday 26th May 1986

Driver training started today, I wasn't that bad on the first day but tempers frayed between friends as the week went on. Shock awaited us on the Wednesday with the news that one of the lads in our intake had lost his fight against leukemia, a sad day.

R.I.P J/Gnr Branson.

Driving continued until Friday and my test was booked for 11.30, my mind wasn't in the right place and I duly failed. The feeling in the troop was generally at a low point and I felt like writing that letter to the Troop Commander, thankfully I didn't. Saturday found us all confined to camp due to someone slashing somebody else's boots. Like I said morale in the troop was low with back biting and face offs becoming a regular occurrence, the heat was on.

Monday 2nd June.

A much-needed PT was a lesson in endurance and then Aikido which we all enjoyed. The evening was block jobs, kit and the long queue at that phone box. Mum tried to reassure me and Dad saying, "Just get on with it"!

Guard duty on Wednesday saw me get stick man for the first and only time of my military service. The following week was Military studies. I got A's in German and Map reading but only scraped up a D grade in military calculations?

Monday 9th June. Introduction to trade training.

The first week was a mixed bag of training for the county fair. Kit and signals for me. The next few weeks were crammed with masses of scribbling, practical/theory tests, the dreaded Batco and masses upon masses of block work.

Some key points over those few weeks were having our No2's fitted, a rare long weekend off and the new recruits arriving on 1st of July 1986. Trade training was tested by a soul-destroying exercise which was followed by cleaning the Sigs hanger and being rewarded with trays of beer for our efforts. We were tired and hungry and the beer didn't take long to take the inevitable effect. Most of the weekend that followed was full of eating, sleeping and kit.

Monday 28th July came quick and it was all about skill at arms/APWT. We reacquainted ourselves with numerous small arms. That day was all about the LMG. Yes LMG, I am that old?

We were granted the weekend off and I went for a flying visit to my Auntie Pat's in Bicester. The train to Banbury cost £7.26 and I enjoyed an evening out with my cousins. Next day I travelled back to camp and prepared for the APWT, which I'm glad to report, I passed on the Thursday.

Leave was due to start on the Friday, Obviously the threat of No Leave was in the air if our kit and blocks weren't deemed good enough but happily we did good, it was summer leave so a decent break, which we all desperately needed and wanted. Before we all set off for all our far-flung destinations morale amongst the troops was at an all-time high. That was Friday 8th of August. We could see the summit.

THE FINAL PUSH!

Thursday 4th September 1986, returned to barracks and sorted out kit for assault course competition on Friday, which turned out to be a really good day. We came fourth but the Sgts were happy we'd given it our all. Saturday saw us packed and heading off to Monmouth for Battery camp. We arrived and were allowed out to explore the local area.

Sunday was filled with rock climbing and abseiling, most enjoyed it but some really didn't! The following day we got to try our hand at horse riding. Not far out of the stables, my horse decided to bolt back to base and I ended up in a conveniently placed bramble bush? The ride continued and I had to suffer the rest of it sharing a saddle with one of the stable girls. As you can imagine, I didn't mind this at all and upon our return to the stables I had to sort of slip off the saddle sideways and make a hasty retreat as most 17yr old lads would do.

Next day we set off on a massive walk and orienteering challenge. It was a good laugh but we were all knackered come close of play and hit the bunks as soon as we could.

Having slept well we awoke to more horse riding, I actually stayed on that time but recall my whole body aching all over. It was now Thursday and time to pack our kit for the return to Gamecock barracks and the huge personal admin task that awaited us.

Friday was consumed by loads of kit and loads of boot work, getting ready for our final training exercise (FTX). I got allocated the MAW/Carl Gustav or 84mm anti-tank weapon, I thought this was cool at the time of issue. I soon wouldn't!

Saturday found us all at Tidworth, we were allowed to go to the NAAFI on the first night, which was a welcome relief. Sunday 14th September, we did fire and movement drills in camp and were put on one hour's notice to move. We were also told we had a practice CFT later?

Monday was patrolling across the plain, then the dreaded CS attack. I was well hacked off carrying the 84 with a noddy-suit and respirator on. My mate carrying the inert rounds for my drainpipe was equally unimpressed.

We headed back to Tidworth for some sort of fair. We were all glad the first stage was over. Wednesday was Grenade drills and throwing which was massively fun until we re-started exercising and had to complete a 22km yomp in the freezing cold, blistering boots and webbing burns seemed to be the order of the day. We made our way to a patrol base and were given a recovery break where we could make a brew and have some scran. We made good use of it. Nightfall made it even colder but we stayed where we were.

Friday saw us worrying about new ration packs and fresh water resupply. We were anxious but were told that we had to go and set up an ambush.

Saturday - This morning we were caught out and force marched to a new position, water was still short but the troop commander really lost his rag earlier that day and didn't we know it. Evening came again, we tabbed back to the FRV (Frozen) then back to camp.

Sunday 21st September, A really exciting day, we did house clearing at Beeches barn then tabbed back to camp (House clearance was supreme fun).

Monday, Start of the BCs exercise, I had the 84mm all day. I was almost broken and felt like I had the arms of an orangutan. Tuesday, very early in the morning we had an NBC attack, then we did section attacks, house clearance, and tabbed to a patrol base. Very early on Wednesday we were bugged-out but it was short lived and we had a brew and breakfast break before being trucked back to Tidworth. Thursday was all about cleaning up and travelling back to Bramcote in the four tonners.

Friday 26th, Back to a parade which went quite well, we got issued our No. 2 dress hats today but it sounded like we were in for a lot of bullshit until Goschen day.

Saturday 27th September, Goshen day parade practice. Kit, drill, kit, drill, phoned home, bed.

Monday 29th September, Military studies and drill dominated our existence. Tuesday 30th, All day drill and kit. Wednesday 1st October, Parade in the morning, drill wasn't bad, then we had an hour with the padre (nice doze) followed by MS, drill and more kit.

Thursday, Church in the morning before drill (I was crap) while marching my t**t hat came off. Not the best move. Evening was fine, a WRVS disco and phoned home. Friday 3rd, We marched well today but a few of us were told we had to totally re-beeswax our boots (gutted). Saturday 4th, Re-done my boots and degreased my locker. Sunday, Church in the morning then given an ultimatum by the Sgts to have the block and lockers immaculate before 18.00 hrs. We cracked on with it and they were happy with the results but the fear of failing was always in the back of our minds.

Monday 6th Military studies. I was told I had enough loaf to take a ACW EPC exam? (Enlighten me fellas if you know/remember what this was)? Then drill, we were on fire. Tuesday 7th, Goschen practice, I was finally getting good at drill & turnout as I didn't get picked up for anything. Wednesday Goschen parade practice again, Not bad. Thursday, Kit exchange in the morning then D&T in the afternoon followed by a full No2 kit inspection with boots and brasses. Friday 10th Goschen practice then more drill and turnout, we did well and were given the rest of the day off to polish and clean stuff. Saturday 11th D&T competition, we came last, the Sgts were well pi**ed off! Sunday 12th, Painting and odd jobs around the block, ready for the new recruits.

MONDAY 13TH OCTOBER 1986 "THE MUSTERING OF THE GUNNERS".

Goschen parade practice, I got a bollocking but overall not bad.

Tuesday, more drill and then Ramsay Troop drinks party. I slept on the barrack room floor.

Wednesday, Admin mainly about postings.

Thursday, Mum and Dad came up from Devon for Goschen. I was in medical centre with suspected concussion, thankfully it was fine.

FRIDAY 17th OCTOBER 1986 GOSCHEN PARADE, PASSING OUT.

The year of training was finally over, after an immaculate parade we were Gunners. I always remember the feelings of achievement and pride were coupled with knowing you wouldn't be seeing your troop mates again for a while, if ever. Nervousness played a part, knowing you were in the man's army now, having to report to your new Regiment was daunting to say the least, Mine was to be 16th Air Defence (The Strathclyde Gunners).

I used my travel warrant and arrived at Doncaster train station on the 10th of November 1986. I was picked up by the duty driver. They were a brilliant bunch of lads to serve with but I never forgot the friends/brothers I made at Bramcote and I don't think I ever will. "UBIQUE" My friends.

**Section 9 – Simon Hutt. Paint – A Boy Soldier's Story. 1989 -
1990**

(Extracted with permission – Copyright © Simon Hutt 2010)

BOY SOLDIER

I had always wanted to be in the Army for as long as I could
remember. The Falklands War was a strong memory, but it was of
the Royal Marines marching with their rifles and Union Jacks and the
liberation of the Islands that stuck in my mind, not the sinking of
HMS Coventry or Simon Weston's horrific injuries.

My toys were all Action Men and small plastic toy soldiers who
always ended up spread all over the garden after a summer of epic
battles. The posters on my wall were of soldiers and military stuff, I
never thought of any other option than joining the Army.

At the age of 14-and-a-half I had enquired about joining and sat some
tests and watched some videos, then at the earliest opportunity, aged
fifteen, I took the Queen's shilling (eight pounds), swore an oath for
God, Queen and Country and signed up. My parents had to give their
permission, and also sign the papers, as they were still my legal
guardians until I was eighteen. They knew this was always my
dream, but still didn't want to sign the forms and tried to persuade me
to join the Engineers or REME; something where I could learn a
trade.

Eventually, and reluctantly, they signed the forms, reasoning that if I
didn't do it now I'd only get the hump and do it when I was 18
anyway. After signing up, the rest of school seemed even more of a
breeze than usual; I didn't need to worry about exam results or
coursework or the careers advice, I just enjoyed my last year. I did
study for my exams, the bare minimum as I always did, and cruised
through them, getting the average grade, a 'C' in absolutely
everything.

I had turned 16 in May and left school in June, and then, on the 4th of
July 1989, I was driven by my parents to the Junior Leaders'

Regiment Royal Artillery based in Bramcote, which coincidentally enough, was just outside my hometown of Nuneaton. I didn't really choose to join the Artillery; the recruitment officer said he wouldn't let me join the Infantry as I had a high score in the intelligence tests, and the Artillery covered loads of different types of jobs that I would be more suited to, or so he said.

That first day was a mad buzz of activity being divided into troops of 50 men, with eight troops per intake, and two intakes per year. So, I was amongst around 400 other 16-year-olds from all over the country. Some of them looked much older than 16, there were tattoos, smoke breaks and impenetrable accents. I could tell that a lot of them were hard as fuck. Somehow, I found myself in the band troop by virtue of being able to make a sound with the flute, and I had my hair shaved off by the same bloke who did my hair in Nuneaton, in his shop above the bus station.

The accommodation consisted of three large rooms containing 15 to 20 men, each man having his own bed and wardrobe. Our equipment was issued over the next few days, everything from helmets to bedding and all of it had a brand-new Army smell to it.

The first week was mainly kit issue and being measured for clothing. The stuff we did have was meant to be placed in a locker a certain way, pressed and folded, boxed off or rolled-up exactly the same as everyone else's. We were woken at 5:30 every morning and bedding was stripped down and made into neat blocks of sheets, and blankets topped off with the pillow at the top of the mattress.

We were taught how to wash and clean and iron correctly, we were even taught how to shave; for most people, including myself, it was the first time we had done it and from then on it would mean shaving every day.

The accommodation was kept spotless. Every morning each of us had a certain area of responsibility, mine was the brass pipes under the sink and urinals, which had to be polished first thing in the morning, before all of us would join in to polish the wooden floor by hand with thick, bright-yellow floor wax and dusters. Every morning there would be a room inspection followed by a parade whereupon we were inspected. There were two troop sergeants in charge of our training; there was no 'Good Cop, Bad Cop' routine, it was purely a very angry and shouty double act, one of them a Geordie and one from Nottingham. We could tell early-on the type of people who wouldn't make it, the ones with a bad attitude to discipline or the ones who were simply a bit weedy.

I absolutely loved it. For some reason everything came naturally, and I had no problem with all the bullshit and being shouted at, or the Sergeants throwing my bed-block everywhere, or tipping out the contents of my locker that took hours of painstaking attention to detail. It only happened rarely anyway as, just like school, I could still manage to do the minimum to get by and it was always good enough, but they still had to make sure everyone at some point got a bollocking. A few weeks into my training they must have realised I was cruising. It was a Sunday, and everyone had to go to church following a parade and inspection.

"You haven't shaved today have you Hutt?" said the Geordie Sergeant looking at my chin.

"Yes sergeant!" I shouted, knowing full well this would be a no-win situation.

"Are you calling me a liar?"

"No sergeant!"

"So, have you shaved today Hutt?" he shouted in my ear.

"No sergeant!" I lied, wanting it over with.

"HUTT, GET YOURSELF DOWN THE GUARDROOM AND ASK FOR AN ALMIGHTY BEASTING COURTESY OF SERGEANT HEADLEY. DO YOU UNDERSTAND?" he screamed into my face.

"YES SERGEANT!" I shouted back.

I marched out of the ranks of other men seeing their faces, which were a mixture of relief that it wasn't them and of trying not to laugh, before running off to the guardroom. The Regimental Police gave me the required 'Beasting', which was marching at double time in a courtyard the size of a large room:

"Leftrightleftrightmarktimeforwardleftturnmarktimeforwardleftturn."

And so it went on for an hour in the drizzle, soaked to the skin with sweat and rain, the steam rising from me. I was happy in the knowledge that I had shaved and therefore it was just 'my turn'. Besides, I had missed the weekly trying-not-to-fall-asleep competition of church.

The months went on as more of the recruits left or were weeded out, but, in the whole troop, there was one soldier from Liverpool that the two sergeants hated with a passion, purely because he was a Scouser, and they were determined to make him leave. This was the only time I have ever seen what would be termed 'bullying' in the Army and it was horrible. To everyone's amazement and his own credit, he carried on and finished training.

We were taught how to use a rifle, taught infantry tactics, nuclear, biological and chemical warfare drills, marching, fitness and plenty of other bullshit required for a junior leader in the Royal Artillery; including, obviously, leadership skills, and all with the minimum amount of sleep.

Our troop also had to learn their band instruments and the specialist marching that was required. There were plenty of drummers and buglers, but after several months of training we were left with only three flute players, which included myself. We learnt to play 'Congratulations' and the theme tune to 'Van der Valk'. However, nobody would be able to hear us anyway, which was a shame as one of the other flute players was a brilliant musician who had learnt his skills in a marching band in Portadown, Northern Ireland, so it was decided that we would just march around with the band without playing.

I also learned basic signaling. This meant learning how to use a radio and, more importantly, how to send Fire Missions, one of the most important jobs in the Artillery. I enjoyed the radio work, and discovered I was pretty good at it, eventually winning a tankard for getting the highest marks in the test for our class. I also somehow found myself on the Regimental Orienteering Team, probably because I could map-read and run at the same time. Improbable as it sounds, I was the Junior Armies (that's every 16 to 17-year-old soldier in training for that year) Orienteering Champion for 1989-90. My parents were well chuffed. And it's my claim to fame.

The year's training passed quickly. The first six months was the shouting and the bullshit of basic training, getting rid of the wasters and wankers and at the same time turning the rest of us from 16-year-old schoolboys into swearing, shouting and shaving soldiers. Also, though I didn't realise it until I left the Army, they had turned us into very obedient robots.

After the first six months, the sergeants eased off a bit, focusing now on our training, after all, when we got to our adult Regiments, the sergeants would be judged on how well we had been trained.

In May 1990, with my proud parents watching, the 1989 intake of Junior Gunners marched across the parade ground for the last time before becoming Gunners and adult soldiers. And while the other soldiers marched on in polished peak caps and rifles, I was standing in the middle of the ranks of bandsmen with an unplayed flute, wearing the Busby and Artillery uniform of the Napoleonic War. Needless to say, I felt a total idiot. My father was all smiles, and even though I looked a total dick, my family were proud of me.

The Junior Leaders' Regiment Royal Artillery Band stayed at Bramcote for another couple of months touring England, playing at country fairs and carnivals, despite the fact that we could only play half a dozen tunes, and me and my fellow flautists just marched along doing nothing.

We felt like real adult soldiers when we mixed with the civilians at these shows, trying to impress the local girls or getting into fights with the local youths. We spent those months enjoying ourselves, and, when back at Bramcote, watched the heartbreak of England in the Italia '90 World Cup on a TV donated by my Dad, lying on beds with duvets instead of sheets and blankets. It was when I was on leave that I noticed the difference in me compared to my friends, they were starting jobs or A-Levels. I had plenty of money in my pocket and felt taller, more grown up. I had a positive attitude to everything and I was following my dreams of being a soldier. I didn't envy them at the time.

There were only two of us going to 39 Heavy Regiment, myself and a guy from Wolverhampton who also stayed behind with the Physical Training Display Team (like the band only without the stupid uniforms). All Army units recruit locally and 39 were then known as the 'Birmingham Gunners', even though it recruited people from all over the Midlands. Most people went to their local Regiment although a few tried for the Parachute or Royal Marine Artillery, which sounded like too much effort for me as I had fallen into a 'comfort zone' following the intensity of basic training, and 39 Regiment had just been equipped with the brand new Multiple Launch Rocket System.

It was just turning autumn of 1990 when I finally arrived at Dempsey Barracks in Sennelager, West Germany. Playing, or in my case marching, with the band at English Summer shows, was now replaced with the reality of being an adult soldier.

Section 10 - Kidane Cousland, Army Foundation College, Harrogate, 2008 – 2009

This section is from the text of an interview with Lt K Cousland, 29 Commando Regiment, RA

Reproduced with kind permission of Lt Cousland RA.

When I was a kid I grew up on the White Hart Lane Estate in Tottenham. I never really see my childhood as being without challenges. We were a large family with only a single-parent. I struggled at school with dyslexia and not understanding that I had this condition.

Growing up, we moved around a lot. Jamaica, Ghana and back to Tottenham. Growing up was challenging, extremely rewarding and It was filled with a lot of love. But equally, it hardened me and prepared me for serving in the army. I didn't feel I was protected from reality or danger at any point.

When I went to my Army Selection Board I was offered the opportunity I was at that age when I could have waited a few months and gone in as an adult. The major who interviewed me said he thought I should go in and do adult service in the Parachute Regiment instead of joining the Royal Artillery as a junior soldier. He didn't think I would get so much out of the experience. But, for me, I was always of a mind that I wanted to spend time perfecting my military skills. I wanted to give myself the best chance of success. I made the conscious decision to go somewhere that would allow me the longest amount of time to develop my soldiering skills.

RECRUITING

I had a fond experience of the recruitment process. I was working in Covent Garden with my brother. We were flying toy helicopters and trying to sell edible underwear. When I had a break, I walked up to the big tri-Services Recruitment Centre near Oxford Circus.

As long as I can remember, I had always wanted to be in the army. So, I got up there at the age of 15 years and 9 months. I walked in and I told them I wanted to join 29 Commando Regiment Royal Artillery. That was exactly what I wanted to do.

They said alright, but you do realise you are still a child. You'll have to bring your mum here and then we can have a proper conversation about it.

I went and got my mum and she said, "Not on your life! You're not going anywhere near that until you've been to college." She wanted me to get some A-Levels and get a commission. The problem was I had done terribly on my GCSEs. So, I re-took my GCSEs at college as a probation period to appease my mum.

When I went back to the centre the sergeant tried to convince me to do almost any other job than the one I wanted to do. He said I would be a perfect fit for air defence, driver, almost everything. Every possible army trade except what I wanted to do.

I wasn't going to but put off. I kept badgering him and I maintained my own integrity until I got what I wanted.

Once he realised I was going to stick to my guns he set e up with a running club that had been organised for people who were going on army selection. I'd go to the track every Wednesday and do a whole circuit. There were quite a few of us and we built up and nice community of people. That was my prelude to the kind of friendships I was going to create in the army. Although, it seemed to be mainly focussed around suffering.

I sore my Oath of Allegiance in Wembley Stadium. They had one of the private boxes. I went up there with my mum and they had arranged food and refreshments. It was amazing.

ARRIVAL AT HARROGATE

The night before I was due to report to the Army Foundation College I had gone out drinking with my mates. There was a girl I really liked and I was hoping that would be the culmination of all this courting. Except it went all wrong. I was so frustrated that I ended up punching a bus stop and breaking my hand.

I got home a six in the morning and I was due to catch the train a nine. I was, by turns, hung-over, excited and in agony with my broken hand.

When I arrived at Harrogate I was ushered in. One strange thing was that all the others had their parents with them and I was just on my own.

It was strange, once the DS pointed me in the right direction I just forgot about everything to do with home. I was awestruck by everyone around me. I was resolute in my commitment. This was exactly what I wanted to do. I was determined to make the biggest success of this chance as I could. I covered up the fact that I had a broken hand by doing things like press-up leaning over to one side.

For me, the arrival at Harrogate was the fulfilment of many years of dreaming. I could not have been happier.

THE OTHER RECRUITS

I got the impression that my fellow recruits found it really hard to get on with me. I was like a tick-tock soldier. The army was all it was. If I was given an order I would do it. I wasn't all that interested in socialising or using the welfare facilities. I wasn't interested about anything other than being the best that I could possibly be. I think that may have rubbed people up the wrong way.

I think is also rubbed members of the directing staff up the wrong way too. There was no give, there was no bend. My troop sergeant summed it up. He told my mum; "He's too rigid to be likeable. He's too unyielding."

I think, when you set yourself up as trying to be the best you can be, you also set yourself up as a target. People want to see you fail just to know that you're a human being. Although, I think my section did well as a team partly because of all my hard work.

After that I did manage to make cordial relationships with most of the others in my section.

We had a lad who joined two weeks late. I was asked to look after him because I was one of the more responsible recruits. So, I started helping him and showing how to square things away. I had always made sure my space was immaculate and he could see the required standard. When it was time for inspections I helped him sort his space out.

I actually invested quite a lot of time into him. He was very homesick and was crying quite regularly, so I spoke to him a lot. I tried to help him get over it.

After all that, he proceeded to ambush my bed space while I was away. He put 'Minstrels' in my boots so when I put them on I would end up with chocolate in my socks. He left a pizza box underneath my bed so I got picked-up on block inspection.

In the end, I lost patience and confronted him about it. We had a bit of an argument. I couldn't believe what I was hearing. He made some really shocking remarks about my mixed-race origins. I was so outraged I could hardly control myself and ended up nearly strangling him. He ended up having to go into hospital and I got charged for it. I was arrested and marched down to the guardroom.

It was decided he was equally to blame for what had happened, but we both got off with nothing worse than an admonishment. All the same, that little episode followed me all the way through the rest of my training.

All in all, I think I adjusted quite easily to living in a barrack room. We shared a 12-man billet, each with our own bed space. That was fine by me. I'd never had my own room so I was quite used to it. Some of the other lads found it really hard to adjust to living in barracks and sharing facilities.

Because my mum had been so strict about us keeping the flat clean and tidy I always made sure my bed space was clean and tidy. The troop sergeant couldn't believe it. He was always double-checking to see if I had missed anything. And he was always disappointed because I never had.

TRAINING STAFF

The staff structure at Harrogate started with the bombardier who would command your section. They were our direct line-managers. They were our first point of contact. Mother, father, welfare inlet, everything to keep an eye on us. They also doubled as our skill-at-arms instructors, drill instructors and training supervisors.

We also had quite a lot of input from our platoon sergeant. He would get us together on a weekly basis and tell us how we were all completely shit.

The only times we ever saw our troop commander was when we were out on exercise. Occasionally he would give us lessons in some aspect of military activity.

One time, were we being given instruction in eating in the field. They got the ration packs out. On this occasion, the lieutenant was sat at a table, with a white linen table cloth, silver cutlery. Out of the ration box he produced a newspaper, a pot of caviar, some gourmet crackers and a bottle of champagne. At the time, we thought it was hilarious. This was a few years before I encountered the Honourable Artillery Company.

Our troop sergeant, Larry Mater, was a horrible, abrasive Scotsman from the Black Watch. Except he was actually okay. He was in your face, he was harsh, but he wasn't malicious.

My first section NCO was Sharon Kay, a female bombardier from 39 Regiment, RA. I got on with her really well. She was firm but fair. She like me because I got things done and made the section and her look good.

Unfortunately, I didn't get on quite so well with her replacement. I think he just didn't 'get me'. I ended up having a lot of run-ins with him. I found it very difficult. I was struggling to maintain the standards and was frustrated when other members of the section started getting complacent. That caused a lot of friction and he then had to intervene and work to smooth things over. I suppose he was even-handed about things and came down on my side as often as he came down on the side of the rest of the section.

After the first 14 weeks, we got given rank. I was promoted to junior lance corporal. The following term I was promoted to junior corporal. In the final term the decision was made as to who would be selected to be promoted to junior sergeant and junior RSM.

I was keen and ambitious to rise through the junior ranks system. However, a couple of weeks before we were due to go on our second test exercise my step-father died. He had contracted malaria in Ghana. They called me to the office and my mum was on the phone. She was crying and I had a little cry myself. They offered me two weeks compassionate leave.

I thought about it and decided to stick with the training. I didn't want to get behind or let the section down. I was expecting the rest of the section to appreciate I was trying to be the kind of person who makes personal sacrifices for the good of the team. But they didn't see it that way.

MY FAVOURITE BIT.

One of my favourite things in training was the live-firing exercises. We did bayonet drill, live platoon attacks, night exercises. I loved it. I thought it was incredible. At the age of 17 I found it extremely rewarding. I was a junior corporal at the time, which, gave me a lot of personal satisfaction.

When it came to our final exercise I really felt like I was a section commander. I felt I had the license to do what needed to be done for the section to succeed. I felt like I had achieved what I had originally set out to do. I felt like I had actually 'got it!'

After all this training I felt it had clicked and I knew I could lead people. I had felt that I could expect nothing. The army owed me nothing. Therefore, everything that I got, I had to earn.

PASSING OUT PARADE

When it came to my passing out parade I felt I had completely succeeded in all of my ambitions. I had focussed on the positive. I had been promoted within the junior soldier hierarchy and I was going to be posted to the adult regiment of my choice.

My one feeling of frustration was that I didn't make it up to junior sergeant. But, I was well content with my sense of achievement.

You ask me if I would do it again? Yes I would.

Printed in Poland
by Amazon Fulfillment
Poland Sp. z o.o., Wrocław